THE FOUR GEORGES
AND THE
ENGLISH HUMOURISTS

W.M. THACKERAY

THE FOUR GEORGES
AND THE
ENGLISH HUMOURISTS

ALAN SUTTON PUBLISHING LIMITED
in association with
THE GEORGIAN GROUP

The English Humourists of the Eighteenth Century first published 1852

The Four Georges first published 1855

First published in this edition in the United Kingdom in 1995
Alan Sutton Publishing Limited
Phoenix Mill · Far Thrupp · Stroud · Gloucestershire · GL5 2BU
in association with
The Georgian Group

British Library Cataloguing in Publication Data

A catalogue record for this book is available from the British Library.

ISBN 0-7509-0954-4

Cover picture: detail from Scene from 'The Beggar's Opera' *(photograph Tate Gallery Publications)*

Printed in Great Britain by
The Guernsey Press Company Limited,
Guernsey, Channel Islands.

CONTENTS.

INTRODUCTION.

THE ARTS IN GEORGIAN ENGLAND

There are two commonly held opinions about the period spanned by the reigns of the four Georges (1714–1830). The first view is that during this time the modern British state headed by constitutional monarchy emerged. This was achieved against a backdrop of Jacobite rebellions, wars with America and France and the increasing wave of libertarianism, which broke with such resonance with the French Revolution. But at the same time the country benefited from the increased prosperity brought about by the Agrarian and Industrial Revolutions. Thackeray's *The Four Georges* gives a lucid account of the events of this era. For the present-day reader Thackeray provides not only a useful insight into the reigns of these Hanoverian monarchs but he also reveals much about attitudes towards them in the subsequent Victorian period.

The second widely held opinion of the Georgian period is that it witnessed the flowering of the arts in Britain. This epoch saw the rise of academies and learned institutions devoted to the study and furtherance of the arts. And throughout the period attitudes towards and the depiction of nature remained central to artistic theory and debate. During this time national schools of painting and architecture emerged which stood proud among their European counterparts. In architecture the achievements of Lord Burlington, Robert Adam and John Nash equalled those of their continental contemporaries. Holbein, Van Dyck and Rubens dominated the art world of the Tudors and Stuarts. But by the mid-eighteenth century British artists such as Reynolds and Gainsborough had established themselves as world-class painters.

The nation's predilection for European art and architecture was questioned by Lord Shaftesbury, writing from Rome in 1712. His criticism singled out the work of Sir Christopher Wren as typifying what he felt to be the lack of good taste. Partly as a response to this, the prevailing European fashion for baroque architecture was rejected in favour of the restrained classicism of Andrea Palladio and his English follower Inigo Jones. This shift in architectural taste coincided with the accession to the throne of George I in 1714, a date generally identified with the beginning of the growth of the arts in Britain. As a German who spoke little English he was remote from the cultural life of his subjects. Perhaps as a consequence his patronage of the arts was limited. But this new age in Britain's history influenced the arts through the efforts of one of George I's, and later George II's, leading courtiers: Richard Boyle, 3rd Earl of Burlington, 4th Earl of Cork (1694–1753), perhaps Britain's first enlightened patron. Burlington encouraged the admiration of the art and architecture and imagined landscapes of antiquity through the works of his protégés, among whom were William Kent, Henry Flitcroft and Colen Campbell. His London home, Burlington House, Piccadilly, served as a kind of informal academy of arts and home to many of Burlington's protégés. Like many of his contemporaries in the Age of Reason, Burlington believed in an identifiable set of rules from which good art could be derived. These principles should be taught by an academy of art. Yet it was only half a century later, in the reign of George III, that the Royal Academy of Art was founded. Burlington's love of music, first seen in his patronage of the composer George Frederick Handel, did, however, encourage him to help establish the Royal Academy of Music.

The poet Alexander Pope (1688–1744) enjoyed Burlington's patronage. Pope did much to promote the classical tradition of literature through his translations of classical texts and his own poetry. His *Epistle to Lord Burlington* (1731) expresses the admiration felt by many of Burlington's role in the revival of the arts. This also contains a warning to those imitators of Burlington who do not understand the rules of antiquity.

The imitation and veneration of Italy was the focus of criticism for those who objected to Burlington and his followers. This group included the artist William Hogarth and the author Henry Fielding. They objected to the close adherence to antiquity and old master paintings, asserting that the indigenous English trends in the arts were superior to those promoted by Burlington and his coterie. Hogarth (1697–1764) promoted an English style of painting based on truthful observation free of the canon of academic art. His treatise, *The Analysis of Beauty*, although largely ignored in England, had a considerable impact abroad later in the period. Hogarth never received the acclaim he sought from the art establishment. But his pioneering work as an engraver did much to popularize the art world.

Irony and wit were used equally by both pro- and anti-Burlington 'camps'. Pope warned against 'imitating fools' who misapplied Burlington's artistic 'rules' and parodied the social mores of the beau monde. Hogarth lampooned Burlington and his coterie in his cartoon *Masquerades and Operas* (1723), where the gateway to Burlington House bears the inscription 'Accademy of Arts' and is adorned by sculptural figures of Michelangelo and Raphael looking up to Burlington who stands atop the pediment. The foibles of contemporary society did not escape Hogarth's biting satire, as seen in his series of engravings *Marriage A-la-Mode*, which criticized marriages made only for financial convenience. Despite their mutual antagonism both sides celebrated England's past achievements, evidenced by Hogarth's self-portrait with his arm resting on volumes by such Englishmen as Shakespeare and Milton or Kent's *Temple of British Worthies* in the gardens at Stowe.

Landscape real or imagined, and through it nature, assumed increasing importance throughout the period. The creation of an arcadian setting for the villas and country houses of Georgian England drew on the physical examples of ancient Rome, and their reinterpretation in Renaissance Italy, and the paintings of Claude and Poussin. Lord Burlington had done much to introduce Italianate ideas into his gardens at Chiswick. The placing of all'antica elements in a landscape setting was also carried out by William Kent in his work at Stowe and Rousham. By the latter half of the century the fashion for creating a landscape setting, following the rules of Claudian composition, was at its height and is best seen in the work of Lancelot 'Capability' Brown, whose designs include the grounds at Blenheim. Landscape painting also began to flourish in the middle years of the century. The artist Richard Wilson imagined himself to be the English Claude, but his work soon became more preoccupied with real nature. This is also seen in the work of Thomas Gainsborough, whose celebration of the English countryside was part of a developing response to the natural world culminating in the work of John Constable and J.M.W. Turner. This direct response to nature is perhaps one of the reasons why portraiture flourished at this time. This, together with landscape, became the backbone of English art in the late eighteenth century.

By the middle years of the eighteenth century a significant national school had emerged which led to the formation of the Royal Academy of Art. Its first president was the celebrated portraitist Sir Joshua Reynolds (1723–92). Reynolds delivered a series of lectures – *The Discourses* – to the students. Here he outlined his belief, shared by fellow intellectuals such as Dr Johnson, that the rules of taste derived from the authority of antiquity and the Italian Renaissance should be used by artists to improve on nature. This was the basis of the teaching at the Royal Academy schools but was rejected by many artists who felt a more direct response to nature was appropriate.

In architecture the authority of antiquity endured. The Society of Dilettanti, founded in 1723, developed from a social club for Grand

Tourists to a serious scholastic institution. The appearance of James Athenian Stuart's and Nicholas Revett's volumes *Antiquities of Athens* in the mid-eighteenth century, originally commissioned by the society, heralded a period of greater archaeological study of the remains of ancient Greece and Rome. Direct contact with classical architectural remains revealed licentiousness and variety – in distinct contrast to the order, proportion and rule imposed by its Renaissance interpreters. The work of the architect Robert Adam (1728–92), especially his interior designs, shows this fresh approach to antiquity which is typical of the Neo-Classical period. The fascination with the pure forms of ancient Greece springs partly from the Romantic notion of the purity of primitive forms and their proximity to nature. As a result the Greek Revival was the dominant architectural style in the opening years of the nineteenth century.

The reign of George IV is the culmination of the period in both dynastic and artistic terms. His prodigious spending briefly reasserted the monarch's importance as a patron and collector. George IV helped to establish London as a world city – the capital of the British Empire – by enabling the development of Regent's Park and Regent Street, the Metropolitan Improvements, and giving it a royal focus in Carlton House and later Buckingham Palace. The development of the National Gallery and the British Museum finally put the ownership and appreciation of art into the public domain.

William Makepeace Thackeray (1811–62) is best known for his novels, which include *Vanity Fair, The Newcomes* and *The Virginians*. He was editor of the *Cornhill Magazine* from its inception in January 1860. His most famous contribution to this was *The Roundabout Papers*. He also wrote for the magazine *Punch* from which his *Yellowplush Papers* and *The Book of Snobs* were republished and widely read and admired. *The Four Georges* was originally a series of lectures delivered in the United States. These were published with his thumbnail sketches of the *English Humourists*, including Hogarth, Pope and Fielding. These complement each other and create a vivid picture of Georgian Britain. Indeed the pungently powerful appraisal of the Hanoverian monarchs in *The Four Georges* still has resonance today.

DANA ARNOLD

THE FOUR GEORGES:

SKETCHES OF MANNERS, MORALS, COURT, AND TOWN LIFE

GEORGE THE FIRST

GEORGE THE FIRST.

VERY few years since, I knew familiarly a lady, who had been asked in marriage by Horace Walpole, who had been patted on the head by George I. This lady had knocked at Doctor Johnson's door; had been intimate with Fox, the beautiful Georgina of Devonshire, and that brilliant Whig society of the reign of George III.; had known the Duchess of Queensberry, the patroness of Gay and Prior, the admired young beauty of the Court of Queen Anne. I often thought as I took my kind old friend's hand, how with it I held on to the old society of wits and men of the world. I could travel back for seven score years of time—have glimpses of Brummel, Selwyn, Chesterfield, and the men of pleasure; of Walpole and Conway; of Johnson, Reynolds,

Note.—The initial letter is from an old Dutch print of Herrenhausen.

Goldsmith ; of North, Chatham, Newcastle ; of the fair maids of honour of George II.'s Court ; of the German retainers of George I.'s : where Addison was secretary of state ; where Dick Steele held a place ; whither the great Marlborough came with his fiery spouse ; when Pope, and Swift, and Bolingbroke yet lived and wrote. Of a society so vast, busy, brilliant, it is impossible in four brief chapters to give a complete notion ; but we may peep here and there into that bygone world of the Georges, see what they and their Courts were like ; glance at the people round about them ; look at past manners, fashions, pleasures, and contrast them with our own. I have to say thus much by way of preface, because the subject of these lectures has been misunderstood, and I have been taken to task for not having given grave historical treatises, which it never was my intention to attempt. Not about battles, about politics, about statesmen and measures of state, did I ever think to lecture you : but to sketch the manners and life of the old world ; to amuse for a few hours with talk about the old society ; and, with the result of many a day's and night's pleasant reading, to try and while away a few winter evenings for my hearers.

Among the German princes who sat under Luther at Wittenberg, was Duke Ernest of Celle, whose younger son, William of Lüneburg, was the progenitor of the illustrious Hanoverian house at present reigning in Great Britain. Duke William held his Court at Celle, a little town of ten thousand people that lies on the railway line between Hamburg and Hanover, in the midst of great plains of sand, upon the river Aller. When Duke William had it, it was a very humble wood-built place, with a great brick church, which he sedulously frequented, and in which he and others of his house lie buried. He was a very religious lord, and was called William the Pious by his small circle of subjects, over whom he ruled till fate deprived him both of sight and reason. Sometimes, in his latter days, the good Duke had glimpses of mental light, when he would bid his musicians play the psalm-tunes which he loved. One thinks of a descendant of his, two hundred years afterwards, blind, old, and lost of wits, singing Handel in Windsor Tower.

William the Pious had fifteen children, eight daughters and seven sons, who, as the property left among them was small, drew lots to determine which one of them should marry, and continue the stout race of the Guelphs. The lot fell on Duke George, the sixth brother. The others remained single, or contracted left-handed marriages after the princely fashion of those days. It is a queer picture—that of the old Prince dying in his little wood-built capital, and his seven sons tossing up which should inherit and transmit the crown of Brentford. Duke George, the lucky prizeman, made the tour of Europe, during which he visited the Court of Queen Elizabeth ; and in the year 1617, came back and settled at Zell, with a wife out of Darmstadt. His remaining brothers all kept their house at Zell, for economy's sake. And presently, in due course, they all died—all the honest Dukes ; Ernest, and Christian, and Augustus, and Magnus, and George, and John—and they are buried in the brick church of Brentford yonder, by the sandy banks of the Aller.

Dr. Vehse gives a pleasant glimpse of the way of life of our Dukes in Zell. "When the trumpeter on the tower has blown," Duke Christian orders—viz. at nine o'clock in the morning, and four in the evening—every one must be present at meals, and those who are not must go without. None of the servants, unless it be a knave who has been ordered to ride out, shall eat or drink in the kitchen or cellar ; or, without special leave, fodder his horses at the Prince's cost. When the meal is served in the court-room, a page shall go round and bid every one be quiet and orderly, forbidding all cursing, swearing, and rudeness ; all throwing about of bread, bones, or roast, or pocketing of the same. Every morning, at seven, the squires shall have their morning soup, along with which, and dinner, they shall be served with their under-drink—every morning, except Friday morning, when there was sermon, and no drink. Every evening they shall have their beer, and at night their sleep-drink. The butler is especially warned not to allow noble or simple to go into the cellar : wine shall only be served at the Prince's or councillors' table ; and every Monday, the honest old Duke Christian ordains the accounts shall be ready, and the expenses in the kitchen, the wine and beer cellar, the bakehouse and stable, made out.

Duke George, the marrying Duke, did not stop at home to partake of the beer and wine, and the sermons. He went about fighting wherever there was profit to be had. He served as general in the army of the circle of Lower Saxony, the Protestant army; then he went over to the Emperor, and fought in his armies in Germany and Italy ; and when Gustavus Adolphus appeared in Germany, George took service as a Swedish general, and seized the Abbey of Hildesheim, as his share of the plunder. Here, in the year 1641, Duke George died, leaving four sons behind him, from the youngest of whom descend our royal Georges.

Under these children of Duke George, the old God-fearing, simple

ways of Zell appear to have gone out of mode. The second brother
was constantly visiting Venice, and leading a jolly, wicked life there.
It was the most jovial of all places at the end of the seventeenth
century; and military men, after a campaign, rushed thither, as the
warriors of the Allies rushed to Paris in 1814, to gamble, and rejoice,
and partake of all sorts of godless delights. This Prince, then,
loving Venice and its pleasures, brought Italian singers and dancers
back with him to quiet old Zell; and, worse still, demeaned himself
by marrying a French lady of birth quite inferior to his own—Eleanor
d'Olbreuse, from whom our Queen is descended. Eleanor had a
pretty daughter, who inherited a great fortune, which inflamed her
cousin, George Louis of Hanover, with a desire to marry her; and
so, with her beauty and her riches, she came to a sad end.

It is too long to tell how the four sons of Duke George divided
his territories amongst them, and how, finally, they came into possession of the son of the youngest of the four. In this generation
the Protestant faith was very nearly extinguished in the family: and
then where should we in England have gone for a king? The third
brother also took delight in Italy, where the priests converted him
and his Protestant chaplain too. Mass was said in Hanover once
more; and Italian soprani piped their Latin rhymes in place of the
hymns which William the Pious and Doctor Luther sang. Louis XIV.
gave this and other converts a splendid pension. Crowds of Frenchmen and brilliant French fashions came to his Court. It is incal-
culable how much that royal bigwig cost Germany. Every prince
imitated the French King, and had his Versailles, his Wilhelmshöhe
or Ludwigslust; his Court and its splendours; his gardens laid out
with statues; his fountains, and water-works, and Tritons; his actors,
and dancers, and singers, and fiddlers; his harem, with its inhabitants; his diamonds and duchies for these latter; his enormous
festivities, his gaming-tables, tournaments, masquerades, and banquets
lasting a week long, for which the people paid with their money,
when the poor wretches had it; with their bodies and very blood
when they had none; being sold in thousands by their lords and
masters, who gaily dealt in soldiers, staked a regiment upon the red
at the gambling-table; swapped a battalion against a dancing-girl's
diamond necklace; and, as it were, pocketed their people.

As one views Europe, through contemporary books of travel in
the early part of the last century, the landscape is awful—wretched
wastes, beggarly and plundered; half-burned cottages and trembling
peasants gathering piteous harvests; gangs of such tramping along

with bayonets behind them, and corporals with canes and cats-of-nine-tails to flog them to barracks. By these passes my lord's gilt carriage floundering through the ruts, as he swears at the postilions, and toils on to the Residenz. Hard by, but away from the noise and brawling of the citizens and buyers, is Wilhelmslust or Ludwigsruhe, or Monbijou, or Versailles—it scarcely matters which,—near to the city, shut out by woods from the beggared country, the enormous, hideous, gilded, monstrous marble palace, where the Prince is, and the Court, and the trim gardens, and huge fountains, and the forest where the ragged peasants are beating the game in (it is death to them to touch a feather); and the jolly hunt sweeps by with its uniform of crimson and gold; and the Prince gallops ahead puffing his royal horn; and his lords and mistresses ride after him; and the stag is pulled down; and the grand huntsman gives the knife in the midst of a chorus of bugles; and 'tis time the Court go home to dinner; and our noble traveller, it may be the Baron of Pöllnitz, or the Count de Königsmarck, or the excellent Chevalier de Seingalt, sees the procession gleaming through the trim avenues of the wood, and hastens to the inn, and sends his noble name to the marshal of the Court. Then our nobleman arrays himself in green and gold, or pink and silver, in the richest Paris mode, and is introduced by the chamberlain, and makes his bow to the jolly Prince, and the gracious Princess; and is presented to the chief lords and ladies, and then comes supper and a bank at Faro, where he loses or wins a thousand pieces by daylight. If it is a German Court, you may add not a little drunkenness to this picture of high life; but German, or French, or Spanish, if you can see out of your palace-windows beyond the trim-cut forest vistas, misery is lying outside; hunger is stalking about the bare villages, listlessly following precarious husbandry; ploughing stony fields with starved cattle; or fearfully taking in scanty harvests. Augustus is fat and jolly on his throne; he can knock down an ox, and eat one almost; his mistress, Aurora von Königsmarck, is the loveliest, the wittiest creature; his diamonds are the biggest and most brilliant in the world, and his feasts as splendid as those of Versailles. As for Louis the Great, he is more than mortal. Lift up your glances respectfully, and mark him eyeing Madame de Fontanges or Madame de Montespan from under his sublime periwig, as he passes through the great gallery where Villars and Vendôme, and Berwick, and Bossuet, and Massillon are waiting. Can Court be more splendid; nobles and knights more gallant and superb; ladies more lovely? A grander monarch, or a more miserable starved

wretch than the peasant his subject, you cannot look on. Let us
bear both these types in mind, if we wish to estimate the old society
properly. Remember the glory and the chivalry? Yes! Remember
the grace and beauty, the splendour and lofty politeness; the gallant
courtesy of Fontenoy, where the French line bids the gentlemen of
the English guard to fire first; the noble constancy of the old King
and Villars his general, who fits out the last army with the last crown-
piece from the treasury, and goes to meet the enemy and die or
conquer for France at Denain. But round all that royal splendour
lies a nation enslaved and ruined : there are people robbed of their
rights—communities laid waste—faith, justice, commerce trampled
upon, and well-nigh destroyed—nay, in the very centre of royalty
itself, what horrible stains and meanness, crime and shame ! It is
but to a silly harlot that some of the noblest gentlemen, and some of
the proudest women in the world, are bowing down ; it is the price
of a miserable province that the King ties in diamonds round his
mistress's white neck. In the first half of the last century, I say,
this is going on all Europe over. Saxony is a waste as well as
Picardy or Artois; and Versailles is only larger and not worse than
Herrenhausen.

It was the first Elector of Hanover who made the fortunate match
which bestowed the race of Hanoverian Sovereigns upon us Britons.
Nine years after Charles Stuart lost his head, his niece Sophia,
one of many children of another luckless dethroned sovereign, the
Elector Palatine, married Ernest Augustus of Brunswick, and brought
the reversion to the crown of the three kingdoms in her scanty
trousseau.

One of the handsomest, the most cheerful, sensible, shrewd,
accomplished of women, was Sophia,* daughter of poor Frederick,
the winter king of Bohemia. The other daughters of lovely, unhappy
Elizabeth Stuart went off into the Catholic Church ; this one, luckily
for her family, remained, I cannot say faithful to the Reformed
Religion, but at least she adopted no other. An agent of the French
King's, Gourville, a convert himself, strove to bring her and her
husband to a sense of the truth ; and tells us that he one day asked
Madame the Duchess of Hanover, of what religion her daughter was,
then a pretty girl of thirteen years old. The duchess replied that the
princess *was of no religion as yet*. They were waiting to know of

---

* The portraits on the next page are from contemporary prints of this
Princess, before her marriage and in her old age.

what religion her husband would be, Protestant or Catholic, before instructing her! And the Duke of Hanover having heard all Gourville's proposal, said that a change would be advantageous to his house, but that he himself was too old to change.

This shrewd woman had such keen eyes that she knew how to shut them upon occasion, and was blind to many faults which it appeared that her husband the Bishop of Osnaburg and Duke of Hanover committed. He loved to take his pleasure like other sovereigns—was a merry prince, fond of dinner and the bottle; liked

to go to Italy, as his brothers had done before him; and we read how he jovially sold 6,700 of his Hanoverians to the seigniory of Venice. They went bravely off to the Morea, under command of Ernest's son, Prince Max, and only 1,400 of them ever came home again. The German princes sold a good deal of this kind of stock. You may remember how George III.'s Government purchased Hessians, and the use we made of them during the War of Independence.

The ducats Duke Ernest got for his soldiers he spent in a series of the most brilliant entertainments. Nevertheless, the jovial Prince was economical, and kept a steady eye upon his own interests. He achieved the electoral dignity for himself : he married his eldest son George to his beautiful cousin of Zell ; and sending his sons out in command of armies to fight—now on this side, now on that—he lived on, taking his pleasure, and scheming his schemes, a merry, wise prince enough, not, I fear, a moral prince, of which kind we shall have but very few specimens in the course of these lectures.

Ernest Augustus had seven children in all, some of whom were scapegraces, and rebelled against the parental system of primogeniture and non-division of property which the Elector ordained. " Gustchen," the Electress writes about her second son :—" Poor Gus is thrust out, and his father will give him no more keep. I laugh in the day, and cry all night about it ; for I am a fool with my children." Three of the six died fighting against Turks, Tartars, Frenchmen. One of them conspired, revolted, fled to Rome, leaving an agent behind him, whose head was taken off. The daughter, of whose early education we have made mention, was married to the Elector of Brandenburg, and so her religion settled finally on the Protestant side.

A niece of the Electress Sophia—who had been made to change her religion, and marry the Duke of Orleans, brother of the French King ; a woman whose honest heart was always with her friends and dear old Deutschland, though her fat little body was confined at Paris, or Marly, or Versailles—has left us, in her enormous correspondence (part of which has been printed in German and French), recollections of the Electress, and of George her son. Elizabeth Charlotte was at Osnaburg when George was born (1660). She narrowly escaped a whipping for being in the way on that auspicious day. She seems not to have liked little George, nor George grown up ; and represents him as odiously hard, cold, and silent. Silent he may have been : not a jolly prince like his father before him, but a prudent, quiet, selfish potentate, going his own way, managing his own affairs, and understanding his own interests remarkably well.

In his father's lifetime, and at the head of the Hanover forces of 8,000 or 10,000 men, George served the Emperor, on the Danube against Turks, at the siege of Vienna, in Italy, and on the Rhine. When he succeeded to the Electorate, he handled its affairs with great prudence and dexterity. He was very much liked by his people of Hanover. He did not show his feelings much, but he cried heartily on leaving them ; as they used for joy when he came back. He showed an uncommon prudence and coolness of behaviour when he came into his kingdom ; exhibiting no elation ; reasonably doubtful whether he should not be turned out some day; looking upon himself only as a lodger, and making the most of his brief tenure of St. James's and Hampton Court; plundering, it is true, somewhat, and dividing amongst his German followers; but what could be expected of a sovereign who at home could sell his subjects at so many ducats per head, and make no scruple in so disposing of them? I fancy a considerable shrewdness, prudence, and even moderation in his ways. The German Protestant was a cheaper, and better, and kinder king than the Catholic Stuart in whose chair he sat, and so far loyal to England, that he let England govern herself.

Having these lectures in view, I made it my business to visit that ugly cradle in which our Georges were nursed. The old town of Hanover must look still pretty much as in the time when George Louis left it. The gardens and pavilions of Herrenhausen are scarce changed since the day when the stout old Electress Sophia fell down in her last walk there, preceding by but a few weeks to the tomb James II.'s daughter, whose death made way for the Brunswick Stuarts in England.

The first two royal Georges, and their father, Ernest Augustus, had quite royal notions regarding marriage; and Louis XIV. and Charles II. scarce distinguished themselves more at Versailles or St. James's, than these German sultans in their little city on the banks of the Leine. You may see at Herrenhausen the very rustic theatre in which the Platens danced and performed masques, and sang before the Elector and his sons. There are the very fauns and dryads of stone still glimmering through the branches, still grinning and piping their ditties of no tone, as in the days when painted nymphs hung garlands round them; appeared under their leafy arcades with gilt crooks, guiding rams with gilt horns; descended from "machines" in the guise of Diana or Minerva; and delivered immense allegorical compliments to the princes returned home from the campaign.

That was a curious state of morals and politics in Europe; a queer consequence of the triumph of the monarchical principle. Feudalism was beaten down. The nobility, in its quarrels with the crown, had pretty well succumbed, and the monarch was all in all. He became almost divine: the proudest and most ancient gentry of the land did menial service for him. Who should carry Louis XIV.'s candle when he went to bed? what prince of the blood should hold the King's shirt when his Most Christian Majesty changed that garment?—the French memoirs of the seventeenth century are full of such details and squabbles. The tradition is not yet extinct in Europe. Any of you who were present, as myriads were, at that splendid pageant, the opening of our Crystal Palace in London, must have seen two noble lords, great officers of the household, with ancient pedigrees, with embroidered coats, and stars on their breasts and wands in their hands, walking backwards for near the space of a mile, while the royal procession made its progress. Shall we wonder—shall we be angry—shall we laugh at these old-world ceremonies? View them as you will, according to your mood; and with scorn or with respect, or with anger and sorrow, as your temper leads you. Up goes Gessler's hat upon the pole. Salute that symbol of sovereignty with heartfelt awe; or with a sulky shrug of acquiescence, or with a grinning obeisance; or with a stout rebellious No—clap your own beaver down on your pate, and refuse to doff it to that spangled velvet and flaunting feather. I make no comment upon the spectators' behaviour; all I say is, that Gessler's cap is still up in the market-place of Europe, and not a few folks are still kneeling to it.

Put clumsy, High Dutch statues in place of the marbles of Versailles: fancy Herrenhausen waterworks in place of those of Marly: spread the tables with Schweinskopf, Specksuppe, Leberkuchen, and the like delicacies, in place of the French *cuisine;* and fancy Frau von Kielmansegge dancing with Count Kammerjunker Quirini, or singing French songs with the most awful German accent: imagine a coarse Versailles, and we have a Hanover before us. " I am now got into the region of beauty," writes Mary Wortley, from Hanover in 1716; " all the women have literally rosy cheeks, snowy foreheads and necks, jet eye-brows, to which may generally be added coal-black hair. These perfections never leave them to the day of their death, and have a very fine effect by candle-light; but I could wish they were handsome with a little variety. They resemble one another as Mrs. Salmon's Court of Great Britain, and are in as much danger of melting away by too nearly approaching the fire." The sly Mary Wortley saw this painted seraglio of the first George at Hanover, the year after his accession to the British throne. There were great doings and feasts there. Here Lady Mary saw George II. too. " I can tell you, without flattery or partiality," she says, " that our young prince has all the accomplishments that it is possible to have at his age, with an air of sprightliness and understanding, and a something so very engaging in his behaviour that needs not the advantage of his rank to appear charming." I find elsewhere similar panegyrics upon Frederick Prince of Wales, George II.'s son; and upon George III., of course, and upon George IV. in an eminent degree. It was the rule to be

dazzled by princes, and people's eyes winked quite honestly at that
royal radiance.

The Electoral Court of Hanover was numerous—pretty well paid,
as times went ; above all, paid with a regularity which few other
European courts could boast of. Perhaps you will be amused to
know how the Electoral Court was composed. There were the
princes of the house in the first class ; in the second, the single field-
marshal of the army (the contingent was 18,000, Pöllnitz says, and
the Elector had other 14,000 troops in his pay). Then follow, in due
order, the authorities civil and military, the working privy councillors,
the generals of cavalry and infantry, in the third class ; the high
chamberlain, high marshals of the court, high masters of the horse,
the major-generals of cavalry and infantry, in the fourth class ; down
to the majors, the hofjunkers or pages, the secretaries or assessors, of
the tenth class, of whom all were noble.

We find the master of the horse had 1,090 thalers of pay ; the high
chamberlain, 2,000—a thaler being about three shillings of our money.
There were two chamberlains, and one for the Princess ; five gentlemen
of the chamber, and five gentlemen ushers ; eleven pages and personages to educate these young noblemen—such as a governor, a
preceptor, a fecht-meister, or fencing master, and a dancing ditto, this
latter with a handsome salary of 400 thalers. There were three body
and Court physicians, with 800 and 500 thalers ; a Court barber, 600
thalers ; a Court organist ; two musikanten ; four French fiddlers ;
twelve trumpeters, and a bugler ; so that there was plenty of music,
profane and pious, in Hanover. There were ten chamber waiters,
and twenty-four lacqueys in livery ; a maître-d'hôtel, and attendants of
the kitchen ; a French cook ; a body cook ; ten cooks ; six cooks'
assistants ; two Braten masters, or masters of the roast—(one fancies
enormous spits turning slowly, and the honest masters of the roast
beladling the dripping) ; a pastry-baker ; a pie-baker ; and finally,
three scullions, at the modest remuneration of eleven thalers. In the
sugar-chamber there were four pastrycooks (for the ladies, no doubt) ;
seven officers in the wine and beer cellars ; four bread-bakers ; and five
men in the plate-room. There were 600 horses in the Serene stables—
no less than twenty teams of princely carriage horses, eight to a team ;
sixteen coachmen ; fourteen postilions ; nineteen ostlers ; thirteen
helps, besides smiths, carriage-masters, horse-doctors, and other
attendants of the stable. The female attendants were not so numerous : I grieve to find but a dozen or fourteen of them about the
Electoral premises, and only two washerwomen for all the Court.

These functionaries had not so much to do as in the present age. I own to finding a pleasure in these small-beer chronicles. I like to people the old world, with its every-day figures and inhabitants—not so much with heroes fighting immense battles and inspiring repulsed battalions to engage; or statesmen locked up in darkling cabinets and meditating ponderous laws or dire conspiracies—as with people occupied with their every-day work or pleasure : my lord and lady hunting in the forest, or dancing in the Court, or bowing to their Serene Highnesses as they pass in to dinner ; John Cook and his procession bringing the meal from the kitchen ; the jolly butlers bearing in the flagons from the cellar ; the stout coachman driving the ponderous gilt waggon, with eight cream-coloured horses in housings of scarlet velvet and morocco leather ; a postilion on the leaders, and a pair or a half-dozen of running footmen scudding along by the side of the vehicle, with conical caps, long silver-headed maces, which they poised as they ran, and splendid jackets laced all over with silver and gold. I fancy the citizens' wives and their daughters looking out from the balconies ; and the burghers over their beer and mumm, rising up, cap in hand, as the cavalcade passes through the town with torch-bearers, trumpeters blowing their lusty cheeks out, and squadrons of jack-booted lifeguardsmen, girt with shining cuirasses, and bestriding thundering chargers, escorting his Highness's coach from Hanover to Herrenhausen ; or halting, mayhap, at Madame Platen's country house of Monplaisir, which lies half-way between the summer-palace and the Residenz.

In the good old times of which I am treating, whilst common men were driven off by herds, and sold to fight the Emperor's enemies on the Danube, or to bayonet King Louis's troops of common men on the Rhine, noblemen passed from Court to Court, seeking service with one prince or the other, and naturally taking command of the ignoble vulgar of soldiery which battled and died almost without hope of promotion. Noble adventurers travelled from Court to Court in search of employment ; not merely noble males, but noble females too ; and if these latter were beauties, and obtained the favourable notice of princes, they stopped in the courts, became the favourites of their Serene or Royal Highnesses ; and received great sums of money and splendid diamonds ; and were promoted to be duchesses, marchionesses, and the like ; and did not fall much in public esteem for the manner in which they won their advancement. In this way Mdlle. de Querouailles, a beautiful French lady, came to London on a special mission of Louis XIV., and was adopted by our grateful country and sovereign, and figured as Duchess of Portsmouth. In this way the beautiful Aurora of Königsmarck travelling about found favour in the eyes of Augustus of Saxony, and became the mother of Marshal Saxe, who gave us a beating at Fontenoy ; and in this manner the lovely sisters Elizabeth and Melusina of Meissenbach (who had actually been driven out of Paris, whither they had travelled on a like errand, by the wise jealousy of the female favourite there in possession) journeyed to Hanover, and became favourites of the serene house there reigning.

That beautiful Aurora von Königsmarck and her brother are wonderful as types of bygone manners, and strange illustrations of the morals of old days. The Königsmarcks were descended from an ancient noble family of Brandenburg, a branch of which passed into Sweden, where it enriched itself and produced several mighty men of valour.

The founder of the race was Hans Christof, a famous warrior and plunderer of the Thirty Years' War. One of Hans' sons, Otto, appeared as ambassador at the Court of Louis XIV., and had to make a Swedish speech at his reception before the Most Christian King. Otto was a famous dandy and warrior, but he forgot the speech, and what do you think he did? Far from being disconcerted, he recited a portion of the Swedish Catechism to his Most Christian Majesty and his Court, not one of whom understood his lingo with the exception of his own suite, who had to keep their gravity as best they might.

Otto's nephew, Aurora's elder brother, Carl Johann of Königsmarck, a favourite of Charles II., a beauty, a dandy, a warrior, a rascal of more than ordinary mark, escaped but deserved being hanged in England, for the murder of Tom Thynne of Longleat. He had a little brother in London with him at this time :—as great a beauty, as great a dandy, as great a villain as his elder. This lad, Philip of Königsmarck, also was implicated in the affair ; and perhaps it is a pity he ever brought his pretty neck out of it. He went over to Hanover, and was soon appointed colonel of a regiment of H. E. Highness's dragoons. In early life he had been page in the Court of Celle ; and it was said that he and the pretty Princess Sophia Dorothea, who by this time was married to her cousin George the Electoral Prince, had been in love with each other as children. Their loves were now to be renewed, not innocently, and to come to a fearful end.

A biography of the wife of George I., by Doctor Doran, has lately

appeared, and I confess I am astounded at the verdict which that
writer has delivered, and at his acquittal of this most unfortunate
lady.   That she had a cold selfish libertine of a husband no one can
doubt ; but that the bad husband had a bad wife is equally clear.   She
was married to her cousin for money or convenience, as all princesses
were married.   She was most beautiful, lively, witty, accomplished :
his brutality outraged her : his silence and coldness chilled her : his
cruelty insulted her.   No wonder she did not love him.   How could
love be a part of the compact in such a marriage as that ?   With this
unlucky heart to dispose of, the poor creature bestowed it on Philip of
Königsmarck, than whom a greater scamp does not walk the history
of the seventeenth century.   A hundred and eighty years after the
fellow was thrust into his unknown grave, a Swedish professor lights
upon a box of letters in the University Library at Upsala, written by
Philip and Dorothea to each other, and telling their miserable story.

The bewitching Königsmarck had conquered two female hearts
in Hanover.   Besides the Electoral Prince's lovely young wife Sophia
Dorothea, Philip had inspired a passion in a hideous old Court lady,
the Countess of Platen.   The Princess seems to have pursued him
with the fidelity of many years.   Heaps of letters followed him on
his campaigns, and were answered by the daring adventurer.   The
Princess wanted to fly with him ; to quit her odious husband at any
rate.   She besought her parents to receive her back ; had a notion of
taking refuge in France and going over to the Catholic religion ; had
absolutely packed her jewels for flight, and very likely arranged its
details with her lover, in that last long night's interview, after which
Philip of Königsmarck was seen no more.

Königsmarck, inflamed with drink—there is scarcely any vice of
which, according to his own showing, this gentleman was not a
practitioner—had boasted at a supper at Dresden of his intimacy
with the two Hanoverian ladies, not only with the Princess, but with
another lady powerful in Hanover.   The Countess Platen, the old
favourite of the Elector, hated the young Electoral Princess.   The
young lady had a lively wit, and constantly made fun of the old one.
The Princess's jokes were conveyed to the old Platen just as our idle
words are carried about at this present day : and so they both hated
each other.

The characters in the tragedy, of which the curtain was now
about to fall, are about as dark a set as eye ever rested on.   There is
the jolly Prince, shrewd, selfish, scheming, loving his cups and his
ease (I think his good-humour makes the tragedy but darker) ; his

Princess, who speaks little but observes all ; his old painted Jezebel of a mistress ; his son, the Electoral Prince, shrewd too, quiet, selfish, not ill-humoured, and generally silent, except when goaded into fury by the intolerable tongue of his lovely wife ; there is poor Sophia Dorothea, with her coquetry and her wrongs, and her passionate attachment to her scamp of a lover, and her wild imprudences, and her mad artifices, and her insane fidelity, and her furious jealousy regarding her husband (though she loathed and cheated him), and her prodigious falsehoods ; and the confidante, of course, into whose hands the letters are slipped; and there is Lothario, finally, than whom, as I have said, one can't imagine a more handsome, wicked, worthless reprobate.

How that perverse fidelity of passion pursues the villain ! How madly true the woman is, and how astoundingly she lies ! She has bewitched two or three persons who have taken her up, and they won't believe in her wrong. Like Mary of Scotland, she finds adherents ready to conspire for her even in history, and people who have to deal with her are charmed, and fascinated, and bedevilled. How devotedly Miss Strickland has stood by Mary's innocence ! Are there not scores of ladies in this audience who persist in it too? Innocent ! I remember as a boy how a great party persisted in declaring Caroline of Brunswick was a martyred angel. So was Helen of Greece innocent. She never ran away with Paris, the dangerous young Trojan. Menelaus, her husband, ill-used her ; and there never was any siege of Troy at all. So was Bluebeard's wife innocent. She never peeped into the closet where the other wives were with their heads off. She never dropped the key, or stained it with blood ; and her brothers were quite right in finishing Bluebeard, the cowardly brute ! Yes, Caroline of Brunswick was innocent ; and Madame Laffarge never poisoned her husband ; and Mary of Scotland never blew up hers ; and poor Sophia Dorothea was never unfaithful ; and Eve never took the apple—it was a cowardly fabrication of the serpent's.

George Louis has been held up to execration as a murderous Blue-beard, whereas the Electoral Prince had no share in the transaction in which Philip of Königsmarck was scuffled out of this mortal scene. The Prince was absent when the catastrophe came. The Princess had had a hundred warnings ; mild hints from her husband's parents ; grim remonstrances from himself—but took no more heed of this advice than such besotted poor wretches do. On the night of Sunday, the 1st of July, 1694, Königsmarck paid a long visit to the Princess, and

left her to get ready for flight.   Her husband was away at Berlin ; her
carriages and horses were prepared and ready for the elopement.

Meanwhile, the spies of Countess Platen had brought the news to their
mistress. She went to Ernest Augustus, and procured from the

Elector an order for the arrest of the Swede. On the way by which he was to come, four guards were commissioned to take him. He strove to cut his way through the four men, and wounded more than one of them. They fell upon him ; cut him down ; and, as he was lying wounded on the ground, the Countess, his enemy, whom he had betrayed and insulted, came out and beheld him prostrate. He cursed her with his dying lips, and the furious woman stamped upon his mouth with her heel. He was despatched presently ; his body burnt the next day ; and all traces of the man disappeared. The guards who killed him were enjoined silence under severe penalties. The Princess was reported to be ill in her apartments, from which she was taken in October of the same year, being then eight-and-twenty years old, and consigned to the castle of Ahlden, where she remained a prisoner for no less than thirty-two years. A separation had been pronounced previously between her and her husband. She was called henceforth the " Princess of Ahlden," and her silent husband no more uttered her name.

Four years after the Königsmarck catastrophe, Ernest Augustus, the first Elector of Hanover, died, and George Louis, his son, reigned in his stead. Sixteen years he reigned in Hanover, after which he became, as we know, King of Great Britain, France, and Ireland, Defender of the Faith. The wicked old Countess Platen died in the year 1706. She had lost her sight, but nevertheless the legend says that she constantly saw Königsmarck's ghost by her wicked old bed. And so there was an end of her.

In the year 1700, the little Duke of Gloucester, the last of poor Queen Anne's children, died, and the folks of Hanover straightway became of prodigious importance in England. The Electress Sophia was declared the next in succession to the English throne. George Louis was created Duke of Cambridge ; grand deputations were sent over from our country to Deutschland ; but Queen Anne, whose weak heart hankered after her relatives at St. Germains, never could be got to allow her cousin, the Elector Duke of Cambridge, to come and pay his respects to her Majesty, and take his seat in her House of Peers. Had the Queen lasted a month longer; had the English Tories been as bold and resolute as they were clever and crafty ; had the Prince whom the nation loved and pitied been equal to his fortune, George Louis had never talked German in St. James's Chapel Royal.

When the crown did come to George Louis he was in no hurry about putting it on. He waited at home for awhile ; took an affecting farewell of his dear Hanover and Herrenhausen ; and set out in the most leisurely manner to ascend "the throne of his ancestors," as he called it in his first speech to Parliament. He brought with him a compact body of Germans, whose society he loved, and whom he kept round the royal person. He had his faithful German chamberlains ; his German secretaries ; his negroes, captives of his bow and spear in Turkish wars ; his two ugly, elderly German favourites, Mesdames of Kielmansegge and Schulenberg, whom he created respectively Countess of Darlington and Duchess of Kendal. The Duchess was tall, and lean of stature, and hence was irreverently nicknamed the Maypole. The Countess was a large-sized noblewoman, and this elevated personage was denominated the Elephant. Both of these ladies loved Hanover and its delights ; clung round the linden-trees of the great Herrenhausen avenue, and at first would not quit the place. Schulenberg, in fact, could not come on account of her debts ; but finding the Maypole would not come, the Elephant packed up her trunk and slipped out of Hanover, unwieldy as she was. On this the Maypole straightway put herself in motion, and followed her beloved George Louis. One seems to be speaking of Captain Macheath, and Polly, and Lucy. The King we had selected ; the courtiers who came in his train ; the English nobles who came to welcome him, and on many of whom the shrewd old cynic turned his back—I protest it is a wonderful satirical picture. I am a citizen waiting at Greenwich pier, say, and crying hurrah for King George ; and yet I can scarcely keep my countenance, and help laughing at the enormous absurdity of this advent !

Here we are, all on our knees. Here is the Archbishop of Canterbury prostrating himself to the head of his Church, with Kiel-mansegge and Schulenberg with their ruddled cheeks grinning behind the Defender of the Faith. Here is my Lord Duke of Marlborough kneeling too, the greatest warrior of all times ; he who betrayed King William—betrayed King James II.—betrayed Queen Anne—betrayed England to the French, the Elector to the Pretender, the Pretender to the Elector ; and here are my Lords Oxford and Bolingbroke, the latter of whom has just tripped up the heels of the former ; and if a month's more time had been allowed him, would have had King James at Westminster. The great Whig gentlemen made their bows and congées with proper decorum and ceremony ; but yonder keen old schemer knows the value of their loyalty. " Loyalty," he must think, " as applied to me—it is absurd ! There are fifty nearer heirs to the throne than I am. I am but an accident, and you fine Whig gentle-men take me for your own sake, not for mine. You Tories hate me ;

you archbishop, smirking on your knees, and prating about Heaven, you know I don't care a fig for your Thirty-nine Articles, and can't understand a word of your stupid sermons. You, my Lords Boling-broke and Oxford—you know you were conspiring against me a month ago ; and you, my Lord Duke of Marlborough—you would sell me or any man else, if you found your advantage in it. Come, my good Melusina, come, my honest Sophia, let us go into my private room, and have some oysters and some Rhine wine, and some pipes after-wards : let us make the best of our situation ; let us take what we can get, and leave these bawling, brawling, lying English to shout, and fight, and cheat, in their own way ! "

If Swift had not been committed to the statesmen of the losing side, what a fine satirical picture we might have had of that general *sauve qui peut* amongst the Tory party ! How mum the Tories became ; how the House of Lords and House of Commons chopped round ; and how decorously the majorities welcomed King George !

Bolingbroke, making his last speech in the House of Lords, pointed out the shame of the peerage, where several lords concurred to condemn in one general vote all that they had approved in former parliaments by many particular resolutions. And so their conduct was shameful. St. John had the best of the argument, but the worst of the vote. Bad times were come for him. He talked philosophy, and pro-fessed innocence. He courted retirement, and was ready to meet persecution ; but, hearing that honest Mat Prior, who had been re-called from Paris, was about to peach regarding the past transactions, the philosopher bolted, and took that magnificent head of his out of the ugly reach of the axe. Oxford, the lazy and good-humoured, had more courage, and awaited the storm at home. He and Mat Prior both had lodgings in the Tower, and both brought their heads safe out of that dangerous menagerie. When Atterbury was carried off to the same den a few years afterwards, and it was asked, what next should be done with him ? " Done with him ? Fling him to the lions," Cadogan said, Marlborough's lieutenant. But the British lion of those days did not care much for drinking the blood of peaceful peers and poets, or crunching the bones of bishops. Only four men were executed in London for the rebellion of 1715 ; and twenty-two in Lancashire. Above a thousand taken in arms, submitted to the King's mercy, and petitioned to be transported to his Majesty's colonies in America. I have heard that their descendants took the loyalist side in the disputes which arose sixty years after. It is pleasant to find that a

friend of ours, worthy Dick Steele, was for letting off the rebels with
their lives.

As one thinks of what might have been, how amusing the speculation is ! We know how the doomed Scottish gentlemen came out
at Lord Mar's summons, mounted the white cockade, that has been a
flower of sad poetry ever since, and rallied round the ill-omened
Stuart standard at Braemar. Mar, with 8,000 men, and but 1,500
opposed to him, might have driven the enemy over the Tweed, and
taken possession of the whole of Scotland ; but that the Pretender's
Duke did not venture to move when the day was his own. Edinburgh
Castle might have been in King James's hands ; but that the men
who were to escalade it stayed to drink his health at the tavern, and
arrived two hours too late at the rendezvous under the castle wall.
There was sympathy enough in the town—the projected attack seems
to have been known there—Lord Mahon quotes Sinclair's account of
a gentleman not concerned, who told Sinclair, that he was in a house
that evening where eighteen of them were drinking, as the facetious
landlady said, " powdering their hair," for the attack on the castle.
Suppose they had not stopped to powder their hair ? Edinburgh
Castle, and town, and all Scotland were King James's. The north
of England rises, and marches over Barnet Heath upon London.
Wyndham is up in Somersetshire ; Packington in Worcestershire ; and
Vivian in Cornwall. The Elector of Hanover, and his hideous
mistresses, pack up the plate, and perhaps the crown jewels in
London, and are off *via* Harwich and Helvoetsluys, for dear old
Deutschland. The King—God save him !—lands at Dover, with
tumultuous applause ; shouting multitudes, roaring cannon, the Duke
of Marlborough weeping tears of joy, and all the bishops kneeling in
the mud. In a few years, mass is said in St. Paul's ; matins and
vespers are sung in York Minster ; and Doctor Swift is turned out
of his stall and deanery house at St. Patrick's, to give place to
Father Dominic, from Salamanca. All these changes were possible then, and once thirty years afterwards—all this we might
have had, but for the *pulveris exigui jactu*, that little toss of powder
for the hair which the Scotch conspirators stopped to take at the
tavern.

You understand the distinction I would draw between history—
of which I do not aspire to be an expounder—and manners and life
such as these sketches would describe. The rebellion breaks out in
the north ; its story is before you in a hundred volumes, in none
more fairly than in the excellent narrative of Lord Mahon. The

clans are up in Scotland ; Derwentwater, Nithsdale and Forster are in arms in Northumberland—these are matters of history, for which you are referred to the due chroniclers. The Guards are set to watch the streets, and prevent the people wearing white roses. I read presently of a couple of soldiers almost flogged to death for wearing oakboughs in their hats on the 29th of May—another badge of the beloved Stuarts. It is with these we have to do, rather than the marches and battles of the armies to which the poor fellows belonged—with statesmen, and how they looked, and how they lived, rather than with measures of State, which belong to history alone. For example, at the close of the old Queen's reign, it is known that the Duke of Marlborough left the kingdom—after what menaces, after what prayers, lies, bribes offered, taken, refused, accepted ; after what dark doubling and tacking, let history, if she can or dare, say. The Queen dead ; who so eager to return as my lord duke ? Who shouts God save the King ! so lustily as the great conqueror of Blenheim and Malplaquet ? (By the way, he will send over some more money for the Pretender yet, on the sly.) Who lays his hand on his blue ribbon, and lifts his eyes more gracefully to heaven than this hero? He makes a quasi-triumphal entrance into London, by Temple Bar, in his enormous gilt coach—and the enormous gilt coach breaks down somewhere by Chancery Lane, and his highness is obliged to get another. There it is we have him. We are with the mob in the crowd, not with the great folks in the procession. We are not the Historic Muse, but her ladyship's attendant, tale-bearer—*valet de chambre*—for whom no man is a hero ; and, as yonder one steps from his carriage to the next handy conveyance, we take the number of the hack ; we look all over at his stars, ribbons, embroidery; we think within ourselves, O you unfathomable schemer ! O you warrior invincible ! O you beautiful smiling Judas ! What master would you not kiss or betray? What traitor's head, blackening on the spikes on yonder gate, ever hatched a tithe of the treason which has worked under your periwig ?

We have brought our Georges to London city, and if we would behold its aspect, may see it in Hogarth's lively perspective of Cheapside, or read of it in a hundred contemporary books which paint the manners of that age. Our dear old *Spectator* looks smiling upon the streets, with their innumerable signs, and describes them with his charming humour. "Our streets are filled with Blue Boars, Black Swans, and Red Lions, not to mention Flying Pigs and Hogs in Armour, with other creatures more extraordinary than any in the deserts of Africa." A few of these quaint old figures still remain in London town. You may still see there, and over its old hostel in Ludgate Hill, the " Belle Sauvage" to whom the *Spectator* so pleasantly alludes in that paper ; and who was, probably, no other than the sweet American Pocahontas, who rescued from death the daring Captain Smith. There is the " Lion's Head," down whose jaws the *Spectator's* own letters were passed ; and over a great banker's in Fleet Street, the effigy of the wallet, which the founder of the firm bore when he came into London a country boy. People this street, so ornamented, with crowds of swinging chairmen, with servants bawling to clear the way, with Mr. Dean in his cassock, his lacquey marching before him ; or Mrs. Dinah in her sack, tripping to chapel, her footboy carrying her ladyship's great prayer-book ; with itinerant tradesmen, singing their hundred cries (I remember forty years ago, as boy in London city, a score of cheery, familiar cries that are silent now). Fancy the beaux thronging to the chocolate-houses, tapping their snuff-boxes as they issue thence, their periwigs appearing over the red curtains. Fancy Saccharissa, beckoning and smiling from the upper windows, and a crowd of soldiers brawling and bustling at the door—gentlemen of the Life Guards, clad in scarlet, with blue facings, and laced with gold at the seams ; gentlemen of the Horse Grenadiers, in their caps of sky-blue cloth, with the garter embroidered on the front in gold and silver ; men of the Halberdiers, in their long red coats, as bluff Harry left them, with their ruff and velvet flat caps. Perhaps the King's Majesty himself is going to St. James's as we pass. If he is going to Parliament, he is in his coach-and-eight, surrounded by his guards and the high officers of his crown. Otherwise his Majesty only uses a chair, with six footmen walking before, and six yeomen of the guard at the sides of the sedan. The officers in waiting follow the King in coaches. It must be rather slow work.

Our *Spectator* and *Tatler* are full of delightful glimpses of the town life of those days. In the company of that charming guide, we may go to the opera, the comedy, the puppet-show, the auction, even the cockpit : we can take boat at Temple Stairs, and accompany Sir Roger de Coverley and Mr. Spectator to Spring Garden—it will be called Vauxhall a few years hence, when Hogarth will paint for it. Would you not like to step back into the past, and be introduced to Mr. Addison ?—not the Right Honourable Joseph Addison, Esq., George I.'s Secretary of State, but to the delightful painter of contemporary manners ; the man who, when in good-humour himself, was the pleasantest companion in all England. I should like to go into

Lockit's with him, and drink a bowl along with Sir R. Steele (who has just been knighted by King George, and who does not happen to have any money to pay his share of the reckoning). I should not care to follow Mr. Addison to his secretary's office in Whitehall. There we get into politics. Our business is pleasure, and the town, and the coffee-house, and the theatre, and the Mall. Delightful Spectator! kind friend of leisure hours! happy companion! true Christian gentleman! How much greater, better, you are than the King Mr. Secretary kneels to!

You can have foreign testimony about old-world London, if you like; and my before-quoted friend, Charles Louis, Baron de Pöllnitz, will conduct us to it. "A man of sense," says he, "or a fine gentleman, is never at a loss for company in London, and this is the way the latter passes his time. He rises late, puts on a frock, and, leaving his sword at home, takes his cane, and goes where he pleases. The park is commonly the place where he walks, because 'tis the Exchange for men of quality. 'Tis the same thing as the Tuileries at Paris, only the park has a certain beauty of simplicity which cannot be described. The grand walk is called the Mall; is full of people at every hour of the day, but especially at morning and evening, when their Majesties often walk with the royal family, who are attended only by a half-dozen yeomen of the guard, and permit all persons to walk at the same time with them. The ladies and gentlemen always appear in rich dresses, for the English, who, twenty years ago, did not wear gold lace but in their army, are now embroidered and bedaubed as much as the French. I speak of persons of quality; for the citizen still contents himself with a suit of fine cloth, a good hat and wig, and fine linen. Everybody is well clothed here, and even the beggars don't make so ragged an appearance as they do elsewhere." After our friend, the man of quality, has had his morning or undress walk in the Mall, he goes home to dress, and then saunters to some coffee-house or chocolate-house frequented by the persons he would see. "For 'tis a rule with the English to go once a day at least to houses of this sort, where they talk of business and news, read the papers, and often look at one another without opening their lips. And 'tis very well they are so mute: for were they all as talkative as people of other nations, the coffee-houses would be intolerable, and there would be no hearing what one man said where they are so many. The chocolate-house in St. James's Street, where I go every morning to pass away the time, is always so full that a man can scarce turn about in it."

Delightful as London city was, King George I. liked to be out of it as much as ever he could ; and when there, passed all his time with his Germans. It was with them as with Blucher, a hundred years afterwards, when the bold old Reiter looked down from St. Paul's, and sighed out, " Was für Plunder ! " The German women plundered ; the German secretaries plundered ; the German cooks and intendants plundered ; even Mustapha and Mahomet, the German negroes, had a share of the booty. Take what you can get, was the old monarch's maxim. He was not a lofty monarch, certainly : he was not a patron of the fine arts : but he was not a hypocrite, he was not revengeful, he was not extravagant. Though a despot in Hanover, he was a moderate ruler in England. His aim was to leave it to itself as much as possible, and to live out of it as much as he could. His heart was in Hanover. When taken ill on his last journey, as he was passing through Holland, he thrust his livid head out of the coach-window, and gasped out, " Osnaburg, Osnaburg ! " He was more than fifty years of age when he came amongst us : we took him because we wanted him, because he served our turn ; we laughed at his uncouth German ways, and sneered at him. He took our loyalty for what it was worth ; laid hands on what money he could ; kept us assuredly from Popery and wooden shoes. I, for one, would have been on his side in those days. Cynical, and selfish, as he was, he was better than a king out of St. Germains with the French King's orders in his pocket, and a swarm of Jesuits in his train.

The Fates are supposed to interest themselves about royal personages ; and so this one had omens and prophecies specially regarding him. He was said to be much disturbed at a prophecy that he should die very soon after his wife ; and sure enough, pallid Death, having seized upon the luckless Princess in her castle of Ahlden, presently pounced upon H. M. King George I., in his travelling chariot, on the Hanover road. What postilion can outride that pale horseman? It is said, George promised one of his left-handed widows to come to her after death, if leave were granted to him to revisit the glimpses of the moon ; and soon after his demise, a great raven actually flying or hopping in at the Duchess of Kendal's window at Twickenham, she chose to imagine the King's spirit inhabited these plumes, and took special care of her sable visitor. Affecting metempsychosis—funereal royal bird ! How pathetic is the idea of the Duchess weeping over it ! When this chaste addition to our English aristocracy died, all her jewels, her plate, her plunder went over to her relations in Hanover I wonder whether her heirs took the bird, and whether it is still flapping its wings over Herrenhausen !

The days are over in England of that strange religion of king-worship, when priests flattered princes in the Temple of God ; when servility was held to be ennobling duty ; when beauty and youth tried eagerly for royal favour ; and woman's shame was held to be no dishonour. Mended morals and mended manners in courts and people, are among the priceless consequences of the freedom which George I. came to rescue and secure. He kept his compact with his English subjects ; and if he escaped no more than other men and monarchs from the vices of his age, at least we may thank him for preserving and transmitting the liberties of ours. In our free air, royal and ₁humble homes have alike been purified ; and Truth, the birthright of high and low among us, which quite fearlessly judges our greatest personages, can only speak of them now in words of respect and regard. There are stains in the portrait of the first George, and traits in it which none of us need admire ; but, among the nobler features, are justice, courage, moderation—and these we may recognize ere we turn the picture to the wall.

GEORGE THE SECOND

GEORGE THE SECOND.

IN the afternoon of the 14th of June, 1727, two horsemen might have been perceived galloping along the road from Chelsea to Richmond. The foremost, cased in the jackboots of the period, was a broad-faced, jolly-looking, and very corpulent cavalier; but, by the manner in which he urged his horse, you might see that he was a bold as well as a skilful rider. Indeed, no man loved sport better; and in the hunting-fields of Norfolk, no squire rode more boldly after the fox, or cheered Ringwood and Sweetlips more lustily, than he who now thundered over the Richmond road.

He speedily reached Richmond Lodge, and asked to see the owner of the mansion. The mistress of the house and her ladies, to whom our friend was admitted, said he could not be introduced to the master, however pressing the business might be. The master was asleep after his dinner; he always slept after his dinner: and woe be to the person who interrupted him! Nevertheless, our stout friend of the jackboots put the affrighted ladies aside, opened the forbidden

door of the bedroom, wherein upon the bed lay a little gentleman;
and here the eager messenger knelt down in his jackboots.

He on the bed started up, and with many oaths and a strong German accent asked who was there, and who dared to disturb him ?

" I am Sir Robert Walpole," said the messenger. The awakened sleeper hated Sir Robert Walpole. " I have the honour to announce to your Majesty that your royal father, King George I., died at Osnaburg, on Saturday last, the 10th inst."

" Dat is one big lie!" roared out his sacred Majesty King George II. : but Sir Robert Walpole stated the fact, and from that day until three-and-thirty years after, George, the second of the name, ruled over England.

How the King made away with his father's will under the astonished nose of the Archbishop of Canterbury ; how he was a choleric little sovereign ; how he shook his fist in the face of his father's courtiers ; how he kicked his coat and wig about in his rages, and called everybody thief, liar, rascal, with whom he differed : you will read in all the history books ; and how he speedily and shrewdly reconciled himself with the bold minister, whom he had hated during his father's life, and by whom he was served during fifteen years of his own with admirable prudence, fidelity, and success. But for Sir Robert Walpole, we should have had the Pretender back again. But for his obstinate love of peace, we should have had wars, which the nation was not strong enough nor united enough to endure. But for his resolute counsels and good-humoured resistance, we might have had German despots attempting a Hanoverian regimen over us : we should have had revolt, commotion, want, and tyrannous misrule, in place of a quarter of a century of peace, freedom, and material prosperity, such as the country never enjoyed, until that corrupter of parliaments, that dissolute tipsy cynic, that courageous lover of peace and liberty, that great citizen, patriot, and statesman governed it. In religion he was little better than a heathen ; cracked ribald jokes at bigwigs and bishops, and laughed at High Church and Low. In private life the old pagan revelled in the lowest pleasures : he passed his Sundays tippling at Richmond ; and his holidays bawling after dogs, or boozing at Houghton with boors over beef and punch. He cared for letters no more than his master did : he judged human nature so meanly that one is ashamed to have to own that he was right, and that men could be corrupted by means so base. But, with his hireling House of Commons, he defended liberty for us ; with his incredulity he kept Church-craft down. There were parsons at Oxford as double-dealing and dangerous as any priests out of Rome, and he routed them both. He gave Englishmen no conquests, but he gave them peace, and ease, and freedom ; the Three per Cents. nearly at par ; and wheat at five and six and twenty shillings a quarter.

It was lucky for us that our first Georges were not more high-minded men ; especially fortunate that they loved Hanover so much as to leave England to have her own way. Our chief troubles began when we got a king who gloried in the name of Briton, and, being born in the country, proposed to rule it. He was no more fit to govern England than his grandfather and great-grandfather, who did not try. It was righting itself during their occupation. The dangerous, noble old spirit of cavalier loyalty was dying out ; the stately old English High Church was emptying itself : the questions dropping which, on one side and the other ;—the side of loyalty, prerogative, church, and king ;—the side of right, truth, civil and religious freedom, —had set generations of brave men in arms. By the time when George III. came to the throne, the combat between loyalty and liberty was come to an end ; and Charles Edward, old, tipsy, and childless, was dying in Italy.

Those who are curious about European Court history of the last age know the memoirs of the Margravine of Bayreuth, and what a Court was that of Berlin, where George II.'s cousins ruled sovereign. Frederick the Great's father knocked down his sons, daughters, officers of state ; he kidnapped big men all Europe over to make grenadiers of : his feasts, his parades, his wine-parties, his tobacco-parties, are all described. Jonathan Wild the Great in language, pleasures, and behaviour, is scarcely more delicate than this German sovereign. Louis XV., his life, and reign, and doings, are told in a thousand French memoirs. Our George II., at least, was not a worse king than his neighbours. He claimed and took the royal exemption from doing right which sovereigns assumed. A dull little man of low tastes he appears to us in England; yet Hervey tells us that this choleric prince was a great sentimentalist, and that his letters—of which he wrote prodigious quantities—were quite dangerous in their powers of fascination. He kept his sentimentalities for his Germans and his queen. With us English, he never chose to be familiar. He has been accused of avarice, yet he did not give much money, and did not leave much behind him. He did not love the fine arts, but he did not pretend to love them. He was no more a hypocrite about religion than his father. He judged men by a low standard ; yet, with such men as were near him, was he wrong in judging as he did ? He readily detected lying and flattery, and liars and flatterers were perforce his companions. Had he been more of a dupe he might

have been more amiable. A dismal experience made him cynical.
No boon was it to him to be clear-sighted, and see only selfishness

and flattery round about him. What could Walpole tell him about
his Lords and Commons, but that they were all venal? Did not his
clergy, his courtiers, bring him the same story? Dealing with men

and women in his rude, sceptical way, he came to doubt about honour, male and female, about patriotism, about religion. "He is wild, but he fights like a man," George I., the taciturn, said of his son and successor. Courage George II. certainly had. The Electoral Prince, at the head of his father's contingent, had approved himself a good and brave soldier under Eugene and Marlborough. At Oudenarde he specially distinguished himself. At Malplaquet the other claimant to the English throne won but little honour. There was always a question about James's courage. Neither then in Flanders, nor afterwards in his own ancient kingdom of Scotland, did the luckless Pretender show much resolution. But dapper little George had a famous tough spirit of his own, and fought like a Trojan. He called out his brother of Prussia, with sword and pistol; and I wish, for the interest of romancers in general, that that famous duel could have taken place. The two sovereigns hated each other with all their might; their seconds were appointed; the place of meeting was settled; and the duel was only prevented by strong representations made to the two, of the European laughter which would have been caused by such a transaction.

Whenever we hear of dapper George at war, it is certain that he demeaned himself like a little man of valour. At Dettingen his horse ran away with him, and with difficulty was stopped from carrying him into the enemy's lines. The King, dismounting from the fiery quadruped, said bravely, "Now I know I shall not run away;" and placed himself at the head of the foot, drew his sword, brandishing it at the whole of the French army, and calling out to his own men to come on, in bad English, but with the most famous pluck and spirit. In '45, when the Pretender was at Derby, and many people began to look pale, the King never lost his courage—not he. "Pooh! don't talk to me that stuff!" he said, like a gallant little prince as he was, and never for one moment allowed his equanimity, or his business, or his pleasures, or his travels, to be disturbed. On public festivals he always appeared in the hat and coat he wore on the famous day of Oudenarde; and the people laughed, but kindly, at the odd old garment, for bravery never goes out of fashion.

In private life the Prince showed himself a worthy descendant of his father. In this respect, so much has been said about the first George's manners, that we need not enter into a description of the son's German harem. In 1705 he married a princess remarkable for beauty, for cleverness, for learning, for good temper—one of the truest and fondest wives ever prince was blessed with, and who loved him and was faithful to him, and he, in his coarse fashion, loved her to the last. It must be told to the honour of Caroline of Anspach, that, at the time when German princes thought no more of changing their religion than you of altering your cap, she refused to give up Protestantism for the other creed, although an archduke, afterwards to be an emperor, was offered to her for a bridegroom. Her Protestant relations in Berlin were angry at her rebellious spirit; it was they who tried to convert her (it is droll to think that Frederick the Great, who had no religion at all, was known for a long time in England as the Protestant hero), and these good Protestants set upon Caroline a certain Father Urban, a very skilful Jesuit, and famous winner of souls. But she routed the Jesuit; and she refused Charles VI.; and she married the little Electoral Prince of Hanover, whom she tended with love, and with every manner of sacrifice, with artful kindness, with tender flattery, with entire self-devotion, thenceforward until her life's end.

When George I. made his first visit to Hanover, his son was appointed regent during the royal absence. But this honour was never again conferred on the Prince of Wales; he and his father fell out presently. On the occasion of the christening of his second son, a royal row took place, and the Prince, shaking his fist in the Duke of Newcastle's face, called him a rogue, and provoked his august father. He and his wife were turned out of St. James's, and their princely children taken from them, by order of the royal head of the family. Father and mother wept piteously at parting from their little ones. The young ones sent some cherries, with their love, to papa and mamma; the parents watered the fruit with tears. They had no tears thirty-five years afterwards, when Prince Frederick died—their eldest son, their heir, their enemy.

The King called his daughter-in-law "*cette diablesse madame la princesse.*" The frequenters of the latter's Court were forbidden to appear at the King's: their Royal Highnesses going to Bath, we read how the courtiers followed them thither, and paid that homage in Somersetshire which was forbidden in London. That phrase of "*cette diablesse madame la princesse*" explains one cause of the wrath of her royal papa. She was a very clever woman: she had a keen sense of humour: she had a dreadful tongue: she turned into ridicule the antiquated sultan and his hideous harem. She wrote savage letters about him home to members of her family. So, driven out from the royal presence, the Prince and Princess set up for themselves in Leicester Fields, "where," says Walpole, "the most promising of the young gentlemen of the next party, and the prettiest and liveliest of the young ladies, formed the new court." Besides Leicester House, they had their lodge at Richmond, frequented by some of the pleasantest company of those days. There were the Herveys, and Chesterfield, and little Mr. Pope from Twickenham, and with him, sometimes, the savage Dean of St. Patrick's, and quite a bevy of young ladies, whose pretty faces smile on us out of history. There was Lepell, famous in ballad song; and the saucy, charming Mary Bellenden, who would have none of the Prince of Wales's fine compliments, who folded her arms across her breast, and bade H.R.H. keep off; and knocked his purse of guineas into his face, and told him she was tired of seeing him count them. He was not an august

monarch, this Augustus. Walpole tells how, one night at the royal card-table, the playful princesses pulled a chair away from under Lady Deloraine, who, in revenge, pulled the King's from under him, so that his Majesty fell on the carpet. In whatever posture one sees this royal George, he is ludicrous somehow; even at Dettingen, where he fought so bravely, his figure is absurd—calling out in his broken English, and lunging with his rapier, like a fencing-master. In contemporary caricatures, George's son, "the Hero of Culloden," is also made an object of considerable fun, as witness the preceding picture of him defeated by the French (1757) at Hastenbeck.

I refrain to quote from Walpole regarding George—for those charming volumes are in the hands of all who love the gossip of the

last century. Nothing can be more cheery than Horace's letters.
Fiddles sing all through them : wax-lights, fine dresses, fine jokes, fine
plate, fine equipages, glitter and sparkle there: never was such a
brilliant, jigging, smirking Vanity Fair as that through which he leads
us. Hervey, the next great authority, is a darker spirit. About him
there is something frightful : a few years since his heirs opened the lid
of the Ickworth box; it was as if a Pompeii was opened to us—the
last century dug up, with its temples and its games, its chariots, its
public places—lupanaria. Wandering through that city of the dead,
that dreadfully selfish time, through those godless intrigues and feasts,
through those crowds, pushing and eager, and struggling—rouged, and
lying, and fawning—I have wanted some one to be friends with. I
have said to friends conversant with that history, "Show me some
good person about that Court; find me, among those selfish courtiers,
those dissolute, gay people, some one being that I can love and regard."
There is that strutting little sultan George II.; there is that hunchbacked, beetle-browed Lord Chesterfield : there is John Hervey, with
his deadly smile, and ghastly, painted face—I hate them. There is
Hoadly, cringing from one bishopric to another : yonder comes little
Mr. Pope, from Twickenham, with his friend, the Irish Dean, in his
new cassock, bowing too, but with rage flashing from under his bushy
eyebrows, and scorn and hate quivering in his smile. Can you be
fond of these? Of Pope I might : at least I might love his genius, his
wit, his greatness, his sensibility—with a certain conviction that at
some fancied slight, some sneer which he imagined, he would turn
upon me and stab me. Can you trust the Queen? She is not of our
order : their very position makes kings and queens lonely. One inscrutable attachment that inscrutable woman has. To that she is
faithful, through all trial, neglect, pain, and time. Save her husband,
she really cares for no created being. She is good enough to her
children, and even fond enough of them : but she would chop them all
up into little pieces to please him. In her intercourse with all around
her, she was perfectly kind, gracious, and natural: but friends may
die, daughters may depart, she will be as perfectly kind and gracious
to the next set. If the King wants her, she will smile upon him, be
she ever so sad ; and walk with him, be she ever so weary ; and
laugh at his brutal jokes, be she in ever so much pain of body or
heart. Caroline's devotion to her husband is a prodigy to read of.
What charm had the little man ? What was there in those wonderful letters of thirty pages long, which he wrote to her when he was
absent, and to his mistresses at Hanover, when he was in London with

his wife? Why did Caroline, the most lovely and accomplished princess of Germany, take a little red-faced staring princeling for a husband, and refuse an emperor? Why, to her last hour, did she love him so? She killed herself because she loved him so. She had the gout, and would plunge her feet in cold water in order to walk with him. With the film of death over her eyes, writhing in intolerable pain, she yet had a livid smile and a gentle word for her master. You have read the wonderful history of that death-bed? How she bade him marry again, and the reply the old King blubbered out, " *Non, non : j'aurai des maîtresses.*" There never was such a ghastly farce. I watch the astonishing scene—I stand by that awful bedside, wondering at the ways in which God has ordained the lives, loves, rewards, successes, passions, actions, ends of his creatures—and can't but laugh, in the presence of death, and with the saddest heart. In that often-quoted passage from Lord Hervey, in which the Queen's death-bed is described, the grotesque horror of the details surpasses all satire : the dreadful humour of the scene is more terrible than Swift's blackest pages, or Fielding's fiercest irony. The man who wrote the story had something diabolical about him : the terrible verses which Pope wrote respecting Hervey, in one of his own moods of almost fiendish malignity, I fear are true. I am frightened as I look back into the past, and fancy I behold that ghastly, beautiful face ; as I think of the Queen writhing on her death-bed, and crying out, " Pray !—pray ! "— of the royal old sinner by her side, who kisses her dead lips with frantic grief, and leaves her to sin more ;—of the bevy of courtly clergymen, and the archbishop, whose prayers she rejects, and who are obliged for propriety's sake to shuffle off the anxious inquiries of the public, and vow that her Majesty quitted this life "in a heavenly frame of mind." What a life!—to what ends devoted ! What a vanity of vanities ! It is a theme for another pulpit than the lecturer's. For a pulpit ?—I think the part which pulpits play in the deaths of kings is the most ghastly of all the ceremonial : the lying eulogies, the blinking of disagreeable truths, the sickening flatteries, the simulated grief, the falsehood and sycophancies—all uttered in the name of Heaven in our State churches : these monstrous threnodies have been sung from time immemorial over kings and queens, good, bad, wicked, licentious. The State parson must bring out his commonplaces ; his apparatus of rhetorical black-hangings. Dead king or live king, the clergyman must flatter him—announce his piety whilst living, and when dead, perform the obsequies of " our most religious and gracious king."

I read that Lady Yarmouth (my most religious and gracious King's favourite) sold a bishopric to a clergyman for 5,000*l.* (He betted her 5,000*l.* that he would not be made a bishop, and he lost, and paid her.) Was he the only prelate of his time led up by such hands for consecration? As I peep into George II.'s St. James's, I see crowds of cassocks rustling up the back-stairs of the ladies of the Court; stealthy clergy slipping purses into their laps; that godless old King yawning under his canopy in his Chapel Royal, as the chaplain before him is discoursing. Discoursing about what?—about righteousness and judgment? Whilst the chaplain is preaching, the King is chattering in German almost as loud as the preacher; so loud that the clergyman— it may be one Doctor Young, he who wrote " Night Thoughts," and discoursed on the splendours of the stars, the glories of heaven, and utter vanities of this world—actually burst out crying in his pulpit because the Defender of the Faith and dispenser of bishoprics would not listen to him! No wonder that the clergy were corrupt and indifferent amidst this indifference and corruption. No wonder that sceptics multiplied and morals degenerated, so far as they depended on the influence of such a King. No wonder that Whitfield cried out in the wilderness, that Wesley quitted the insulted temple to pray on the hill-side. I look with reverence on those men at that time. Which is the sublimer spectacle—the good John Wesley, surrounded by his congregation of miners at the pit's mouth, or the Queen's chaplains mumbling through their morning office in their ante-room, under the picture of the great Venus, with the door opened into the adjoining chamber, where the Queen is dressing, talking scandal to Lord Hervey, or uttering sneers at Lady Suffolk, who is kneeling with the basin at her mistress's side? I say I am scared as I look round at this society—at this King, at these courtiers, at these politicians, at these bishops—at this flaunting vice and levity. Whereabouts in this Court is the honest man? Where is the pure person one may like? The air stifles one with its sickly perfumes. There are some old-world follies and some absurd ceremonials about our Court of the present day, which I laugh at, but as an Englishman, contrasting it with the past, shall I not acknowledge the change of to-day? As the mistress of St. James's passes me now, I salute the sovereign, wise, moderate, exemplary of life; the good mother; the good wife; the accomplished lady; the enlightened friend of art; the tender sympathizer in her people's glories and sorrows.

Of all the Court of George and Caroline, I find no one but Lady Suffolk with whom it seems pleasant and kindly to hold converse. Even the misogynist Croker, who edited her letters, loves her, and has that regard for her with which her sweet graciousness seems to have inspired almost all men and some women who came near her. I have noted many little traits which go to prove the charms of her character (it is not merely because she is charming, but because she is characteristic, that I allude to her). She writes delightfully sober letters. Addressing Mr. Gay at Tunbridge (he was, you know, a poet, penniless and in disgrace), she says : " The place you are in, has strangely filled your head with physicians and cures ; but, take my word for it, many a fine lady has gone there to drink the waters without being sick ; and many a man has complained of the loss of his heart, who had it in his own possession. I desire you will keep yours ; for I shall not be very fond of a friend without one, and I have a great mind you should be in the number of mine."

When Lord Peterborough was seventy years old, that indomitable youth addressed some flaming love, or rather gallantry, letters to Mrs. Howard—curious relics they are of the romantic manner of wooing sometimes in use in those days. It is not passion ; it is not love ; it is gallantry : a mixture of earnest and acting ; high-flown compliments, profound bows, vows, sighs and ogles, in the manner of the Clelie romances, and Millamont and Doricourt in the comedy. There was a vast elaboration of ceremonies and etiquette, of raptures—a regulated form for kneeling and wooing which has quite passed out of our downright manners. Henrietta Howard accepted the noble old earl's philandering ; answered the queer love-letters with due acknowledgment ; made a profound curtsey to Peterborough's profound bow ; and got John Gay to help her in the composition of her letters in reply to her old knight. He wrote her charming verses, in which there was truth as well as grace. " O wonderful creature ! " he writes :—

> " O wonderful creature, a woman of reason !
> Never grave out of pride, never gay out of season !
> When so easy to guess who this angel should be,
> Who would think Mrs. Howard ne'er dreamt it was she ?"

The great Mr. Pope also celebrated her in lines not less pleasant, and painted a portrait of what must certainly have been a delightful lady :—

> " I know a thing that's most uncommon —
> Envy, be silent and attend !—
> I know a reasonable woman,
> Handsome, yet witty, and a friend :

" Not warp'd by passion, aw'd by rumour,
    Not grave through pride, or gay through folly :
An equal mixture of good-humour
    And exquisite soft melancholy.

" Has she no faults, then (Envy says), sir?
    Yes, she has one, I must aver—
When all the world conspires to praise her,
    The woman's deaf, and does not hear ! "

Even the women concurred in praising and loving her. The Duchess of Queensberry bears testimony to her amiable qualities, and writes to her : " I tell you so and so, because you love children, and to have children love you." The beautiful, jolly Mary Bellenden, represented by contemporaries as " the most perfect creature ever known," writes very pleasantly to her "dear Howard," her "dear Swiss," from the country, whither Mary had retired after her marriage, and when she gave up being a maid of honour. " How do you do, Mrs. Howard ? " Mary breaks out. " How do you do, Mrs. Howard ? that is all I have to say. This afternoon I am taken with a fit of writing ; but as to matter, I have nothing better to entertain you, than news of my farm. I therefore give you the following list of the stock of eatables that I am fatting for my private tooth. It is well known to the whole county of Kent, that I have four fat calves, two fat hogs, fit for killing, twelve promising black pigs, two young chickens, three fine geese, with thirteen eggs under each (several being duck-eggs, else the others do not come to maturity) ; all this, with rabbits, and pigeons, and carp in plenty, beef and mutton at reasonable rates. Now, Howard, if you have a mind to stick a knife into anything I have named, say so ! "

A jolly set must they have been, those maids of honour. Pope introduces us to a whole bevy of them, in a pleasant letter. " I went," he says, " by water to Hampton Court, and met the Prince, with all his ladies, on horseback, coming from hunting. Mrs. Bellenden and Mrs. Lepell took me into protection, contrary to the laws against harbouring Papists, and gave me a dinner, with something I liked better, an opportunity of conversation with Mrs. Howard. We all agreed that the life of a maid of honour was of all things the most miserable, and wished that all women who envied it had a specimen of it. To eat Westphalia ham of a morning, ride over hedges and ditches on borrowed hacks, come home in the heat of the day with a fever, and (what is worse a hundred times) with a red mark on the forehead from an uneasy hat—all this may qualify them to make excellent wives for hunters. As soon as they wipe off the heat of the day, they must simper an hour and catch cold in the Princess's apartment; from thence to dinner with what appetite they may; and after that till midnight, work, walk, or think which way they please. No lone house in Wales, with a mountain and rookery, is more contemplative than this Court. Miss Lepell walked with me three or four hours by moonlight, and we met no creature of any quality but the King, who gave audience to the vice-chamberlain all alone under the garden wall."

I fancy it was a merrier England, that of our ancestors, than the island which we inhabit. People high and low amused themselves very much more. I have calculated the manner in which statesmen and persons of condition passed their time—and what with drinking, and dining, and supping, and cards, wonder how they got through their business at all. They played all sorts of games, which, with the exception of cricket and tennis, have quite gone out of our manners now. In the old prints of St. James's Park, you still see the marks along the walk, to note the balls when the Court played at Mall. Fancy Birdcage Walk now so laid out, and Lord John and Lord Palmerston knocking balls up and down the avenue! Most of those jolly sports belong to the past, and the good old games of England are only to be found in old novels, in old ballads, or the columns of dingy old newspapers, which say how a main of cocks is to be fought at Winchester between the Winchester men and the Hampton men; or how the Cornwall men and the Devon men are going to hold a great wrestling-match at Totnes, and so on.

A hundred and twenty years ago there were not only country towns in England, but people who inhabited them. We were very much more gregarious; we were amused by very simple pleasures. Every town had its fair, every village its wake. The old poets have sung a hundred jolly ditties about great cudgel-playings, famous grinning through horse-collars, great maypole meetings, and morris-dances. The girls used to run races clad in very light attire; and the kind gentry and good parsons thought no shame in looking on. Dancing bears went about the country with pipe and tabor. Certain well-known tunes were sung all over the land for hundreds of years, and high and low rejoiced in that simple music. Gentlemen who wished to entertain their female friends constantly sent for a band. When Beau Fielding, a mighty fine gentleman, was courting the lady whom he married, he treated her and her companion at his lodgings to a supper from the tavern, and after supper they sent out for a fiddler—three of them. Fancy the three, in a great wainscoted room,

in Covent Garden or Soho, lighted by two or three candles in silver
sconces, some grapes and a bottle of Florence wine on the table, and

the honest fiddler playing old tunes in quaint old minor keys, as the
Beau takes out one lady after the other, and solemnly dances with her!

The very great folks, young noblemen, with their governors, and the like, went abroad and made the great tour; the home satirists jeered at the Frenchified and Italian ways which they brought back; but the greater number of people never left the country. The jolly squire often had never been twenty miles from home. Those who did go went to the baths, to Harrogate, or Scarborough, or Bath, or Epsom. Old letters are full of these places of pleasure. Gay writes to us about the fiddlers at Tunbridge; of the ladies having merry little private balls amongst themselves; and the gentlemen entertaining them by turns with tea and music. One of the young beauties whom he met did not care for tea: "We have a young lady here," he says, "that is very particular in her desires. I have known some young ladies, who, if ever they prayed, would ask for some equipage or title, a husband or matadores: but this lady, who is but seventeen, and has 30,000*l.* to her fortune, places all her wishes on a pot of good ale. When her friends, for the sake of her shape and complexion, would dissuade her from it, she answers, with the truest sincerity, that by the loss of shape and complexion she could only lose a husband, whereas ale is her passion."

Every country town had its assembly-room—mouldy old tenements, which we may still see in deserted inn-yards, in decayed provincial cities, out of which the great wen of London has sucked all the life. York, at assize-times, and throughout the winter, harboured a large society of northern gentry. Shrewsbury was celebrated for its festivities. At Newmarket, I read of "a vast deal of good company, besides rogues and blacklegs;" at Norwich, of two assemblies, with a prodigious crowd in the hall, the rooms, and the gallery. In Cheshire (it is a maid of honour of Queen Caroline who writes, and who is longing to be back at Hampton Court, and the fun there) I peep into a country house, and see a very merry party: "We meet in the work-room before nine, eat, and break a joke or two till twelve, then we repair to our own chambers and make ourselves ready, for it cannot be called dressing. At noon the great bell fetches us into a parlour, adorned with all sorts of fine arms, poisoned darts, several pair of old boots and shoes worn by men of might, with the stirrups of King Charles I., taken from him at Edgehill,"—and there they have their dinner, after which comes dancing and supper.

As for Bath, all history went and bathed and drank there. George II. and his Queen, Prince Frederick and his Court, scarce a character one can mention of the early last century, but was seen in that famous Pump Room where Beau Nash presided, and his picture hung between the busts of Newton and Pope:

> " This picture, placed these busts between,
>   Gives satire all its strength :
> Wisdom and Wit are little seen,
>   But Folly at full length."

I should like to have seen the Folly. It was a splendid, embroidered, beruffled, snuff-boxed, red-heeled, impertinent Folly, and knew how to make itself respected. I should like to have seen that noble old madcap Peterborough in his boots (he actually had the audacity to walk about Bath in boots !), with his blue ribbon and stars, and a cabbage under each arm, and a chicken in his hand, which he had been cheapening for his dinner. Chesterfield came there many a time and gambled for hundreds, and grinned through his gout. Mary Wortley was there, young and beautiful ; and Mary Wortley, old, hideous, and snuffy. Miss Chudleigh came there, slipping away from one husband, and on the look-out for another. Walpole passed many a day there ; sickly, supercilious, absurdly dandified, and affected ; with a brilliant wit, a delightful sensibility ; and for his friends, a most tender, generous, and faithful heart. And if you and I had been alive then, and strolling down Milsom Street —hush ! we should have taken our hats off, as an awful, long, lean, gaunt figure, swathed in flannels, passed by in its chair, and a livid face looked out from the window—great fierce eyes staring from under a bushy, powdered wig, a terrible frown, a terrible Roman nose —and we whisper to one another, " There he is ! There's the great commoner ! There is Mr. Pitt ! " As we walk away, the abbey bells are set a-ringing ; and we meet our testy friend Toby Smollett, on the arm of James Quin the actor, who tells us that the bells ring for Mr. Bullock, an eminent cowkeeper from Tottenham, who has just arrived to drink the waters ; and Toby shakes his cane at the door of Colonel Ringworm—the Creole gentleman's lodgings next his own—where the colonel's two negroes are practising on the French horn.

When we try to recall social England, we must fancy it playing at cards for many hours every day. The custom is well nigh gone out among us now, but fifty years ago was general, fifty years before that almost universal, in the country. "Gaming has become so much the fashion," writes Seymour, the author of the "Court Gamester," "that he who in company should be ignorant of the games in vogue, would be reckoned low-bred, and hardly fit for conversation." There were cards everywhere. It was considered ill-bred to read in company. "Books were not fit articles for drawing-rooms," old ladies used to say. People were jealous, as it were, and angry with them. You will find in Hervey that George II. was always furious at the sight of books; and his Queen, who loved reading, had to practise it in secret in her closet. But cards were the resource of all the world. Every night, for hours, kings and queens of England sat down and handled their majesties of spades and diamonds. In European Courts, I believe the practice still remains, not for gambling, but for pastime. Our ancestors generally adopted it. " Books ! prithee, don't talk to me about books," said old Sarah Marlborough. " The only books I know are men and cards." " Dear old Sir Roger de Coverley sent all his tenants a string of hogs' puddings and a pack of cards at Christmas," says the *Spectator*, wishing to depict a kind landlord. One of the good old lady writers in whose letters I have been dipping cries out, " Sure, cards have kept us women from a great deal of scandal !" Wise old Johnson regretted that he had not learnt to play. " It is very useful in life," he says ; "it generates kindness, and consolidates society." David Hume never went to bed without his whist. We have Walpole, in one of his letters, in a transport of gratitude for the cards. " I shall build an altar to Pam," says he, in his pleasant dandified way, " for the escape of my charming Duchess of Grafton." The Duchess had been playing cards at Rome, when she ought to have been at a cardinal's concert, where the floor fell in, and all the monsignors were precipitated into the cellar. Even the Nonconformist clergy looked not unkindly on the practice. " I do not think," says one of them, "that honest Martin Luther committed sin by playing at back-gammon for an hour or two after dinner, in order by unbending his mind to promote digestion." As for the High Church parsons, they all played, bishops and all. On Twelfth-day the Court used to play in state. " This being Twelfth-day, his Majesty, the Prince of Wales, and the Knights Companions of the Garter, Thistle, and Bath, appeared in the collars of their respective orders. Their Majesties, the Prince of Wales, and three eldest Princesses, went to the Chapel Royal, preceded by the heralds. The Duke of Manchester carried the sword of State. The King and Prince made offering at the altar of gold, frankincense, and myrrh, according to the annual custom. At night their Majesties played at hazard with the nobility, for the benefit of the groom-porter ; and 'twas said the King won 600 guineas ; the Queen, 360 ; Princess Amelia, twenty ; Princess Caroline, ten ; the Duke of Grafton and the Earl of Portmore, several thousands."

Let us glance at the same chronicle, which is of the year 1731, and see how others of our forefathers were engaged.

"Cork, 15th January.—This day, one Tim Croneen was, for the murder and robbery of Mr. St. Leger and his wife, sentenced to be hanged two minutes, then his head to be cut off, and his body divided in four quarters, to be placed in four cross-ways. He was servant to Mr. St. Leger, and committed the murder with the privity of the servant-maid, who was sentenced to be burned; also of the gardener, whom he knocked on the head, to deprive him of his share of the booty."

"January 3.—A postboy was shot by an Irish gentleman on the road near Stone, in Staffordshire, who died in two days, for which the gentleman was imprisoned."

"A poor man was found hanging in a gentleman's stables at Bungay, in Suffolk, by a person who cut him down, and running for assistance, left his penknife behind him. The poor man recovering, cut his throat with the knife; and a river being nigh, jumped into it; but company coming, he was dragged out alive, and was like to remain so."

"The Honourable Thomas Finch, brother to the Earl of Nottingham, is appointed ambassador at the Hague, in the room of the Earl of Chesterfield, who is on his return home."

"William Cowper, Esq., and the Rev. Mr. John Cowper, chaplain in ordinary to her Majesty, and rector of Great Berkhampstead, in the county of Hertford, are appointed clerks of the Commissioners of Bankruptcy."

"Charles Creagh, Esq., and —— Macnamara, Esq., between whom an old grudge of three years had subsisted, which had occasioned their being bound over about fifty times for breaking the peace, meeting in company with Mr. Eyres, of Galloway, they discharged their pistols, and all three were killed on the spot—to the great joy of their peaceful neighbours, say the Irish papers."

"Wheat is 26s. to 28s., and barley 20s. to 22s. a quarter; three per cents., 92; best loaf sugar, 9¼d.; Bohea, 12s. to 14s.; Pekoe, 18s.; and Hyson, 35s. per pound."

"At Exon was celebrated with great magnificence the birthday of the son of Sir W. Courtney, Bart., at which more than 1,000 persons were present. A bullock was roasted whole; a butt of wine and several tuns of beer and cider were given to the populace. At the same time Sir William delivered to his son, then of age, Powdram Castle, and a great estate."

"Charlesworth and Cox, two solicitors, convicted of forgery, stood on the pillory at the Royal Exchange. The first was severely handled by the populace, but the other was very much favoured, and protected by six or seven fellows who got on the pillory to protect him from the insults of the mob."

"A boy killed by falling upon iron spikes, from a lamp-post, which he climbed to see Mother Needham stand in the pillory."

"Mary Lynn was burnt to ashes at the stake for being concerned in the murder of her mistress."

"Alexander Russell, the foot soldier, who was capitally convicted for a street robbery in January sessions, was reprieved for transportation; but having an estate fallen to him, obtained a free pardon."

"The Lord John Russell married to the Lady Diana Spencer, at Marlborough House. He has a fortune of 30,000l. down, and is to have 100,000l. at the death of the Duchess Dowager of Marlborough, his grandmother."

"March 1 being the anniversary of the Queen's birthday, when her Majesty entered the forty-ninth year of her age, there was a splendid appearance of nobility at St. James's. Her Majesty was magnificently dressed, and wore a flowered muslin head-edging, as did also her Royal Highness. The Lord Portmore was said to have had the richest dress, though an Italian Count had twenty-four diamonds instead of buttons."

New clothes on the birthday were the fashion for all loyal people. Swift mentions the custom several times. Walpole is constantly speaking of it; laughing at the practice, but having the very finest clothes from Paris, nevertheless. If the King and Queen were unpopular, there were very few new clothes at the drawing-room. In a paper in the *True Patriot*, No. 3, written to attack the Pretender, the Scotch, French, and Popery, Fielding supposes the Scotch and the Pretender in possession of London, and himself about to be hanged for loyalty,—when, just as the rope is round his neck, he says: "My little girl entered my bed-chamber, and put an end to my dream by pulling open my eyes, and telling me that the tailor had just brought home my clothes for his Majesty's birthday." In his "Temple Beau," the beau is dunned "for a birthday suit of velvet, 40l." Be sure that Mr. Harry Fielding was dunned too.

The public days, no doubt, were splendid, but the private Court life must have been awfully wearisome. "I will not trouble you," writes Hervey to Lady Sandon, "with any account of our occupations at Hampton Court. No mill-horse ever went in a more constant track, or a more unchanging circle; so that, by the assistance of an almanack for the day of the week, and a watch for the hour of the day, you may inform yourself fully, without any other intelligence but your memory, of every transaction within the verge of the Court. Walking, chaises, levées, and audiences fill the morning. At night the King plays at commerce and backgammon, and the Queen at quadrille, where poor Lady Charlotte runs her usual nightly gauntlet, the Queen pulling her hood, and the Princess Royal rapping her knuckles. The Duke of Grafton takes his nightly opiate of lottery, and sleeps as usual between the Princesses Amelia and Caroline. Lord Grantham strolls from one room to another (as Dryden says), like some discontented ghost that oft appears, and is forbid to speak; and stirs himself about as people stir a fire, not with any design, but in hopes to make it burn brisker. At last the King gets up; the pool finishes; and everybody has their dismission. Their Majesties retire to Lady Charlotte and my Lord Lifford; my Lord Grantham, to Lady Frances and Mr. Clark: some to supper, some to bed; and thus the evening and the morning make the day."

The King's fondness for Hanover occasioned all sorts of rough jokes among his English subjects, to whom *sauerkraut* and sausages have ever been ridiculous objects. When our present Prince Consort came among us, the people bawled out songs in the streets indicative of the absurdity of Germany in general. The sausage-shops produced enormous sausages which we might suppose were the daily food and delight of German princes. I remember the caricatures at the marriage of Prince Leopold with the Princess Charlotte. The bridegroom was drawn in rags. George III.'s wife was called by the people a beggarly German duchess; the British idea being that all princes were beggarly except British princes. King George paid us back. He thought there were no manners out of Germany. Sarah Marlborough once coming to visit the Princess, whilst her Royal Highness was whipping one of the roaring royal children, "Ah!" says George, who was standing by, "you have no good manners in England, because you are not properly brought up when you are young." He insisted that no English cook could roast, no English coachman could drive: he actually questioned the superiority of our nobility, our horses, and our roast beef!

Whilst he was away from his beloved Hanover, everything remained there exactly as in the Prince's presence. There were 800 horses in the stables, there was all the apparatus of chamberlains, court-marshals, and equerries; and court assemblies were held every

Saturday, where all the nobility of Hanover assembled at what I can't but think a fine and touching ceremony. A large arm-chair was placed in the assembly-room, and on it the King's portrait. The nobility advanced, and made a bow to the arm-chair, and to the image which Nebuchadnezzar the king had set up; and spoke under their voices before the august picture, just as they would have done had the King Churfürst been present himself.

He was always going back to Hanover. In the year 1729, he went for two whole years, during which Caroline reigned for him in England, and he was not in the least missed by his British subjects. He went again in '35 and '36; and between the years 1740 and 1755 was no less than eight times on the Continent, which amusement he was obliged to give up at the outbreak of the Seven Years' War. Here every day's amusement was the same. "Our life is as uniform as that of a monastery," writes a courtier whom Vehse quotes. "Every morning at eleven, and every evening at six, we drive in the heat to Herrenhausen, through an enormous linden avenue; and twice a day cover our coats and coaches with dust. In the King's society there never is the least change. At table, and at cards, he sees always the same faces, and at the end of the game retires into his chamber. Twice a week there is a French theatre; the other days there is play in the gallery. In this way, were the King always to stop in Hanover, one could make a ten years' calendar of his proceedings; and settle beforehand what his time of business, meals, and pleasure would be."

The old pagan kept his promise to his dying wife. Lady Yarmouth was now in full favour, and treated with profound respect by the Hanover society, though it appears rather neglected in England when she came among us. In 1740, a couple of the King's daughters went to see him at Hanover; Anna, the Princess of Orange (about whom, and whose husband and marriage-day, Walpole and Hervey have left us the most ludicrous descriptions), and Maria of Hesse-Cassel, with their respective lords. This made the Hanover court very brilliant. In honour of his high guests, the King gave several *fêtes;* among others, a magnificent masked ball, in the green theatre at Herrenhausen—the garden theatre, with linden and box for screen, and grass for a carpet, where the Platens had danced to George and his father the late sultan. The stage and a great part of the garden were illuminated with coloured lamps. Almost the whole Court appeared in white dominoes, "like," says the describer of the scene, "like spirits in the Elysian fields. At night, supper was served in the gallery with three great tables, and the King was very merry. After supper dancing was resumed, and I did not get home till five o'clock by full daylight to Hanover. Some days afterwards we had, in the opera-house at Hanover, a great assembly. The King appeared in a Turkish dress; his turban was ornamented with a magnificent agraffe of diamonds; the Lady Yarmouth was dressed as a sultana; nobody was more beautiful than the Princess of Hesse." So, while poor Caroline is resting in her coffin, dapper little George, with his red face and his white eyebrows and goggle-eyes, at sixty years of age, is dancing a pretty dance with Madame Walmoden, and capering about dressed up like a Turk! For twenty years more, that little old Bajazet went on in this Turkish fashion, until the fit came which choked the old man, when he ordered the side of his coffin to be taken out, as well as that of poor Caroline's who had preceded him, so that his sinful old bones and ashes might mingle with those of the faithful creature. O strutting Turkey-cock of Herrenhausen! O naughty little Mahomet! in what Turkish paradise are you now, and where be your painted houris? So Countess Yarmouth appeared as a sultana, and his Majesty in a Turkish dress wore an agraffe of diamonds, and was very merry, was he? Friends! he was your fathers' King as well as mine—let us drop a respectful tear over his grave.

He said of his wife that he never knew a woman who was worthy to buckle her shoe: he would sit alone weeping before her portrait, and when he had dried his eyes, he would go off to his Walmoden and talk of her. On the 25th day of October, 1760, he being then in the seventy-seventh year of his age, and the thirty-fourth of his reign, his page went to take him his royal chocolate, and behold! the most religious and gracious King was lying dead on the floor. They went and fetched Walmoden; but Walmoden could not wake him. The sacred Majesty was but a lifeless corpse. The King was dead; God save the King! But, of course, poets and clergymen decorously bewailed the late one. Here are some artless verses, in which an English divine deplored the famous departed hero, and over which you may cry or you may laugh, exactly as your humour suits:—

> " While at his feet expiring Faction lay,
> No contest left but who should best obey;
> Saw in his offspring all himself renewed;
> The same fair path of glory still pursued;
> Saw to young George Augusta's care impart
> Whate'er could raise and humanize the heart;

> Blend all his grandsire's virtues with his own,
> And form their mingled radiance for the throne—
> No farther blessing could on earth be given—
> The next degree of happiness was—heaven ! "

If he had been good, if he had been just, if he had been pure in life, and wise in council, could the poet have said much more? It was a parson who came and wept over this grave, with Walmoden sitting on it, and claimed heaven for the poor old man slumbering below. Here was one who had neither dignity, learning, morals, nor wit—who tainted a great society by a bad example ; who in youth, manhood, old age, was gross, low, and sensual ; and Mr. Porteus, afterwards my Lord Bishop Porteus, says the earth was not good enough for him, and that his only place was heaven ! Bravo, Mr. Porteus ! The divine who wept these tears over George the Second's memory wore George the Third's lawn.   I don't know whether people still admire his poetry or his sermons.

GEORGE THE THIRD

GEORGE THE THIRD.

WE have to glance over sixty years in as many minutes. To read the mere catalogue of characters who figured during that long period, would occupy our allotted time, and we should have all text and no sermon. England has to undergo the revolt of the American colonies ; to submit to defeat and separation ; to shake under the volcano of the French Revolution ; to grapple and fight for the life with her gigantic enemy Napoleon ; to gasp and rally after that tremendous struggle. The old society, with its courtly splendours, has to pass away ; generations of statesmen to rise and disappear ; Pitt to follow Chatham to the tomb ; the memory of Rodney and Wolfe to be superseded by Nelson's and Wellington's glory ; the old poets who unite us to Queen Anne's time to sink into their graves ; Johnson to die, and Scott and Byron to arise ; Garrick to delight the world with his dazzling dramatic genius, and Kean to leap on the stage and take possession of the astonished theatre. Steam has to be invented ; kings to be beheaded, banished, deposed, restored. Napoleon is to be but an episode, and George III. is to be alive through all these varied changes, to accompany his people through all these revolutions of thought, government, society ; to survive out of the old world into ours.

When I first saw England, she was in mourning for the young Princess Charlotte, the hope of the empire. I came from India as a child, and our ship touched at an island on the way home, where my black servant took me a long walk over rocks and hills until we reached a garden, where we saw a man walking. "That is he," said the black man : "that is Bonaparte ! He eats three sheep every day, and all the little children he can lay hands on !" There were people in the British dominions besides that poor Calcutta serving-man, with an equal horror of the Corsican ogre.

With the same childish attendant, I remember peeping through the colonnade at Carlton House, and seeing the abode of the great Prince Regent. I can see yet the Guards pacing before the gates of the place. The place! What place? The palace exists no more than the palace of Nebuchadnezzar. It is but a name now. Where be the sentries who used to salute as the Royal chariots drove in and out ? The chariots, with the kings inside, have driven to the realms of Pluto ; the tall Guards have marched into darkness, and the echoes of their drums are rolling in Hades. Where the palace once stood, a hundred little children are paddling up and down the steps to St. James's Park. A score of grave gentlemen are taking their tea at the " Athenæum Club ;" as many grisly warriors are garrisoning the " United Service Club " opposite. Pall Mall is the great social Exchange of London now—the mart of news, of politics, of scandal, of rumour—the English Forum, so to speak, where men discuss the last despatch from the Crimea, the last speech of Lord Derby, the next move of Lord John. And, now and then, to a few antiquarians whose thoughts are with the past rather than with the present, it is a memorial of old times and old people, and Pall Mall is our Palmyra. Look ! About this spot Tom of Ten Thousand was killed by Königsmarck's gang. In that great red house Gainsborough lived, and Culloden Cumberland, George III.'s uncle. Yonder is Sarah Marlborough's palace, just as it stood when that termagant occupied it. At 25, Walter Scott used to live ; at the house, now No. 79,* and occupied by the Society for the Propagation of the Gospel in Foreign Parts, resided Mistress Eleanor Gwynn, comedian. How often has Queen Caroline's chair issued from under yonder arch ! All the men of the Georges have passed up and down the street. It has seen Walpole's chariot and Chatham's sedan ; and Fox, Gibbon, Sheridan, on their way to Brookes's ; and stately William Pitt stalking on the arm of Dundas ; and Hanger and Tom Sheridan reeling out of Raggett's ; and Byron limping into Wattier's ; and Swift striding out of Bury Street ; and Mr. Addison and Dick Steele, both perhaps a

* 1856.

little the better for liquor ; and the Prince of Wales and the Duke of York clattering over the pavement ; and Johnson counting the posts along the streets, after dawdling before Dodsley's window ; and Horry Walpole hobbling into his carriage, with a gimcrack just bought at Christie's ; and George Selwyn sauntering into White's.

In the published letters to George Selwyn we get a mass of correspondence by no means so brilliant and witty as Walpole's, or so bitter and bright as Hervey's, but as interesting, and even more descriptive of the time, because the letters are the work of many hands. You hear more voices speaking, as it were, and more natural than Horace's dandified treble, and Sporus's malignant whisper. As one reads the Selwyn letters—as one looks at Reynolds's noble pictures illustrative of those magnificent times and voluptuous people—one almost hears the voice of the dead past ; the laughter and the chorus ; the toast called over the brimming cups ; the shout at the racecourse or the gaming-table ; the merry joke frankly spoken to the laughing fine lady. How fine those ladies were, those ladies who heard and spoke such coarse jokes ; how grand those gentlemen!

I fancy that peculiar product of the past, the fine gentleman, has almost vanished off the face of the earth, and is disappearing like the beaver or the Red Indian. We can't have fine gentlemen any more, because we can't have the society in which they lived. The people will not obey : the parasites will not be as obsequious as formerly : children do not go down on their knees to beg their parents' blessing : chaplains do not say grace and retire before the pudding : servants do not say " your honour " and " your worship " at every moment : tradesmen do not stand hat in hand as the gentleman passes : authors do not wait for hours in gentlemen's anterooms with a fulsome dedication, for which they hope to get five guineas from his lordship. In the days when there were fine gentlemen, Mr. Secretary Pitt's under-secretaries did not dare to sit down before him ; but Mr. Pitt, in his turn, went down on his gouty knees to George II. ; and when George III. spoke a few kind words to him, Lord Chatham burst into tears of reverential joy and gratitude ; so awful was the idea of the monarch, and so great the distinctions of rank. Fancy Lord John Russell or Lord Palmerston on their knees whilst the Sovereign was reading a despatch, or beginning to cry because Prince Albert said something civil !

At the accession of George III., the patricians were yet at the height of their good fortune. Society recognized their superiority, which they themselves pretty calmly took for granted. They inherited not only titles and estates, and seats in the House of Peers, but seats in the House of Commons. There were a multitude of Government places, and not merely these, but bribes of actual 500*l.* notes, which members of the House took not much shame in receiving. Fox went into Parliament at twenty : Pitt when just of age : his father when not much older. It was the good time for patricians. Small blame to them if they took and enjoyed, and over-enjoyed, the prizes of politics, the pleasures of social life.

In these letters to Selwyn, we are made acquainted with a whole society of these defunct fine gentlemen : and can watch with a curious interest a life which the novel-writers of that time, I think, have scarce touched upon. To Smollett, to Fielding even, a lord was a lord : a gorgeous being with a blue ribbon, a coroneted chair, and an immense star on his bosom, to whom commoners paid reverence. Richardson, a man of humbler birth than either of the above two, owned that he was ignorant regarding the manners of the aristocracy, and besought Mrs. Donnellan, a lady who had lived in the great world, to examine a volume of Sir Charles Grandison, and point out any errors which she might see in this particular. Mrs. Donnellan found so many faults, that Richardson changed colour ; shut up the book ; and muttered that it were best to throw it in the fire. Here, in Selwyn, we have the real original men and women of fashion of the early time of George III. We can follow them to the new club at Almack's : we can travel over Europe with them : we can accompany them not only to the public places, but to their country-houses and private society. Here is a whole company of them ; wits and prodigals ; some persevering in their bad ways : some repentant, but relapsing ; beautiful ladies, parasites, humble chaplains, led captains. Those fair creatures whom we love in Reynolds's portraits, and who still look out on us from his canvases with their sweet calm faces and gracious smiles— those fine gentlemen who did us the honour to govern us ; who inherited their boroughs ; took their ease in their patent places ; and slipped Lord North's bribes so elegantly under their ruffles—we make acquaintance with a hundred of these fine folks, hear their talk and laughter, read of their loves, quarrels, intrigues, debts, duels, divorces ; can fancy them alive if we read the book long enough. We can attend at Duke Hamilton's wedding, and behold him marry his bride with the curtain-ring : we can peep into her poor sister's death-bed : we can see Charles Fox cursing over the cards, or March bawling out the odds at Newmarket : we can imagine Burgoyne tripping off from St. James's Street to conquer the Americans, and slinking back into the club somewhat crestfallen after his beating ; we can see the young

King dressing himself for the drawing-room and asking ten thousand questions regarding all the gentlemen : we can have high life or low, the struggle at the Opera to behold the Violetta or the Zamperini—the Macaronies and fine ladies in their chairs trooping to the masquerade or Madame Cornelys's—the crowd at Drury Lane to look at the body of Miss Ray, whom Parson Hackman has just pistolled—or we can peep into Newgate, where poor Mr. Rice the forger is waiting his fate and his supper. "You need not be particular about the sauce for his fowl," says one turnkey to another : "for you know he is to be hanged in the morning." "Yes," replies the second janitor, "but the chaplain sups with him, and he is a terrible fellow for melted butter."

Selwyn has a chaplain and parasite, one Doctor Warner, than whom Plautus, or Ben Jonson, or Hogarth, never painted a better character. In letter after letter he adds fresh strokes to the portrait of himself, and completes a portrait not a little curious to look at now that the man has passed away; all the foul pleasures and gambols in which he revelled, played out ; all the rouged faces into which he leered, worms and skulls ; all the fine gentlemen whose shoebuckles he kissed, laid in their coffins. This worthy clergyman takes care to tell us that he does not believe in his religion, though, thank heaven, he is not so great a rogue as a lawyer. He goes on Mr. Selwyn's errands, any errands, and is proud, he says, to be that gentleman's proveditor. He waits upon the Duke of Queensberry—old Q.—and exchanges pretty stories with that aristocrat. He comes home "after a hard day's christening," as he says, and writes to his patron before sitting down to whist and partridges for supper. He revels in the thoughts of ox-cheek and burgundy—he is a boisterous, uproarious parasite, licks his master's shoes with explosions of laughter and cunning smack and gusto, and likes the taste of that blacking as much as the best claret in old Q.'s cellar. He has Rabelais and Horace at his greasy fingers' ends. He is inexpressibly mean, curiously jolly; kindly and good-natured in secret—a tender-hearted knave, not a venomous lickspittle. Jesse says, that at his chapel in Long Acre, "he attained a considerable popularity by the pleasing, manly, and eloquent style of his delivery." Was infidelity endemic, and corruption in the air? Around a young king, himself of the most exemplary life and undoubted piety, lived a court society as dissolute as our country ever knew. George II.'s bad morals bore their fruit in George III.'s early years; as I believe that a knowledge of that good man's example, his moderation, his frugal simplicity, and God-fearing life, tended infinitely to improve the morals of the country and purify the whole nation.

After Warner, the most interesting of Selwyn's correspondents is the Earl of Carlisle, grandfather of the amiable nobleman at present* Viceroy in Ireland. The grandfather, too, was Irish Viceroy, having previously been treasurer of the King's household; and, in 1778, the principal commissioner for treating, consulting, and agreeing upon the means of quieting the divisions subsisting in his Majesty's colonies, plantations, and possessions in North America. You may read his lordship's manifestoes in the *Royal New York Gazette.* He returned to England, having by no means quieted the colonies; and speedily afterwards the *Royal New York Gazette* somehow ceased to be published.

This good, clever, kind, highly-bred Lord Carlisle was one of the English fine gentlemen who was well-nigh ruined by the awful debauchery and extravagance which prevailed in the great English society of those days. Its dissoluteness was awful: it had swarmed over Europe after the Peace; it had danced, and raced, and gambled in all the Courts. It had made its bow at Versailles; it had run its horses on the plain of Sablons, near Paris, and created the Anglomania there: it had exported vast quantities of pictures and marbles from Rome and Florence: it had ruined itself by building great galleries and palaces for the reception of the statues and pictures: it had brought over singing-women and dancing-women from all the operas of Europe, on whom my lords lavished their thousands, whilst they left their honest wives and honest children languishing in the lonely, deserted splendours of the castle and park at home.

Besides the great London society of those days, there was another unacknowledged world, extravagant beyond measure, tearing about in the pursuit of pleasure; dancing, gambling, drinking, singing; meeting the real society in the public places (at Ranelaghs, Vauxhalls, and Ridottos, about which our old novelists talk so constantly), and outvying the real leaders of fashion in luxury, and splendour, and beauty. For instance, when the famous Miss Gunning visited Paris as Lady Coventry, where she expected that her beauty would meet with the applause which had followed her and her sister through England, it appears she was put to flight by an English lady still more lovely in the eyes of the Parisians. A certain Mrs. Pitt took a box at the opera opposite the Countess; and was so much handsomer than her ladyship, that the parterre cried out that this was the real English angel, whereupon Lady Coventry quitted Paris in a huff. The poor thing died presently of consumption, accelerated, it was said, by the red and white

* 1856.

paint with which she plastered those luckless charms of hers. (We must represent to ourselves all fashionable female Europe, at that time, as plastered with white, and raddled with red.) She left two daughters behind her, whom George Selwyn loved (he was curiously fond of little children), and who are described very drolly and pathetically in these letters, in their little nursery, where passionate little Lady Fanny, if she had not good cards, flung hers into Lady Mary's face; and where they sat conspiring how they should receive a mother-in-law whom their papa presently brought home. They got on very well with their mother-in-law, who was very kind to them; and they grew up, and they were married, and they were both divorced afterwards—poor little souls! Poor painted mother, poor society, ghastly in its pleasures, its loves, its revelries!

As for my lord commissioner, we can afford to speak about him; because, though he was a wild and weak commissioner at one time, though he hurt his estate, though he gambled and lost ten thousand pounds at a sitting—"five times more," says the unlucky gentleman, " than I ever lost before;" though he swore he never would touch a card again; and yet, strange to say, went back to the table and lost still more: yet he repented of his errors, sobered down, and became a worthy peer and a good country gentleman, and returned to the good wife and the good children whom he had always loved with the best part of his heart. He had married at one-and-twenty. He found himself, in the midst of a dissolute society, at the head of a great fortune. Forced into luxury, and obliged to be a great lord and a great idler, he yielded to some temptations, and paid for them a bitter penalty of manly remorse; from some others he fled wisely, and ended by conquering them nobly. But he always had the good wife and children in his mind, and they saved him. " I am very glad you did not come to me the morning I left London," he writes to G. Selwyn, as he is embarking for America. "I can only say, I never knew till that moment of parting, what grief was." There is no parting now, where they are. The faithful wife, the kind, generous gentleman, have left a noble race behind them: an inheritor of his name and titles, who is beloved as widely as he is known; a man most kind, accomplished, gentle, friendly, and pure; and female descendants occupying high stations and embellishing great names; some renowned for beauty, and all for spotless lives, and pious matronly virtues.

Another of Selwyn's correspondents is the Earl of March,

afterwards Duke of Queensberry, whose life lasted into this century ; and who certainly as earl or duke, young man or greybeard, was not an ornament to any possible society. The legends about old Q. are awful. In Selwyn, in Wraxall, and contemporary chronicles, the observer of human nature may follow him, drinking, gambling, intriguing to the end of his career ; when the wrinkled, palsied, tooth-less old Don Juan died, as wicked and unrepentant as he had been at the hottest season of youth and passion. There is a house in Picca-dilly, where they used to show a certain low window at which old Q. sat to his very last days, ogling through his senile glasses the women as they passed by.

There must have been a great deal of good about this lazy, sleepy George Selwyn, which, no doubt, is set to his present credit. "Your friendship," writes Carlisle to him, "is so different from anything I have ever met with or seen in the world, that when I recollect the extraordinary proofs of your kindness, it seems to me like a dream." "I have lost my oldest friend and acquaintance, G. Selwyn," writes Walpole to Miss Berry : "I really loved him, not only for his infinite wit, but for a thousand good qualities." I am glad, for my part, that such a lover of cakes and ale should have had a thousand good qualities—that he should have been friendly, generous, warm-hearted, trustworthy. "I rise at six," writes Carlisle to him, from Spa (a great resort of fashionable people in our ancestors' days), "play at cricket till dinner, and dance in the evening, till I can scarcely crawl to bed at eleven. There is a life for you ! You get up at nine ; play with Raton your dog till twelve, in your dressing-gown ; then creep down to 'White's ;' are five hours at table ; sleep till supper-time ; and then make two wretches carry you in a sedan-chair, with three pints of claret in you, three miles for a shilling." Occasionally, instead of sleeping at "White's," George went down and snoozed in the House of Commons by the side of Lord North. He represented Gloucester for many years, and had a borough of his own, Ludgershall, for which, when he was too lazy to contest Gloucester, he sat himself. "I have given directions for the election of Ludgershall to be of Lord Melbourne and myself," he writes to the Premier, whose friend he was, and who was himself as sleepy, as witty, and as good-natured as George.

If, in looking at the lives of princes, courtiers, men of rank and fashion, we must perforce depict them as idle, profligate, and criminal, we must make allowances for the rich men's failings, and recollect that we, too, were very likely indolent and voluptuous, had we no motive for work, a mortal's natural taste for pleasure, and the daily temptation of a large income. What could a great peer, with a great castle and park, and a great fortune, do but be splendid and idle ? In these letters of Lord Carlisle's from which I have been quoting, there is many a just complaint made by the kind-hearted young nobleman of the state which he is obliged to keep ; the magnificence in which he must live ; the idleness to which his position as a peer of England bound him. Better for him had he been a lawyer at his desk, or a clerk in his office ;—a thousand times better chance for happiness, education, employment, security from temptation. A few years since the profession of arms was the only one which our nobles could follow. The church, the bar, medicine, literature, the arts, commerce, were below them. It is to the middle class we must look for the safety of England : the working educated men, away from Lord North's bribery in the senate ; the good clergy not corrupted into parasites by hopes of preferment ; the tradesmen rising into manly opulence ; the painters pursuing their gentle calling : the men of letters in their quiet studies ; these are the men whom we love and like to read of in the last age. How small the grandees and the men of pleasure look beside them ! how contemptible the stories of the George III. court squabbles are beside the recorded talk of dear old Johnson ! What is the grandest entertainment at Windsor, compared to a night at the club over its modest cups, with Percy and Langton, and Goldsmith, and poor Bozzy at the table ? I declare I think, of all the polite men of that age, Joshua Reynolds was the finest gentleman. And they were good, as well as witty and wise, those dear old friends of the past. Their minds were not debauched by excess, or effeminate with luxury. They toiled their noble day's labour : they rested, and took their kindly pleasure : they cheered their holiday meetings with generous wit and hearty interchange of thought : they were no prudes, but no blush need follow their conversation : they were merry, but no riot came out of their cups. Ah ! I would have liked a night at the "Turk's Head," even though bad news had arrived from the colonies, and Doctor Johnson was growling against the rebels; to have sat with him and Goldy; and to have heard Burke, the finest talker in the world ; and to have had Garrick flashing in with a story from his theatre !—I like, I say, to think of that society ; and not merely how pleasant and how wise, but how *good* they were. I think it was on going home one night from the club that Edmund Burke—his noble soul full of great thoughts, be sure, for they never left him ; his heart full of gentleness—was accosted by a poor wandering woman, to whom he spoke words of kindness ; and moved by the tears of this Magdalen, perhaps having caused them by the good words he spoke to her, he took her home to the house of his wife and children, and never left her until he had found the means of restoring her to honesty and labour. O you fine gentlemen! you Marches, and Selwyns, and Chesterfields, how small you look by the side of these great men! Good-natured Carlisle plays at cricket all day, and dances in the evening "till he can scarcely crawl," gaily contrasting his superior virtue with George Selwyn's, "carried to bed by two wretches at midnight with three pints of claret in him." Do you remember the verses—the sacred verses—which Johnson wrote on the death of his humble friend, Levett?

> "Well tried through many a varying year,
>   See Levett to the grave descend ;
> Officious, innocent, sincere,
>   Of every friendless name the friend.
>
> "In misery's darkest cavern known,
>   His useful care was ever nigh,
> Where hopeless anguish poured the groan,
>   And lonely want retired to die.
>
> "No summons mocked by chill delay,
>   No petty gain disdained by pride,
> The modest wants of every day
>   The toil of every day supplied.
>
> "His virtues walked their narrow round,
>   Nor made a pause, nor left a void ;
> And sure the Eternal Master found
>   His single talent well employed."

Whose name looks the brightest now, that of Queensberry the wealthy duke, or Selwyn the wit, or Levett the poor physician?

I hold old Johnson (and shall we not pardon James Boswell some errors for embalming him for us?) to be the great supporter of the British monarchy and church during the last age—better than whole benches of bishops, better than Pitts, Norths, and the great Burke himself. Johnson had the ear of the nation : his immense authority reconciled it to loyalty, and shamed it out of irreligion. When George III. talked with him, and the people heard the great author's good opinion of the sovereign, whole generations rallied to the King. Johnson was revered as a sort of oracle ; and the oracle declared for church and king. What a humanity the old man had!

He was a kindly partaker of all honest pleasures : a fierce foe to all

sin, but a gentle enemy to all sinners. "What, boys, are you for a
frolic?" he cries, when Topham Beauclerc comes and wakes him up

at midnight : " I'm with you." And away he goes, tumbles on his homely old clothes, and trundles through Covent Garden with the young fellows. When he used to frequent Garrick's theatre, and had "the liberty of the scenes," he says, "All the actresses knew me, and dropped me a curtsey as they passed to the stage." That would make a pretty picture : it is a pretty picture, in my mind, of youth, folly, gaiety, tenderly surveyed by wisdom's merciful, pure eyes.

George III. and his Queen lived in a very unpretending but elegant-looking house, on the site of the hideous pile under which his granddaughter at present reposes. The King's mother inhabited Carlton House, which contemporary prints represent with a perfect paradise of a garden, with trim lawns, green arcades, and vistas of classic statues. She admired these in company with my Lord Bute, who had a fine classic taste, and sometimes counsel took and sometimes tea in the pleasant green arbours along with that polite nobleman. Bute was hated with a rage of which there have been few examples in English history. He was the butt for everybody's abuse ; for Wilkes's devilish mischief ; for Churchill's slashing satire ; for the hooting of the mob that roasted the boot, his emblem, in a thousand bonfires ; that hated him because he was a favourite and a Scotchman, calling him " Mortimer," " Lothario," I know not what names, and accusing his royal mistress of all sorts of crimes—the grave, lean, demure elderly woman, who, I dare say, was quite as good as her neighbours. Chatham lent the aid of his great malice to influence the popular sentiment against her. He assailed, in the House of Lords, " the secret influence, more mighty than the throne itself, which betrayed and clogged every administration." The most furious pamphlets echoed the cry. " Impeach the King's mother," was scribbled over every wall at the Court end of the town, Walpole tells us. What had she done? What had Frederick, Prince of Wales, George's father, done, that he was so loathed by George II. and never mentioned by George III. ? Let us not seek for stones to batter that forgotten grave, but acquiesce in the contemporary epitaph over him :—

> " Here lies Fred,
>   Who was alive, and is dead.
>   Had it been his father,
>   I had much rather.
>   Had it been his brother,
>   Still better than another.
>   Had it been his sister,
>   No one would have missed her.

> Had it been the whole generation,
> Still better for the nation.
> But since 'tis only Fred,
> Who was alive, and is dead,
> There's no more to be said."

The widow with eight children round her, prudently reconciled herself with the King, and won the old man's confidence and good-will. A shrewd, hard, domineering, narrow-minded woman, she educated her children according to her lights, and spoke of the eldest as a dull, good boy : she kept him very close : she held the tightest rein over him : she had curious prejudices and bigotries. His uncle, the burly Cumberland, taking down a sabre once, and drawing it to amuse the child—the boy started back and turned pale. The Prince felt a generous shock : " What must they have told him about me ? " he asked.

His mother's bigotry and hatred he inherited with the courageous obstinacy of his own race; but he was a firm believer where his fathers had been free-thinkers, and a true and fond supporter of the Church, of which he was the titular defender. Like other dull men, the King was all his life suspicious of superior people. He did not like Fox ; he did not like Reynolds ; he did not like Nelson, Chatham, Burke ; he was testy at the idea of all innovations, and suspicious of all innovators. He loved mediocrities ; Benjamin West was his favourite painter ; Beattie was his poet. The King lamented, not without pathos, in his after life, that his education had been neglected. He was a dull lad brought up by narrow-minded people. The cleverest tutors in the world could have done little probably to expand that small intellect, though they might have improved his tastes, and taught his perceptions some generosity.

But he admired as well as he could. There is little doubt that a letter, written by the little Princess Charlotte of Mecklenburg-Strelitz, —a letter containing the most feeble commonplaces about the horrors of war, and the most trivial remarks on the blessings of peace—struck the young monarch greatly, and decided him upon selecting the young Princess as the sharer of his throne. I pass over the stories of his juvenile loves—of Hannah Lightfoot, the Quakeress, to whom they say he was actually married (though I don't know who has ever seen the register)—of lovely black-haired Sarah Lennox, about whose beauty Walpole has written in raptures, and who used to lie in wait for the young Prince, and make hay at him on the lawn of Holland House. He sighed and he longed, but he rode away from her. Her picture still hangs in Holland House, a magnificent master-piece of Reynolds, a canvas worthy of Titian. She looks from the castle window, holding a bird in her hand, at black-eyed young Charles Fox, her nephew. The royal bird flew away from lovely Sarah. She had to figure as bridesmaid at her little Mecklenburg rival's wedding, and died in our own time a quiet old lady, who had become the mother of the heroic Napiers.

They say the little Princess who had written the fine letter about the horrors of war—a beautiful letter without a single blot, for which she was to be rewarded, like the heroine of the old spelling-book story —was at play one day with some of her young companions in the gardens of Strelitz, and that the young ladies' conversation was, strange to say, about husbands. "Who will take such a poor little princess as me?" Charlotte said to her friend, Ida von Bulow, and at that very moment the postman's horn sounded, and Ida said, "Princess! there is the sweetheart." As she said, so it actually turned out. The postman brought letters from the splendid young King of all England, who said, "Princess! because you have written such a beautiful letter, which does credit to your head and heart, come and be Queen of Great Britain, France, and Ireland, and the true wife of your most obedient servant, George!" So she jumped for joy; and went upstairs and packed all her little trunks; and set off straightway for her kingdom in a beautiful yacht, with a harpsichord on board for her to play upon, and around her a beautiful fleet, all covered with flags and streamers : and the distinguished Madame Auerbach complimented her with an ode, a translation of which may be read in the *Gentleman's Magazine* to the present day :—

> " Her gallant navy through the main
> Now cleaves its liquid way.
> There to their queen a chosen train
> Of nymphs due reverence pay.

> " Europa, when conveyed by Jove
> To Crete's distinguished shore,
> Greater attention scarce could prove,
> Or be respected more."

They met, and they were married, and for years they led the happiest, simplest lives sure ever led by married couple. It is said the King winced when he first saw his homely little bride ; but, how- ever that may be, he was a true and faithful husband to her, as she was a faithful and loving wife. They had the simplest pleasures—the very mildest and simplest—little country dances, to which a dozen couples were invited, and where the honest King would stand up and dance for three hours at a time to one tune ; after which delicious excitement they would go to bed without any supper (the Court people grumbling sadly at that absence of supper), and get up quite early the next morning, and perhaps the next night have another dance ; or the Queen would play on the spinet—she played pretty well, Haydn said —or the King would read to her a paper out of the *Spectator*, or perhaps one of Ogden's sermons. O Arcadia ! what a life it must have been ! There used to be Sunday drawing-rooms at Court ; but the young King stopped these, as he stopped all that godless gambling whereof we have made mention. Not that George was averse to any innocent pleasures, or pleasures which he thought innocent. He was a patron of the arts, after his fashion ; kind and gracious to the artists whom he favoured, and respectful to their calling. He wanted once to establish an Order of Minerva for literary and scientific characters ; the knights were to take rank after the Knights of the Bath, and to sport a straw-coloured ribbon and a star of sixteen points. But there was such a row amongst the *literati* as to the persons who should be appointed, that the plan was given up, and Minerva and her star never came down amongst us.

He objected to painting St. Paul's, as Popish practice ; accordingly, the most clumsy heathen sculptures decorate that edifice at present It is fortunate that the paintings, too, were spared, for painting and drawing were wofully unsound at the close of the last century ; and it is far better for our eyes to contemplate whitewash (when we turn them away from the clergyman) than to look at Opie's pitchy canvases, or Fuseli's livid monsters.

And yet there is one day in the year—a day when old George loved with all his heart to attend it—when I think St. Paul's presents the noblest sight in the whole world : when five thousand charity children, with cheeks like nosegays, and sweet, fresh voices, sing the hymn which makes every heart thrill with praise and happiness. I have seen a hundred grand sights in the world—coronations, Parisian splendours, Crystal Palace openings, Pope's chapels with their processions of long-tailed cardinals and quavering choirs of fat soprani —but think in all Christendom there is no such sight as Charity Children's Day. *Non Angli, sed angeli.* As one looks at that beautiful multitude of innocents : as the first note strikes : indeed one may almost fancy that cherubs are singing.

Of church music the King was always very fond, showing skill in it both as a critic and as a performer. Many stories, mirthful and affecting, are told of his behaviour at the concerts which he ordered. When he was blind and ill he chose the music for the Ancient Concerts once, and the music and words which he selected were from "Samson Agonistes," and all had reference to his blindness, his captivity, and his affliction. He would beat time with his music-roll as they sang the anthem in the Chapel Royal. If the page below was talkative or inattentive, down would come the music-roll on young scapegrace's powdered head. The theatre was always his delight. His bishops and clergy used to attend it, thinking it no shame to appear where that good man was seen. He is said not to have cared for Shakspeare or tragedy much ; farces and pantomimes were his joy ; and especially when clown swallowed a carrot or a string of sausages, he would laugh so outrageously that the lovely Princess by his side would have to say, " My gracious monarch, do compose yourself." But he continued to laugh, and at the very smallest farces, as long as his poor wits were left him.

There is something to me exceedingly touching in that simple early life of the King's. As long as his mother lived—a dozen years after his marriage with the little spinet-player—he was a great, shy, awkward boy, under the tutelage of that hard parent. She must have been a clever, domineering, cruel woman. She kept her household lonely and in gloom, mistrusting almost all people who came about her children. Seeing the young Duke of Gloucester silent and unhappy once, she sharply asked him the cause of his silence. " I am thinking," said the poor child. " Thinking, sir ! and of what ? " " I am thinking if ever I have a son I will not make him so unhappy as you make me." The other sons were all wild, except George. Dutifully every evening George and Charlotte paid their visit to the King's mother at Carlton House. She had a throat-complaint, of which she died ; but to the last persisted in driving about the streets to show she was alive. The night before her death the resolute woman talked with her son and daughter-in-law as usual, went to bed, and was found dead there in the morning. " George, be a king ! " were the words which she was for ever croaking in the ears of her son : and a king the simple, stubborn, affectionate, bigoted man tried to be.

He did his best ; he worked according to his lights ; what virtue he knew, he tried to practise ; what knowledge he could master, he strove to acquire. He was for ever drawing maps, for example, and learned geography with no small care and industry. He knew all about the family histories and genealogies of his gentry, and pretty histories he must have known. He knew the whole *Army List;* and all the facings, and the exact number of the buttons, and all the tags and laces, and the cut of all the cocked hats, pigtails, and gaiters in his army. He knew the *personnel* of the Universities; what doctors were inclined to Socinianism, and who were sound Churchmen; he knew the etiquettes of his own and his grandfather's courts to a nicety, and the smallest particulars regarding the routine of ministers, secretaries, embassies, audiences; the humblest page in the ante-room, or the meanest helper in the stables or kitchen. These parts of the royal business he was capable of learning, and he learned. But, as one thinks of an office, almost divine, performed by any mortal man—of any single being pretending to control the thoughts, to direct the faith, to order the implicit obedience of brother millions, to compel them into war at his offence or quarrel; to command, " In this way you shall trade, in this way you shall think; these neighbours shall be your allies whom you shall help, these others your enemies whom you shall slay at my orders; in this way you shall worship God;"—who can wonder that, when such a man as George took such an office on himself, punishment and humiliation should fall upon people and chief?

Yet there is something grand about his courage. The battle of the King with his aristocracy remains yet to be told by the historian who shall view the reign of George more justly than the trumpery panegyrists who wrote immediately after his decease. It was he, with the people to back him, who made the war with America; it was he and the people who refused justice to the Roman Catholics; and on both questions he beat the patricians. He bribed: he bullied: he darkly dissembled on occasion: he exercised a slippery perseverance, and a vindictive resolution, which one almost admires as one thinks his character over. His courage was never to be beat. It trampled North under foot: it bent the stiff neck of the younger Pitt: even his illness never conquered that indomitable spirit. As soon as his brain was clear, it resumed the scheme, only laid aside when his reason left him: as soon as his hands were out of the strait waistcoat, they took up the pen and the plan which had engaged him up to the moment of his malady. I believe it is by persons believing themselves in the right that nine-tenths of the tyranny of this world has been perpetrated. Arguing on that convenient premiss, the Dey of Algiers would cut off twenty heads of a morning; Father Dominic would burn a score of Jews in the presence of the Most Catholic King, and the

Archbishops of Toledo and Salamanca sing Amen. Protestants were roasted, Jesuits hung and quartered at Smithfield, and witches burned at Salem, and all by worthy people, who believed they had the best authority for their actions.

And so, with respect to old George, even Americans, whom he hated and who conquered him, may give him credit for having quite honest reasons for oppressing them. Appended to Lord Brougham's biographical sketch of Lord North are some autograph notes of the King, which let us most curiously into the state of his mind. " The times certainly require," says he, " the concurrence of all who wish to prevent anarchy. I have no wish but the prosperity of my own dominions, therefore I must look upon all who would not heartily assist me as bad men, as well as bad subjects." That is the way he reasoned. " I wish nothing but good, therefore every man who does not agree with me is a traitor and a scoundrel." Remember that he believed himself anointed by a Divine commission ; remember that he was a man of slow parts and imperfect education ; that the same awful will of Heaven which placed a crown upon his head, which made him tender to his family, pure in his life, courageous and honest, made him dull of comprehension, obstinate of will, and at many times deprived him of reason. He was the father of his people ; his rebellious children must be flogged into obedience. He was the defender of the Protestant faith ; he would rather lay that stout head upon the block than that Catholics should have a share in the government of England. And you do not suppose that there are not honest bigots enough in all countries to back kings in this kind of statesmanship? Without doubt the American war was popular in England. In 1775 the address in favour of coercing the colonies was carried by 304 to 105 in the Commons, by 104 to 29 in the House of Lords. Popular ?—so was the Revocation of the Edict of Nantes popular in France : so was the massacre of St. Bartholomew : so was the Inquisition exceedingly popular in Spain.

Wars and revolutions are, however, the politician's province. The great events of this long reign, the statesmen and orators who illustrated it, I do not pretend to make the subjects of an hour's light talk.* Let us return to our humbler duty of Court gossip. Yonder sits our little Queen, surrounded by many stout sons and fair daughters whom she bore to her faithful George. The history of the daughters,

* On the next page are the figures, as drawn by young Gilray, of Lord North, Mr. Fox, Mr. Pitt, and Mr. Burke.

as little Miss Burney has painted them to us, is delightful. They
were handsome—she calls them beautiful ; they were most kind,
loving, and lady-like ; they were gracious to every person, high and
low, who served them. They had many little accomplishments of
their own. This one drew : that one played the piano : they all
worked most prodigiously, and fitted up whole suites of rooms—pretty,
smiling Penelopes,—with their busy little needles. As we picture to
ourselves the society of eighty years ago, we must imagine hundreds
of thousands of groups of women in great high caps, tight bodies, and
full skirts, needling away, whilst one of the number, or perhaps a
favoured gentleman in a pigtail, reads out a novel to the company. Peep into the cottage at Olney, for example, and see
there Mrs. Unwin and Lady Hesketh, those high-bred ladies, those
sweet, pious women, and William Cowper, that delicate wit, that
trembling pietist, that refined gentleman, absolutely reading out
" Jonathan Wild " to the ladies ! What a change in our manners, in
our amusements, since then !

King George's household was a model of an English gentleman's
household. It was early ; it was kindly ; it was charitable ; it was
frugal ; it was orderly ; it must have been stupid to a degree which I
shudder now to contemplate. No wonder all the princes ran away
from the lap of that dreary domestic virtue. It always rose, rode,
dined at stated intervals. Day after day was the same. At the same
hour at night the King kissed his daughters' jolly cheeks ; the
Princesses kissed their mother's hand ; and Madame Thielke brought
the royal nightcap. At the same hour the equerries and women in
waiting had their little dinner, and cackled over their tea. The King
had his backgammon or his evening concert ; the equerries yawned
themselves to death in the anteroom ; or the King and his family
walked on Windsor slopes, the King holding his darling little Princess
Amelia by the hand ; and the people crowded round quite good-
naturedly ; and the Eton boys thrust their chubby cheeks under the
crowd's elbows ; and the concert over, the King never failed to take
his enormous cocked-hat off, and salute his band, and say, " Thank
you, gentlemen."

A quieter household, a more prosaic life than this of Kew or
Windsor, cannot be imagined. Rain or shine, the King rode every
day for hours ; poked his red face into hundreds of cottages round
about, and showed that shovel hat and Windsor uniform to farmers,
to pig-boys, to old women making apple dumplings ; to all sorts of
people, gentle and simple, about whom countless stories are told.

Nothing can be more undignified than these stories. When Haroun Alraschid visits a subject incog., the latter is sure to be very much the better for the caliph's magnificence. Old George showed no such royal splendour. He used to give a guinea sometimes : sometimes feel in his pockets and find he had no money : often ask a man a hundred questions : about the number of his family, about his oats and beans, about the rent he paid for his house, and ride on. On one occasion he played the part of King Alfred, and turned a piece of meat with a string at a cottager's house. When the old woman came home, she found a paper with an enclosure of money, and a note written by the royal pencil : "Five guineas to buy a jack." It was not splendid, but it was kind and worthy of Farmer George. One day, when the King and Queen were walking together, they met a little boy—they were always fond of children, the good folks—and patted the little white head. "Whose little boy are you?" asks the Windsor uniform. "I am the King's beefeater's little boy," replied the child. On which the King said, "Then kneel down, and kiss the Queen's hand." But the innocent offspring of the beefeater declined this treat. "No," said he, "I won't kneel, for if I do, I shall spoil my new breeches." The thrifty King ought to have hugged him and knighted him on the spot. George's admirers wrote pages and pages of such stories about him. One morning, before anybody else was up, the King walked about Gloucester town ; pushed over Molly the housemaid with her pail, who was scrubbing the doorsteps ; ran upstairs and woke all the equerries in their bedrooms ; and then trotted down to the bridge, where, by this time, a dozen of louts were assembled. "What ! is this Gloucester New Bridge?" asked our gracious monarch ; and the people answered him, "Yes, your Majesty." "Why, then, my boys," said he, "let us have a huzzay!" After giving them which intellectual gratification, he went home to breakfast. Our fathers read these simple tales with fond pleasure ; laughed at these very small jokes ; liked the old man who poked his nose into every cottage ; who lived on plain wholesome roast and boiled ; who despised your French kickshaws ; who was a true hearty old English gentleman. You may have seen Gilray's famous print of him—in the old wig, in the stout old hideous Windsor uniform—as the King of Brobdingnag, peering at a little Gulliver, whom he holds up in his hand, whilst in the other he has an opera-glass, through which he surveys the pigmy? Our fathers chose to set up George as the type of a great king ; and the little Gulliver was the great Napoleon. We prided ourselves on our prejudices ; we blustered

and bragged with absurd vainglory; we dealt to our enemy a
monstrous injustice of contempt and scorn; we fought him with all

weapons, mean as well as heroic. There was no lie we would not believe ; no charge of crime which our furious prejudice would not credit. I thought at one time of making a collection of the lies which the French had written against us, and we had published against them during the war : it would be a strange memorial of popular falsehood.

Their Majesties were very sociable potentates : and the Court Chronicler tells of numerous visits which they paid to their subjects, gentle and simple : with whom they dined ; at whose great country-houses they stopped ; or at whose poorer lodgings they affably partook of tea and bread-and-butter. Some of the great folks spent enormous sums in entertaining their sovereigns. As marks of special favour, the King and Queen sometimes stood as sponsors for the children of the nobility. We find Lady Salisbury was so honoured in the year 1786 ; and in the year 1802, Lady Chesterfield. The *Court News* relates how her ladyship received their Majesties on a state bed "dressed with white satin and a profusion of lace : the counterpane of white satin embroidered with gold, and the bed of crimson satin lined with white." The child was first brought by the nurse to the Marchioness of Bath, who presided as chief nurse. Then the Marchioness handed baby to the Queen. Then the Queen handed the little darling to the Bishop of Norwich, the officiating clergyman ; and, the ceremony over, a cup of caudle was presented by the Earl to his Majesty on one knee, on a large gold waiter, placed on a crimson velvet cushion. Misfortunes would occur in these interesting genuflectory ceremonies of royal worship. Bubb Dodding-ton, Lord Melcombe, a very fat, puffy man, in a most gorgeous court-suit, had to kneel, Cumberland says, and was so fat and so tight that he could not get up again. "Kneel, sir, kneel!" cried my lord in waiting to a country mayor who had to read an address, but who went on with his compliment standing. "Kneel, sir, kneel!" cries my lord, in dreadful alarm. "I can't!" says the mayor, turning round ; "don't you see I have got a wooden leg?" In the capital "Burney Diary and Letters," the home and court life of good old King George and good old Queen Charlotte are presented at portentous length. The King rose every morning at six : and had two hours to himself. He thought it effeminate to have a carpet in his bedroom. Shortly before eight, the Queen and the royal family were always ready for him, and they proceeded to the King's chapel in the castle. There were no fires in the passages : the chapel was scarcely alight ; princesses, governesses, equerries grumbled and caught cold : but cold or hot, it was their duty to go : and, wet or dry, light or dark, the stout old George was always in his place to say amen to the chaplain.

The Queen's character is represented in " Burney " at full length. She was a sensible, most decorous woman ; a very grand lady on state occasions, simple enough in ordinary life ; well read as times went, and giving shrewd opinions about books ; stingy, but not unjust ; not generally unkind to her dependants, but invincible in her notions of etiquette, and quite angry if her people suffered ill-health in her service. She gave Miss Burney a shabby pittance, and led the poor young woman a life which well-nigh killed her. She never thought but that she was doing Burney the greatest favour, in taking her from freedom, fame, and competence, and killing her off with languor in that dreary Court. It was not dreary to her. Had she been servant instead of mistress, her spirit would never have broken down : she never would have put a pin out of place, or been a moment from her duty. *She* was not weak, and she could not pardon those who were. She was perfectly correct in life, and she hated poor sinners with a rancour such as virtue sometimes has. She must have had awful private trials of her own : not merely with her children, but with her husband, in those long days about which nobody will ever know anything now ; when he was not quite insane ; when his incessant tongue was babbling folly, rage, persecution ; and she had to smile and be respectful and attentive under this intolerable ennui. The Queen bore all her duties stoutly, as she expected others to bear them. At a State christening, the lady who held the infant was tired and looked unwell, and the Princess of Wales asked permission for her to sit down. " Let her stand," said the Queen, flicking the snuff off her sleeve. *She* would have stood, the resolute old woman, if she had had to hold the child till his beard was grown. " I am seventy years of age," the Queen said, facing a mob of ruffians who stopped her sedan : " I have been fifty years Queen of England, and I never was insulted before." Fearless, rigid, unforgiving little queen ! I don't wonder that her sons revolted from her.

Of all the figures in that large family group which surrounds George and his Queen, the prettiest, I think, is the father's darling, the Princess Amelia, pathetic for her beauty, her sweetness, her early death, and for the extreme passionate tenderness with which her father loved her. This was his favourite amongst all the children : of his sons, he loved the Duke of York best. Burney tells a sad story of the poor old man at Weymouth, and how eager he was to have this darling son with him. The King's house was not big enough to hold the Prince ; and his father had a portable house erected close to his own, and at huge pains, so that his dear Frederick should be near him. He clung on his arm all the time of his visit : talked to no one else ; had talked of no one else for some time before. The Prince, so long expected, stayed but a single night. He had business in London the next day, he said. The dulness of the old King's Court stupefied York and the other big sons of George III. They scared equerries and ladies, frightened the modest little circle, with their coarse spirits and loud talk. Of little comfort, indeed, were the King's sons to the King.

But the pretty Amelia was his darling ; and the little maiden, prattling and smiling in the fond arms of that old father, is a sweet image to look on. There is a family picture in " Burney," which a man must be very hard-hearted not to like. She describes an after-dinner walk of the royal family at Windsor :—" It was really a mighty pretty procession," she says. " The little Princess, just turned of three years old, in a robe-coat covered with fine muslin, a dressed close cap, white gloves, and fan, walked on alone and first, highly delighted with the parade, and turning from side to side to see everybody as she passed ; for all the terracers stand up against the walls, to make a clear passage for the royal family the moment they come in sight. Then followed the King and Queen, no less delighted with the joy of their little darling. The Princess Royal leaning on Lady Elizabeth Waldegrave, the Princess Augusta holding by the Duchess of Ancaster, the Princess Elizabeth led by Lady Charlotte Bertie, followed. Office here takes place of rank," says Burney,—to explain how it was that Lady E. Waldegrave, as lady of the bedchamber, walked before a duchess ; — " General Bude, and the Duke of Montague, and Major Price as equerry, brought up the rear of the procession." One sees it ; the band playing its old music, the sun shining on the happy, loyal crowd ; and lighting the ancient battlements, the rich elms, and purple landscape, and bright greensward ; the royal standard drooping from the great tower yonder ; as old George passes, followed by his race, preceded by the charming infant, who caresses the crowd with her innocent smiles.

" On sight of Mrs. Delany, the King instantly stopped to speak to her ; the Queen, of course, and the little Princess, and all the rest, stood still. They talked a good while with the sweet old lady, during which time the King once or twice addressed himself to me. I caught the Queen's eye, and saw in it a little surprise, but by no means any displeasure, to see me of the party. The little Princess went up to Mrs. Delany, of whom she is very fond, and behaved like a little angel to her. She then, with a look of inquiry and recollection, came behind Mrs. Delany to look at me. 'I am afraid,' said I, in a whisper, and stooping down, 'your Royal Highness does not remember me?' Her answer was an arch little smile, and a nearer approach, with her lips pouted out to kiss me."

The Princess wrote verses herself, and there are some pretty plaintive lines attributed to her, which are more touching than better poetry :—

> " Unthinking, idle, wild, and young,
>   I laughed, and danced, and talked, and sung :
>   And, proud of health, of freedom vain,
>   Dreamed not of sorrow, care, or pain ;
>   Concluding, in those hours of glee,
>   That all the world was made for me.

> " But when the hour of trial came,
>   When sickness shook this trembling frame,
>   When folly's gay pursuits were o'er,
>   And I could sing and dance no more,
>   It then occurred, how sad 'twould be,
>   Were this world only made for me."

The poor soul quitted it—and ere yet she was dead the agonized father was in such a state, that the officers round about him were obliged to set watchers over him, and from November, 1810, George III. ceased to reign. All the world knows the story of his malady : all history presents no sadder figure than that of the old man, blind and deprived of reason, wandering through the rooms of his palace, addressing imaginary parliaments, reviewing fancied troops, holding ghostly courts. I have seen his picture as it was taken at this time, hanging in the apartment of his daughter, the Landgravine of Hesse Hombourg — amidst books and Windsor furniture, and a hundred fond reminiscences of her English home. The poor old father is represented in a purple gown, his snowy beard falling over his breast—the star of his famous Order still idly shining on it. He was not only sightless : he became utterly deaf. All light, all reason, all sound of human voices, all the pleasures of this world

of God, were taken from him. Some slight lucid moments he had ;
in one of which, the Queen, desiring to see him, entered the room,

and found him singing a hymn, and accompanying himself at the harpsichord. When he had finished, he knelt down and prayed aloud for her, and then for his family, and then for the nation, concluding with a prayer for himself, that it might please God to avert his heavy calamity from him, but if not, to give him resignation to submit. He then burst into tears, and his reason again fled.

What preacher need moralize on this story; what words save the simplest are requisite to tell it? It is too terrible for tears. The thought of such a misery smites me down in submission before the Ruler of kings and men, the Monarch Supreme over empires and republics, the inscrutable Dispenser of life, death, happiness, victory. "O brothers," I said to those who heard me first in America—"O brothers! speaking the same dear mother tongue—O comrades! enemies no more, let us take a mournful hand together as we stand by this royal corpse, and call a truce to battle! Low he lies to whom the proudest used to kneel once, and who was cast lower than the poorest: dead, whom millions prayed for in vain. Driven off his throne; buffeted by rude hands; with his children in revolt; the darling of his old age killed before him untimely; our Lear hangs over her breathless lips and cries, 'Cordelia, Cordelia, stay a little!'

> ' Vex not his ghost—oh! let him pass—he hates him
> That would upon the rack of this tough world
> Stretch him out longer !'

Hush! Strife and Quarrel, over the solemn grave! Sound, trumpets, a mournful march. Fall, dark curtain, upon his pageant, his pride, his grief, his awful tragedy."

GEORGE THE FOURTH

GEORGE THE FOURTH.

IN Twiss's amusing "Life of Eldon," we read how, on the death of the Duke of York, the old chancellor became possessed of a lock of the defunct Prince's hair; and so careful was he respecting the authenticity of the relic, that Bessy Eldon his wife sat in the room with the young man from Hamlet's, who distributed the ringlet into separate lockets, which each of the Eldon family afterwards wore. You know how, when George IV. came to Edinburgh, a better man than he went on board the royal yacht to welcome the King to his kingdom of Scotland, seized a goblet from which his Majesty had just drunk, vowed it should remain for ever as an heirloom in his family, clapped the precious glass in his pocket, and sat down on it and broke it when he got home. Suppose the good sheriff's prize unbroken now at Abbotsford, should we not smile with something like pity as we beheld it ? Suppose one of those lockets of the no-Popery Prince's hair offered for sale at Christie's, *quot libras e duce summo invenies ?* how many pounds would you find for the illustrious Duke ? Madame Tussaud has got King George's coronation robes; is there any man now alive who would kiss the hem of that trumpery ? He sleeps since thirty years : do not any of you, who remember him, wonder that you once respected and huzza'd and admired him ?

To make a portrait of him at first seemed a matter of small difficulty. There is his coat, his star, his wig, his countenance simpering under it : with a slate and a piece of chalk, I could at this very desk perform a recognizable likeness of him. And yet after reading of him in scores of volumes, hunting him through old magazines and newspapers, having him here at a ball, there at a public dinner, there at races and so forth, you find you have nothing—nothing but a coat and a wig and a mask smiling below it—nothing but a great simulacrum. His sire and grandsires were men. One knows what they were like : what they would do in given circumstances : that on occasion they fought and demeaned themselves like tough good soldiers. They had friends whom they liked according to their natures ; enemies whom they hated fiercely ; passions, and actions, and individualities of their own. The sailor King who came after George was a man : the Duke of York was a man, big, burly, loud, jolly, cursing, courageous. But this George, what was he? I look through all his life, and recognize but a bow and a grin. I try and take him to pieces, and find silk stockings, padding, stays, a coat with frogs and a fur collar, a star and blue ribbon, a pocket-handkerchief prodigiously scented, one of Truefitt's best nutty brown wigs reeking with oil, a set of teeth and a huge black stock, underwaistcoats, more underwaistcoats, and then nothing. I know of no sentiment that he ever distinctly uttered. Documents are published under his name, but people wrote them—private letters, but people spelt them. He put a great George P. or George R. at the bottom of the page and fancied he had written the paper : some bookseller's clerk, some poor author, some *man* did the work ; saw to the spelling, cleaned up the slovenly sentences, and gave the lax maudlin slipslop a sort of consistency. He must have had an individuality : the dancing-master whom he emulated, nay, surpassed—the wig-maker who curled his toupee for him—the tailor who cut his coats, had that. But, about George, one can get at nothing actual. That outside, I am certain, is pad and tailor's work ; there may be something behind, but what ? We cannot get at the character ; no doubt never shall. Will men of the future have nothing better to do than to unswathe and interpret that royal old mummy ? I own I once used to think it would be good sport to pursue him, fasten on him, and pull him down. But now I am ashamed to mount and lay good dogs on, to summon a full field, and then to hunt the poor game.

On the 12th August, 1762, the forty-seventh anniversary of the accession of the House of Brunswick to the English throne, all the bells in London pealed in gratulation, and announced that an heir to George

III. was born. Five days afterwards the King was pleased to pass
letters patent under the great seal, creating H. R. H. the Prince of
Great Britain, Electoral Prince of Brunswick Lüneburg, Duke of
Cornwall and Rothsay, Earl of Carrick, Baron of Renfrew, Lord of the
Isles, and Great Steward of Scotland, Prince of Wales and Earl of
Chester.

All the people at his birth thronged to see this lovely child ; and
behind a gilt china-screen railing in St. James's Palace, in a cradle sur-
mounted by the three princely ostrich feathers, the royal infant was
laid to delight the eyes of the lieges. Among the earliest instances of
homage paid to him, I read that "a curious Indian bow and arrows
were sent to the Prince from his father's faithful subjects in New

1780.   1790.

York." He was fond of playing with these toys : an old statesman,
orator, and wit of his grandfather's and great-grandfather's time, never
tired of his business, still eager in his old age to be well at Court, used
to play with the little Prince, and pretend to fall down dead when the
Prince shot at him with his toy bow and arrows—and get up and fall
down dead over and over again—to the increased delight of the child.
So that he was flattered from his cradle upwards ; and before his little
feet could walk, statesmen and courtiers were busy kissing them.

There is a pretty picture of the royal infant—a beautiful buxom
child—asleep in his mother's lap ; who turns round and holds a finger
to her lip, as if she would bid the courtiers around respect the baby's
slumbers. From that day until his decease, sixty-eight years after, I

suppose there were more pictures taken of that personage than of any other human being who ever was born and died—in every kind of uniform and every possible court-dress—in long fair hair, with powder, with and without a pig-tail—in every conceivable cocked-hat—in dragoon uniform—in Windsor uniform—in a field-marshal's clothes— in a Scotch kilt and tartans, with dirk and claymore (a stupendous figure)—in a frogged frock-coat with a fur collar and tight breeches and silk stockings—in wigs of every colour, fair, brown, and black,— in his famous coronation robes finally, with which performance he was so much in love that he distributed copies of the picture to all the Courts and British embassies in Europe, and to numberless clubs, town-halls, and private friends. I remember as a young man how almost every dining-room had his portrait.

THE REGENT.   THE KING.

There is plenty of biographical tattle about the Prince's boyhood. It is told with what astonishing rapidity he learned all languages, ancient and modern ; how he rode beautifully, sang charmingly, and played elegantly on the violoncello. That he was beautiful was patent to all eyes. He had a high spirit : and once, when he had had a difference with his father, burst into the royal closet and called out, " Wilkes and liberty for ever ! " He was so clever, that he confounded his very governors in learning ; and one of them, Lord Bruce, having made a false quantity in quoting Greek, the admirable young Prince instantly corrected him. Lord Bruce could not remain a governor after this humiliation ; resigned his office, and, to soothe his feelings, was actually promoted to be an earl ! It is the most wonderful reason for promoting a man that ever I heard. Lord Bruce was made an earl for a blunder in prosody ; and Nelson was made a baron for the victory of the Nile.

Lovers of long sums have added up the millions and millions which in the course of his brilliant existence this single Prince consumed. Besides his income of 50,000*l.*, 70,000*l.*, 100,000*l.*, 120,000*l.* a year, we read of three applications to Parliament : debts to the amount of 160,000*l.*, of 650,000*l.* ; besides mysterious foreign loans, whereof he pocketed the proceeds. What did he do for all this money? Why was he to have it ? If he had been a manufacturing town, or a populous rural district, or an army of five thousand men, he would not have cost more. He, one solitary stout man, who did not toil, nor spin, nor fight,—what had any mortal done that he should be pampered so ?

In 1784, when he was twenty-one years of age, Carlton Palace was given to him, and furnished by the nation with as much luxury as could be devised. His pockets were filled with money : he said it was not enough ; he flung it out of window : he spent 10,000*l.* a year for the coats on his back. The nation gave him more money, and more, and more. The sum is past counting. He was a prince most lovely to look on, and was christened Prince Florizel on his first appearance in the world. That he was the handsomest prince in the whole world was agreed by men, and alas ! by many women.

I suppose he must have been very graceful. There are so many testimonies to the charm of his manner, that we must allow him great elegance and powers of fascination. He, and the King of France's brother, the Count d'Artois, a charming young Prince who danced deliciously on the tight-rope—a poor old tottering exiled King, who asked hospitality of King George's successor, and lived awhile in the palace of Mary Stuart—divided in their youth the title of first gentleman of Europe. We in England of course gave the prize to *our* gentleman. Until George's death the propriety of that award was scarce questioned, or the doubters voted rebels and traitors. Only the other day I was reading in the reprint of the delightful "Noctes" of Christopher North. The health of THE KING is drunk in large capitals by the loyal Scotsman. You would fancy him a hero, a sage, a statesman, a pattern for kings and men. It was Walter Scott who had that accident with the broken glass I spoke of anon. He was the King's Scottish champion, rallied all Scotland to him, made loyalty the fashion, and laid about him fiercely with his claymore upon all the Prince's enemies. The Brunswicks had no such defenders as those two Jacobite commoners, old Sam Johnson, the Lichfield chapman's son, and Walter Scott, the Edinburgh lawyer's.

Nature and circumstance had done their utmost to prepare the Prince for being spoiled : the dreadful dulness of papa's Court, its stupid amusements, its dreary occupations, the maddening humdrum, the stifling sobriety of its routine, would have made a scapegrace of a much less lively prince. All the big princes bolted from that castle of *ennui* where old King George sat, posting up his books and droning over his Handel ; and old Queen Charlotte over her snuff and her tambour-frame. Most of the sturdy, gallant sons settled down after sowing their wild oats, and became sober subjects of their father and brother—not ill liked by the nation, which pardons youthful irregularities readily enough, for the sake of pluck, and unaffectedness, and good-humour.

The boy is father of the man. Our Prince signalized his entrance into the world by a feat worthy of his future life. He invented a new shoebuckle. It was an inch long and five inches broad. " It covered almost the whole instep, reaching down to the ground on either side of the foot." A sweet invention ! lovely and useful as the Prince on whose foot it sparkled. At his first appearance at a Court ball, we read that " his coat was pink silk, with white cuffs ; his waistcoat white silk, embroidered with various-coloured foil, and adorned with a profusion of French paste. And his hat was ornamented with two rows of steel beads, five thousand in number, with a button and loop of the same metal, and cocked in a new military style." What a Florizel ! Do these details seem trivial? They are the grave incidents of his life. His biographers say that when he commenced housekeeping in that splendid new palace of his, the Prince of Wales had some windy projects of encouraging literature, science, and the arts ; of having assemblies of literary characters ; and societies for the encouragement of geography, astronomy, and botany. Astronomy, geography, and botany ! Fiddlesticks ! French ballet-dancers, French cooks, horse-jockeys, buffoons, procurers, tailors, boxers, fencing-masters, china, jewel, and gimcrack merchants— these were his real companions. At first he made a pretence of having Burke and Fox and Sheridan for his friends. But how could such men be serious before such an empty scapegrace as this lad? Fox might talk dice with him, and Sheridan wine ; but what else had these men of genius in common with their tawdry young host of Carlton House? That fribble the leader of such men as Fox and Burke ! That man's opinions about the constitution, the India Bill,

justice to the Catholics—about any question graver than the button
for a waistcoat or the sauce for a partridge—worth anything ! The
friendship between the Prince and the Whig chiefs was impossible.
They were hypocrites in pretending to respect him, and if he broke
the hollow compact between them, who shall blame him ?   His natural
companions were dandies and parasites.   He could talk to a tailor or
a cook ; but, as the equal of great statesmen, to set up a creature,
lazy, weak, indolent, besotted, of monstrous vanity, and levity incurable
—it is absurd.   They thought to use him, and did for awhile ; but
they must have known how timid he was ; how entirely heartless and
treacherous, and have expected his desertion.   His next set of friends
were mere table companions, of whom he grew tired too ; then we
hear of him with a very few select toadies, mere boys from school or
the Guards, whose sprightliness tickled the fancy of the worn-out
voluptuary.   What matters what friends he had ?   He dropped all his
friends ; he never could have real friends.   An heir to the throne has
flatterers, adventurers who hang about him, ambitious men who use
him ; but friendship is denied him.

And women, I suppose, are as false and selfish in their dealings
with such a character as men.   Shall we take the Leporello part,
flourish a catalogue of the conquests of this royal Don Juan, and tell
the names of the favourites to whom, one after the other, George Prince
flung his pocket-handkerchief ?   What purpose would it answer to say
how Perdita was pursued, won, deserted, and by whom succeeded ?
What good in knowing that he did actually marry Mrs. Fitz-Herbert
according to the rites of the Roman Catholic Church ; that her
marriage settlements have been seen in London ; that the names of
the witnesses to her marriage are known.   This sort of vice that
we are now come to presents no new or fleeting trait of manners.
Debauchees, dissolute, heartless, fickle, cowardly, have been ever since
the world began.   This one had more temptations than most, and so
much may be said in extenuation for him.

It was an unlucky thing for this doomed one, and tending to lead
him yet farther on the road to the deuce, that, besides being lovely,
so that women were fascinated by him ; and heir-apparent, so that all
the world flattered him ; he should have a beautiful voice, which led
him directly in the way of drink : and thus all the pleasant devils
were coaxing on poor Florizel ; desire, and idleness, and vanity, and
drunkenness, all clashing their merry cymbals and bidding him come
on.

We first hear of his warbling sentimental ditties under the walls of

Kew Palace by the moonlit banks of Thames, with Lord Viscount Leporello keeping watch lest the music should be disturbed.

Singing after dinner and supper was the universal fashion of the day. You may fancy all England sounding with choruses, some ribald, some harmless, but all occasioning the consumption of a prodigious deal of fermented liquor.

> " The jolly Muse her wings to try no frolic flights need take,
> But round the bowl would dip and fly, like swallows round a lake,"

sang Morris in one of his gallant Anacreontics, to which the Prince many a time joined in chorus, and of which the burden is,—

> " And that I think's a reason fair to drink and fill again."

This delightful boon companion of the Prince's found " a reason fair " to forego filling and drinking, saw the error of his ways, gave up the bowl and chorus, and died retired and religious. The Prince's table no doubt was a very tempting one. The wits came and did their utmost to amuse him. It is wonderful how the spirits rise, the wit brightens, the wine has an aroma, when a great man is at the head of the table. Scott, the loyal cavalier, the King's true liegeman, the very best *raconteur* of his time, poured out with an endless generosity his store of old-world learning, kindness, and humour. Grattan contributed to it his wondrous eloquence, fancy, feeling. Tom Moore perched upon it for awhile, and piped his most exquisite little love-tunes on it, flying away in a twitter of indignation afterwards, and attacking the Prince with bill and claw. In such society, no wonder the sitting was long, and the butler tired of drawing corks. Remember what the usages of the time were, and that William Pitt, coming to the House of Commons after having drunk a bottle of port-wine at his own house, would go into Bellamy's with Dundas, and help finish a couple more.

You peruse volumes after volumes about our Prince, and find some half-dozen stock stories—indeed not many more—common to all the histories. He was good-natured; an indolent, voluptuous prince, not unkindly. One story, the most favourable to him of all, perhaps, is that as Prince Regent he was eager to hear all that could be said in behalf of prisoners condemned to death, and anxious, if possible, to remit the capital sentence. He was kind to his servants. There is a story common to all the biographies, of Molly the housemaid, who, when his household was to be broken up, owing to some reforms which he tried absurdly to practise, was discovered crying as she dusted the chairs because she was to leave a master who had a kind word for all his servants. Another tale is that of a groom of the Prince's being discovered in corn and oat peculations, and dismissed by the personage at the head of the stables; the Prince had word of John's disgrace, remonstrated with him very kindly, generously reinstated him, and bade him promise to sin no more—a promise which John kept. Another story is very fondly told of the Prince as a young man hearing of an officer's family in distress, and how he straightway borrowed six or eight hundred pounds, put his long fair hair under his hat, and so disguised carried the money to the starving family. He sent money, too, to Sheridan on his death-bed, and would have sent more had not death ended the career of that man of genius. Besides these, there are a few pretty speeches, kind and graceful, to persons with whom he was brought in contact. But he turned upon twenty friends. He was fond and familiar with them one day, and he passed them on the next without recognition. He used them, liked them, loved them perhaps in his way, and then separated from them. On Monday he kissed and fondled poor Perdita, and on Tuesday he met her and did not know her. On Wednesday he was very affectionate with that wretched Brummel, and on Thursday forgot him; cheated him even out of a snuff-box which he owed the poor dandy; saw him years afterwards in his downfall and poverty, when the bankrupt Beau sent him another snuff-box with some of the snuff he used to love, as a piteous token of remembrance and submission, and the King took the snuff, and ordered his horses, and drove on, and had not the grace to notice his old companion, favourite, rival, enemy, superior. In Wraxall there is some gossip about him. When the charming, beautiful, generous Duchess of Devonshire died—the lovely lady whom he used to call his dearest duchess once, and pretend to admire as all English society admired her—he said, "Then we have lost the best-bred woman in England." "Then we have lost the kindest heart in England," said noble Charles Fox. On another occasion, when three noblemen were to receive the Garter, says Wraxall, "A great personage observed that never did three men receive the order in so characteristic a manner. The Duke of A. advanced to the sovereign with a phlegmatic, cold, awkward air like a clown; Lord B. came forward fawning and smiling like a courtier; Lord C. presented himself easy, unembarrassed, like a gentleman!" These are the stories one has to recall about the Prince and King—kindness to a housemaid, generosity to a groom, criticism on a bow. There *are* no better stories about him: they are mean and trivial, and they characterize him. The great

war of empires and giants goes on. Day by day victories are won
and lost by the brave. Torn, smoky flags and battered eagles are
wrenched from the heroic enemy and laid at his feet; and he sits there on
his throne and smiles, and gives the guerdon of valour to the conqueror.
He! Elliston the actor, when the *Coronation* was performed, in which
he took the principal part, used to fancy himself the King, burst into
tears, and hiccup a blessing on the people. I believe it is certain
about George IV., that he had heard so much of the war, knighted so
many people, and worn such a prodigious quantity of marshal's uni-
forms, cocked hats, cock's feathers, scarlet and bullion in general, that
he actually fancied he had been present in some campaigns, and, under
the name of General Brock, led a tremendous charge of the German
legion at Waterloo.

He is dead but thirty years, and one asks how a great society could
have tolerated him? Would we bear him now? In this quarter of a
century, what a silent revolution has been working! how it has separated
us from old times and manners! How it has changed men themselves! I can see old gentlemen now among us, of perfect good
breeding, of quiet lives, with venerable grey heads, fondling their
grandchildren; and look at them, and wonder what they were once.
That gentleman of the grand old school, when he was in the 10th
Hussars, and dined at the Prince's table, would fall under it night
after night. Night after night, that gentleman sat at Brooks' or
Raggett's over the dice. If, in the petulance of play or drink, that gentleman spoke a sharp word to his neighbour, he and the other would
infallibly go out and try to shoot each other the next morning. That
gentleman would drive his friend Richmond the black boxer down to
Moulsey, and hold his coat, and shout and swear, and hurrah with
delight, whilst the black man was beating Dutch Sam the Jew. That
gentleman would take a manly pleasure in pulling his own coat off,
and thrashing a bargeman in a street row. That gentleman has been
in a watch-house. That gentleman, so exquisitely polite with ladies in
a drawing-room, so loftily courteous, if he talked now as he used
among men in his youth, would swear so as to make your hair stand
on end. I met lately a very old German gentleman, who had served
in our army at the beginning of the century. Since then he has lived
on his own estate, but rarely meeting with an Englishman, whose
language—the language of fifty years ago that is—he possesses perfectly. When this highly bred old man began to speak English to
me almost every other word he uttered was an oath: as they used
(they swore dreadfully in Flanders) with the Duke of York before

Valenciennes, or at Carlton House over the supper and cards. Read Byron's letters. So accustomed is the young man to oaths that he employs them even in writing to his friends, and swears by the post. Read his account of the doings of the young men at Cambridge, of the ribald professors, "one of whom could pour out Greek like a drunken Helot," and whose excesses surpassed even those of the young men. Read Matthews' description of the boyish lordling's housekeeping at Newstead, the skull-cup passed round, the monks' dresses from the masquerade warehouse, in which the young scape-graces used to sit until daylight, chanting appropriate songs round their wine. "We come to breakfast at two or three o'clock," Matthews says. "There are gloves and foils for those who like to amuse themselves, or we fire pistols at a mark in the hall, or we worry the wolf." A jolly life truly! The noble young owner of the mansion writes about such affairs himself in letters to his friend, Mr. John Jackson, pugilist, in London.

All the Prince's time tells a similar strange story of manners and pleasure. In Wraxall we find the Prime Minister himself, the re-doubted William Pitt, engaged in high jinks with personages of no less importance than Lord Thurlow the Lord Chancellor, and Mr. Dundas the Treasurer of the Navy. Wraxall relates how these three statesmen, returning after dinner from Addiscombe, found a turnpike open and galloped through it without paying the toll. The turnpike-man, fancying they were highwaymen, fired a blunderbuss after them, but missed them; and the poet sang,—

> " How as Pitt wandered darkling o'er the plain,
>   His reason drown'd in Jenkinson's champagne,
>   A rustic's hand, but righteous fate·withstood,
>   Had shed a premier's for a robber's blood."

Here we have the Treasurer of the Navy, the Lord High Chancellor, and the Prime Minister, all engaged in a most undoubted lark. In Eldon's "Memoirs," about the very same time, I read that the bar loved wine, as well as the woolsack. Not John Scott himself; he was a good boy always; and though he loved port-wine, loved his business and his duty and his fees a great deal better.

He has a Northern Circuit story of those days, about a party at the house of a certain Lawyer Fawcett, who gave a dinner every year to the counsel.

"On one occasion," related Lord Eldon, "I heard Lee say, 'I cannot leave Fawcett's wine. Mind, Davenport, you will go home

immediately after dinner, to read the brief in that cause that we have
to conduct to-morrow.'

"'Not I,' said Davenport. 'Leave my dinner and my wine to
read a brief! No, no, Lee; that won't do.'

"'Then,' said Lee, 'what is to be done? who else is employed?'

"*Davenport.*—'Oh! young Scott.'

"*Lee.*—'Oh! he must go. Mr. Scott, you must go home immediately, and make yourself acquainted with that cause, before our consultation this evening.'

"This was very hard upon me; but I did go, and there was an
attorney from Cumberland, and one from Northumberland, and I do
not know how many other persons. Pretty late, in came Jack Lee, as
drunk as he could be.

"'I cannot consult to-night; I must go to bed,' he exclaimed, and
away he went. Then came Sir Thomas Davenport.

"'We cannot have a consultation to-night, Mr. Wordsworth'
(Wordsworth, I think, was the name; it was a Cumberland name),
shouted Davenport. 'Don't you see how drunk Mr. Scott is? it is
impossible to consult.' Poor me! who had scarce had any dinner,
and lost all my wine—I was so drunk that I could not consult! Well,
a verdict was given against us, and it was all owing to Lawyer
Fawcett's dinner. We moved for a new trial; and I must say, for the
honour of the bar, that those two gentlemen, Jack Lee and Sir Thomas
Davenport, paid all the expenses between them of the first trial. It is
the only instance I ever knew; but they did. We moved for a new
trial (on the ground, I suppose, of the counsel not being in their
senses), and it was granted. When it came on, the following year, the
judge rose and said,—

"'Gentlemen, did any of you dine with Lawyer Fawcett yesterday?
for, if you did, I will not hear this cause till next year.'

"There was great laughter. We gained the cause that time."

On another occasion, at Lancaster, where poor Bozzy must needs
be going the Northern Circuit, "we found him," says Mr. Scott, lying
upon the pavement inebriated. We subscribed a guinea at supper for
him, and a half-crown for his clerk"—(no doubt there was a large bar,
so that Scott's joke did not cost him much),—"and sent him, when he
waked next morning, a brief, with instructions to move for what we
denominated the writ of *quare adhæsit pavimento!* with observations
duly calculated to induce him to think that it required great learning
to explain the necessity of granting it, to the judge before whom he
was to move." Boswell sent all round the town to attorneys for books

that might enable him to distinguish himself—but in vain. He moved, however, for the writ, making the best use he could of the observations in the brief. The judge was perfectly astonished, and the audience amazed. The judge said, " I never heard of such a writ—what can it be that adheres *pavimento?* Are any of you gentlemen at the bar able to explain this ?"

The bar laughed. At last one of them said,—

" My lord, Mr. Boswell last night *adhæsit pavimento.* There was no moving him for some time. At last he was carried to bed, and he has been dreaming about himself and the pavement."

The canny old gentleman relishes these jokes. When the Bishop of Lincoln was moving from the deanery of St. Paul's, he says he asked a learned friend of his, by name Will Hay, how he should move some especially fine claret, about which he was anxious.

" Pray, my lord bishop," says Hay, " how much of the wine have you ?"

The bishop said six dozen.

" If that is all," Hay answered, " you have but to ask me six times to dinner, and I will carry it all away myself."

There were giants in those days ; but this joke about wine is not so fearful as one perpetrated by Orator Thelwall, in the heat of the French Revolution, ten years later, over a frothing pot of porter. He blew the head off, and said, " This is the way I would serve all kings."

Now we come to yet higher personages, and find their doings recorded in the blushing pages of timid little Miss Burney's " Memoirs." She represents a prince of the blood in quite a royal condition. The loudness, the bigness, boisterousness, creaking boots and rattling oaths of the young princes, appear to have frightened the prim household of Windsor, and set all the teacups twittering on the tray. On the night of a ball and birthday, when one of the pretty, kind princesses was to come out, it was agreed that her brother, Prince William Henry, should dance the opening minuet with her, and he came to visit the household at their dinner.

" At dinner, Mrs. Schwellenberg presided, attired magnificently ; Miss Goldsworthy, Mrs. Stanforth, Messrs. Du Luc and Stanhope, dined with us ; and while we were still eating fruit, the Duke of Clarence entered.

" He was just risen from the King's table, and waiting for his equipage to go home and prepare for the ball. To give you an idea of the energy of his Royal Highness's language, I ought to set apart an objection to writing, or rather intimating, certain forcible words, and beg leave to show you in genuine colours a royal sailor.

"We all rose, of course, upon his entrance, and the two gentlemen placed themselves behind their chairs, while the footmen left the room. But he ordered us all to sit down, and called the men back to hand about some wine. He was in exceeding high spirits, and in the utmost good humour. He placed himself at the head of the table, next Mrs. Schwellenberg, and looked remarkably well, gay, and full of sport and mischief; yet clever withal, as well as comical.

"'Well, this is the first day I have ever dined with the King at St. James's on his birthday. Pray, have you all drunk his Majesty's health?'

"'No, your Royal Highness; your Royal Highness might make dem do dat,' said Mrs. Schwellenberg.

"'Oh, by ——, I will! Here, you' (to the footman), 'bring champagne; I'll drink the King's health again, if I die for it. Yes, I have done it pretty well already; so has the King, I promise you! I believe his Majesty was never taken such good care of before; we have kept his spirits up, I promise you; we have enabled him to go through his fatigues; and I should have done more still, but for the ball and Mary;—I have promised to dance with Mary. I must keep sober for Mary.'"

Indefatigable Miss Burney continues for a dozen pages reporting H.R.H.'s conversation, and indicating, with a humour not unworthy of the clever little author of "Evelina," the increasing state of excitement of the young sailor Prince, who drank more and more champagne, stopped old Mrs. Schwellenberg's remonstrances by giving the old lady a kiss, and telling her to hold her potato-trap, and who did not "keep sober for Mary." Mary had to find another partner that night, for the royal William Henry could not keep his legs.

Will you have a picture of the amusements of another royal Prince? It is the Duke of York, the blundering general, the beloved commander-in-chief of the army, the brother with whom George IV. had had many a midnight carouse, and who continued his habits of pleasure almost till death seized his stout body.

In Pückler Muskau's "Letters," that German Prince describes a bout with H.R.H., who in his best time was such a powerful toper that "six bottles of claret after dinner scarce made a perceptible change in his countenance."

"I remember," says Pückler, "that one evening,—indeed, it was past midnight,—he took some of his guests, among whom were the

Austrian ambassador, Count Meervelt, Count Beroldingen, and myself, into his beautiful armoury. We tried to swing several Turkish sabres, but none of us had a very firm grasp ; whence it happened that the Duke and Meervelt both scratched themselves with a sort of straight Indian sword so as to draw blood. Meervelt then wished to try if the sword cut as well as a Damascus, and attempted to cut through one of the wax candles that stood on the table. The experiment answered so ill, that both the candles, candlesticks and all, fell to the ground and were extinguished. While we were groping in the dark and trying to find the door, the Duke's aide-de-camp stammered out in great agitation, ' By G—, sir, I remember the sword is poisoned ! '

"You may conceive the agreeable feelings of the wounded at this intelligence ! Happily, on further examination, it appeared that claret, and not poison, was at the bottom of the colonel's exclamation."

And now I have one more story of the bacchanalian sort, in which Clarence and York, and the very highest personage of the realm, the great Prince Regent, all play parts. The feast took place at the Pavilion at Brighton, and was described to me by a gentleman who was present at the scene. In Gilray's caricatures, and amongst Fox's jolly associates, there figures a great nobleman, the Duke of Norfolk, called Jockey of Norfolk in his time, and celebrated for his table exploits. He had quarrelled with the Prince, like the rest of the Whigs ; but a sort of reconciliation had taken place ; and now, being a very old man, the Prince invited him to dine and sleep at the Pavilion, and the old Duke drove over from his Castle of Arundel with his famous equipage of grey horses, still remembered in Sussex.

The Prince of Wales had concocted with his royal brothers a notable scheme for making the old man drunk. Every person at table was enjoined to drink wine with the Duke—a challenge which the old toper did not refuse. He soon began to see that there was a conspiracy against him ; he drank glass for glass ; he overthrew many of the brave. At last the First Gentleman of Europe proposed bumpers of brandy. One of the royal brothers filled a great glass for the Duke. He stood up and tossed off the drink. " Now," says he, " I will have my carriage, and go home." The Prince urged upon him his previous promise to sleep under the roof where he had been so generously entertained. " No," he said ; he had had enough of such hospitality. A trap had been set for him ; he would leave the place at once and never enter its doors more.

The carriage was called, and came ; but, in the half-hour's interval, the liquor had proved too potent for the old man ; his host's generous purpose was answered, and the Duke's old grey head lay stupefied on the table. Nevertheless, when his post-chaise was announced, he

staggered to it as well as he could, and stumbling in, bade the postilions drive to Arundel. They drove him for half an hour round and round the Pavilion lawn; the poor old man fancied he was going home.

When he awoke that morning he was in bed at the Prince's hideous house at Brighton. You may see the place now for sixpence : they have fiddlers there every day ; and sometimes buffoons and mountebanks hire the Riding House and do their tricks and tumbling there. The trees are still there, and the gravel walks round which the poor old sinner was trotted. I can fancy the flushed faces of the royal Princes as they support themselves at the portico pillars, and look on at old Norfolk's disgrace ; but I can't fancy how the man who perpetrated it continued to be called a gentleman.

From drinking, the pleased Muse now turns to gambling, of which in his youth our Prince was a great practitioner. He was a famous pigeon for the play-men ; they lived upon him. Egalité Orleans, it was believed, punished him severely. A noble lord, whom we shall call the Marquis of Steyne, is said to have mulcted him in immense sums. He frequented the clubs, where play was then almost universal ; and, as it was known his debts of honour were sacred, whilst he was gambling Jews waited outside to purchase his notes of hand. His transactions on the turf were unlucky as well as discreditable : though I believe he, and his jockey, and his horse, Escape, were all innocent in that affair which created so much scandal.

Arthur's, Almack's, Bootle's, and White's were the chief clubs of the young men of fashion. There was play at all, and decayed noblemen and broken-down senators fleeced the unwary there. In Selwyn's "Letters" we find Carlisle, Devonshire, Coventry, Queensberry, all undergoing the probation. Charles Fox, a dreadful gambler, was cheated in very late times—lost 200,000*l.* at play. Gibbon tells of his playing for twenty-two hours at a sitting, and losing 500*l.* an hour. That indomitable punter said that the greatest pleasure in life, after winning, was losing. What hours, what nights, what health did he waste over the devil's books ! I was going to say what peace of mind ; but he took his losses very philosophically. After an awful night's play, and the enjoyment of the greatest pleasure but *one* in life, he was found on a sofa tranquilly reading an Eclogue of Virgil.

Play survived long after the wild Prince and Fox had given up the dice-box. The dandies continued it. Byron, Brummel—how many names could I mention of men of the world who have suffered by it ! In 1837 occurred a famous trial which pretty nigh put an end to gambling in England. A peer of the realm was found cheating at whist, and repeatedly seen to practise the trick called *sauter la coupe.* His friends at the clubs saw him cheat, and went on playing with him. One greenhorn, who had discovered his foul play, asked an old hand

what he should do. " Do !" said the Mammon of Unrighteousness.
"*Back him, you fool.*" The best efforts were made to screen him.
People wrote him anonymous letters and warned him ; but he would
cheat, and they were obliged to find him out. Since that day, when
my lord's shame was made public, the gaming-table has lost all its
splendour. Shabby Jews and blacklegs prowl about racecourses and
tavern parlours, and now and then inveigle silly yokels with greasy
packs of cards in railroad cars ; but Play is a deposed goddess, her
worshippers bankrupt and her table in rags.

So is another famous British institution gone to decay—the Ring :
the noble practice of British boxing, which in my youth was still almost
flourishing.

The Prince, in his early days, was a great patron of this national
sport, as his grand-uncle Culloden Cumberland had been before him ;
but, being present at a fight at Brighton, where one of the combatants
was killed, the Prince pensioned the boxer's widow, and declared he
never would attend another battle. " But, nevertheless,"—I read in
the noble language of Pierce Egan (whose smaller work on Pugilism
I have the honour to possess),—" he thought it a manly and decided
English feature, which ought not to be destroyed. His Majesty had
a drawing of the sporting characters in the Fives' Court placed in his
boudoir, to remind him of his former attachment and support of true
courage ; and when any fight of note occurred after he was king,
accounts of it were read to him by his desire." That gives one a fine
image of a king taking his recreation ;—at ease in a royal dressing-
gown ;—too majestic to read himself, ordering the prime minister to
read him accounts of battles : how Cribb punched Molyneux's eye, or
Jack Randall thrashed the Game Chicken.

Where my Prince *did* actually distinguish himself was in driving.
He drove once in four hours and a half from Brighton to Carlton
House—fifty-six miles. All the young men of that day were fond of
that sport. But the fashion of rapid driving deserted England ; and,
I believe, trotted over to America. Where are the amusements of our
youth? I hear of no gambling now but amongst obscure ruffians ; of
no boxing but amongst the lowest rabble. One solitary four-in-hand
still drove round the parks in London last year ; but that charioteer
must soon disappear. He was very old ; he was attired after the
fashion of the year 1825. He must drive to the banks of Styx ere
long,—where the ferry-boat waits to carry him over to the defunct
revellers who boxed and gambled and drank and drove with King
George.

The bravery of the Brunswicks, that all the family must have it, that George possessed it, are points which all English writers have agreed to admit ; and yet I cannot see how George IV. should have been endowed with this quality. Swaddled in feather-beds all his life, lazy, obese, perpetually eating and drinking, his education was quite unlike that of his tough old progenitors. His grandsires had confronted hardship and war, and ridden up and fired their pistols undaunted into the face of death. His father had conquered luxury and overcome indolence. Here was one who never resisted any temptation ; never had a desire but he coddled and pampered it ; if ever he had any nerve, frittered it away among cooks, and tailors, and barbers, and furniture-mongers, and opera-dancers. What muscle would not grow flaccid in such a life—a life that was never strung up to any action—an endless Capua without any campaign—all fiddling and flowers, and feasting, and flattery, and folly ? When George III. was pressed by the Catholic question and the India Bill, he said he would retire to Hanover rather than yield upon either point ; and he would have done what he said. But, before yielding, he was determined to fight his Ministers and Parliament ; and he did, and he beat them. The time came when George IV. was pressed too upon the Catholic claims ; the cautious Peel had slipped over to that side : the grim old Wellington had joined it ; and Peel tells us, in his " Memoirs," what was the conduct of the King. He at first refused to submit ; whereupon Peel and the Duke offered their resignations, which their gracious master accepted. He did these two gentlemen the honour, Peel says, to kiss them both when they went away. (Fancy old Arthur's grim countenance and eagle beak as the monarch kisses it !) When they were gone he sent after them, surrendered, and wrote to them a letter begging them to remain in office, and allowing them to have their way. Then his Majesty had a meeting with Eldon, which is related at curious length in the latter's " Memoirs." He told Eldon what was not true about his interview with the new Catholic converts ; utterly misled the old ex-Chancellor ; cried, whimpered, fell on his neck, and kissed him too. We know old Eldon's own tears were pumped very freely. Did these two fountains gush together ? I can't fancy a behaviour more unmanly, imbecile, pitiable. This a defender of the faith ! This a chief in the crisis of a great nation ! This an inheritor of the courage of the Georges !

Many of my hearers no doubt have journeyed to the pretty old town of Brunswick, in company with that most worthy, prudent, and polite gentleman, the Earl of Malmesbury, and fetched away Princess

Caroline, for her longing husband, the Prince of Wales. Old Queen Charlotte would have had her eldest son marry a niece of her own, that famous Louisa of Strelitz, afterwards Queen of Prussia, and who shares with Marie Antoinette in the last age the sad pre-eminence of beauty and misfortune. But George III. had a niece at Brunswick ; she was a richer Princess than her Serene Highness of Strelitz :—in fine, the Princess Caroline was selected to marry the heir to the English throne. We follow my Lord Malmesbury in quest of her ; we are introduced to her illustrious father and royal mother ; we witness the balls and fêtes of the old Court ; we are presented to the Princess herself, with her fair hair, her blue eyes, and her impertinent shoulders—a lively, bouncing, romping Princess, who takes the advice of her courtly English mentor most generously and kindly. We can be present at her very toilette, if we like ; regarding which, and for very good reasons, the British courtier implores her to be particular. What a strange Court ! What a queer privacy of morals and manners do we look into ! Shall we regard it as preachers and moralists, and cry Woe, against the open vice and selfishness and corruption ; or look at it as we do at the king in the pantomime, with his pantomime wife and pantomime courtiers, whose big heads he knocks together, whom he pokes with his pantomime sceptre, whom he orders to prison under the guard of his pantomime beefeaters, as he sits down to dine on his pantomime pudding? It is grave, it is sad : it is theme most curious for moral and political speculation ; it is monstrous, grotesque, laughable, with its prodigious littlenesses, etiquettes, cere-monials, sham moralities ; it is as serious as a sermon, and as absurd and outrageous as Punch's puppet-show.

Malmesbury tells us of the private life of the Duke, Princess Caroline's father, who was to die, like his warlike son, in arms against the French ; presents us to his courtiers, his favourite ; his Duchess, George III.'s sister, a grim old Princess, who took the British envoy aside and told him wicked old stories of wicked old dead people and times ; who came to England afterwards when her nephew was Regent, and lived in a shabby furnished lodging, old, and dingy, and deserted, and grotesque, but somehow royal. And we go with him to the Duke to demand the Princess's hand in form, and we hear the Brunswick guns fire their adieux of salute, as H.R.H. the Princess of Wales departs in the frost and snow ; and we visit the domains of the Prince Bishop of Osnaburg—the Duke of York of our early time ; and we dodge about from the French revolutionists, whose ragged legions are pouring over Holland and Germany, and gaily

trampling down the old world to the tune of "*Ça ira;*" and we take
shipping at Stade, and we land at Greenwich, where the Princess's
ladies and the Prince's ladies are in waiting to receive her Royal
Highness.

What a history follows! Arrived in London, the bridegroom

hastened eagerly to receive his bride. When she was first presented
to him, Lord Malmesbury says she very properly attempted to kneel.
" He raised her gracefully enough, embraced her, and turning round
to me, said,—

" ' Harris, I am not well ; pray get me a glass of brandy.'

" I said, ' Sir, had you not better have a glass of water?'

"Upon which, much out of humour, he said, with an oath, 'No ; I will go to the Queen.'"

What could be expected from a wedding which had such a beginning—from such a bridegroom and such a bride? I am not going to carry you through the scandal of that story, or follow the poor Princess through all her vagaries ; her balls and her dances, her travels to Jerusalem and Naples, her jigs, and her junketings, and her tears. As I read her trial in history, I vote she is not guilty. I don't say it is an impartial verdict ; but as one reads her story the heart bleeds for the kindly, generous, outraged creature. If wrong there be, let it lie at his door who wickedly thrust her from it. Spite of her follies, the great hearty people of England loved, and protected, and pitied her. "God bless you ! we will bring your husband back to you," said a mechanic one day, as she told Lady Charlotte Bury with tears streaming down her cheeks. They could not bring that husband back ; they could not cleanse that selfish heart. Was hers the only one he had wounded? Steeped in selfishness, impotent for faithful attachment and manly enduring love,—had it not survived remorse, was it not accustomed to desertion?

Malmesbury gives us the beginning of the marriage story ;—how the Prince reeled into chapel to be married ; how he hiccupped out his vows of fidelity—you know how he kept them : how he pursued the woman whom he had married ; to what a state he brought her ; with what blows he struck her ; with what malignity he pursued her ; what his treatment of his daughter was ; and what his own life. *He* the first gentleman of Europe ! There is no stronger satire on the proud English society of that day, than that they admired George.

No, thank God, we can tell of better gentlemen ; and whilst our eyes turn away, shocked, from this monstrous image of pride, vanity, weakness, they may see in that England over which the last George pretended to reign, some who merit indeed the title of gentlemen, some who make our hearts beat when we hear their names, and whose memory we fondly salute when that of yonder imperial mannikin is tumbled into oblivion. I will take men of my own profession of letters. I will take Walter Scott, who loved the King, and who was his sword and buckler, and championed him like that brave Highlander in his own story, who fights round his craven chief. What a good gentleman ! What a friendly soul, what a generous hand, what an amiable life was that of the noble Sir Walter ! I will take another man of letters, whose life I admire even more,—an English worthy, doing his duty for fifty noble years of labour, day by day storing up learning, day by day working for scant wages, most charitable out of his small means, bravely faithful to the calling which he had chosen, refusing to turn from his path for popular praise or princes' favour ;—I mean *Robert Southey*. We have left his old political landmarks miles and miles behind ; we protest against his dogmatism ; nay, we begin to forget it and his politics : but I hope his life will not be forgotten, for it is sublime in its simplicity, its energy, its honour, its affection. In the combat between Time and Thalaba, I suspect the former destroyer has conquered. Kehama's Curse frightens very few readers now ; but Southey's private letters are worth piles of epics, and are sure to last among us, as long as kind hearts like to sympathize with goodness and purity, and love and upright life. " If your feelings are like mine," he writes to his wife, " I will not go to Lisbon without you, or I will stay at home, and not part from you. For though not unhappy when away, still without you I am not happy. For your sake, as well as my own and little Edith's, I will not consent to any separation ; the growth of a year's love between her and me, if it please God she should live, is a thing too delightful in itself, and too valuable in its consequences, to be given up for any light inconvenience on your part or mine. . . On these things we will talk at leisure ; only, dear, dear Edith, *we must not part !* "

This was a poor literary gentleman. The First Gentleman in Europe had a wife and daughter too. Did he love them so ? Was he faithful to them ? Did he sacrifice ease for them, or show them the sacred examples of religion and honour ? Heaven gave the Great English Prodigal no such good fortune. Peel proposed to make a baronet of Southey ; and to this advancement the King agreed. The poet nobly rejected the offered promotion.

" I have," he wrote, " a pension of 200*l.* a year, conferred upon me by the good offices of my old friend C. Wynn, and I have the laureate-ship. The salary of the latter was immediately appropriated, as far as it went, to a life-insurance for 3,000*l.*, which, with an earlier insurance, is the sole provision I have made for my family. All beyond must be derived from my own industry. Writing for a livelihood, a livelihood is all that I have gained ; for, having also something better in view, and never, therefore, having courted popularity, nor written for the mere sake of gain, it has not been possible for me to lay by anything. Last year, for the first time in my life, I was provided with a year's expenditure beforehand. This exposition may show how unbecoming and unwise it would be to accept the rank which, so greatly to my honour, you have solicited for me."

How noble his poverty is, compared to the wealth of his master ! His acceptance even of a pension was made the object of his opponents' satire : but think of the merit and modesty of this State pensioner ; and that other enormous drawer of public money, who receives 100,000*l.* a year, and comes to Parliament with a request for 650,000*l.* more !

Another true knight of those days was Cuthbert Collingwood ; and I think, since heaven made gentlemen, there is no record of a better one than that. Of brighter deeds, I grant you, we may read performed by others ; but where of a nobler, kinder, more beautiful life of duty, of a gentler, truer heart ? Beyond dazzle of success and blaze of genius, I fancy shining a hundred and a hundred times higher, the sublime purity of Collingwood's gentle glory. His heroism stirs British hearts when we recall it. His love, and goodness, and piety make one thrill with happy emotion. As one reads of him and his great comrade going into the victory with which their names are immortally connected, how the old English word comes up, and that old English feeling of what I should like to call Christian honour ! What gentlemen they were, what great hearts they had ! "We can, my dear Coll," writes Nelson to him, "have no little jealousies ; we have only one great object in view,—that of meeting the enemy, and getting a glorious peace for our country." At Trafalgar, when the "Royal Sovereign" was pressing alone into the midst of the combined fleets, Lord Nelson said to Captain Blackwood : "See how that noble fellow, Collingwood, takes his ship into action ! How I envy him !" The very same throb and impulse of heroic generosity was beating in Collingwood's honest bosom. As he led into the fight, he said : "What would Nelson give to be here !"

After the action of the 1st of June, he writes :—"We cruised for a few days, like disappointed people looking for what they could not find, *until the morning of little Sarah's birthday*, between eight and nine o'clock, when the French fleet, of twenty-five sail of the line, was discovered to windward. We chased them, and they bore down within about five miles of us. The night was spent in watching and preparation for the succeeding day ; and many a blessing did I send forth to my Sarah, lest I should never bless her more. At dawn, we made our approach on the enemy, then drew up, dressed our ranks, and it was about eight when the admiral made the signal for each ship to engage her opponent, and bring her to close action ; and then down we went under a crowd of sail, and in a manner that would have animated the coldest heart, and struck terror into the most intrepid enemy. The ship we were to engage was two ahead of the French admiral, so we had to go through his fire and that of two ships next to him, and received all their broadsides two or three times before we fired a gun. It was then near ten o'clock. I observed to the admiral that about that time our wives were going to church, but that I thought the peal we should ring about the Frenchman's ear would outdo their parish bells."

There are no words to tell what the heart feels in reading the simple phrases of such a hero. Here is victory and courage, but love sublimer and superior. Here is a Christian soldier spending the night before battle in watching and preparing for the succeeding day, thinking of his dearest home, and sending many blessings forth to his Sarah, "lest he should never bless her more." Who would not say Amen to his supplication? It was a benediction to his country—the prayer of that intrepid loving heart.

We have spoken of a good soldier and good men of letters as specimens of English gentlemen of the age just past : may we not also —many of my elder hearers, I am sure, have read, and fondly remember his delightful story—speak of a good divine, and mention Reginald Heber as one of the best of English gentlemen? The charming poet, the happy possessor of all sorts of gifts and accomplishments, birth, wit, fame, high character, competence—he was the beloved parish priest in his own home of Hodnet, "counselling his people in their troubles, advising them in their difficulties, comforting them in distress, kneeling often at their sick beds at the hazard of his own life ; exhorting, encouraging where there was need : where there was strife the peace-maker ; where there was want the free giver."

When the Indian bishopric was offered to him he refused at first ; but after communing with himself (and committing his case to the quarter whither such pious men are wont to carry their doubts), he withdrew his refusal, and prepared himself for his mission and to leave his beloved parish. "Little children, love one another, and forgive one another," were the last sacred words he said to his weeping people. He parted with them, knowing, perhaps, he should see them no more. Like those other good men of whom we have just spoken, love and duty were his life's aim. Happy he, happy they who were so gloriously faithful to both ! He writes to his wife those charming lines on his journey :—

> " If thou, my love, wert by my side, my babies at my knee,
> How gladly would our pinnace glide o'er Gunga's mimic sea !

I miss thee at the dawning gray, when, on our deck reclined,
In careless ease my limbs I lay and woo the cooler wind.

I miss thee when by Gunga's stream my twilight steps I guide ;
But most beneath the lamp's pale beam I miss thee by my side.

I spread my books, my pencil try, the lingering noon to cheer ;
But miss thy kind approving eye, thy meek attentive ear.

But when of morn and eve the star beholds me on my knee,
I feel, though thou art distant far, thy prayers ascend for me.

Then on ! then on ! where duty leads my course be onward still,—
O'er broad Hindostan's sultry meads, or bleak Almorah's hill.

That course nor Delhi's kingly gates, nor wild Malwah detain,
For sweet the bliss us both awaits by yonder western main.

Thy towers, Bombay, gleam bright, they say, across the dark blue sea :
But ne'er were hearts so blithe and gay as then shall meet in thee ! "

Is it not Collingwood and Sarah, and Southey and Edith? His affection is part of his life. What were life without it ? Without love, I can fancy no gentleman.

How touching is a remark Heber makes in his "Travels through India," that on inquiring of the natives at a town, which of the governors of India stood highest in the opinion of the people, he found that, though Lord Wellesley and Warren Hastings were honoured as the two greatest men who had ever ruled this part of the world, the people spoke with chief affection of Judge Cleveland, who had died, aged twenty-nine, in 1784. The people have built a monument over him, and still hold a religious feast in his memory. So does his own country still tend with a heart's regard the memory of the gentle Heber.

And Cleveland died in 1784, and is still loved by the heathen, is he? Why, that year 1784 was remarkable in the life of our friend the First Gentleman of Europe. Do you not know that he was twenty-one in that year, and opened Carlton House with a grand ball to the nobility and gentry, and doubtless wore that lovely pink coat which we have described. I was eager to read about the ball, and looked to the old magazines for information. The entertainment took place on the 10th February. In the *European Magazine* of March, 1784, I came straightway upon it :—

" The alterations at Carlton House being finished, we lay before our readers a description of the state apartments as they appeared on the 10th instant, when H.R.H. gave a grand ball to the principal nobility and gentry. . . . . . The entrance to the state room fills the mind with an inexpressible idea of greatness and splendour.

"The state chair is of a gold frame, covered with crimson damask; on each corner of the feet is a lion's head, expressive of fortitude and strength; the feet of the chair have serpents twining round them, to denote wisdom. Facing the throne, appears the helmet of Minerva; and over the windows, glory is represented by Saint George with a superb gloria.

"But the saloon may be styled the *chef d'œuvre*, and in every ornament discovers great invention. It is hung with a figured lemon satin. The window-curtains, sofas, and chairs are of the same colour. The ceiling is ornamented with emblematical paintings, representing the Graces and Muses, together with Jupiter, Mercury, Apollo, and Paris. Two *ormolu* chandeliers are placed here. It is impossible by expression to do justice to the extraordinary workmanship, as well as design, of the ornaments. They each consist of a palm, branching out in five directions for the reception of lights. A beautiful figure of a rural nymph is represented entwining the stems of the tree with wreaths of flowers. In the centre of the room is a rich chandelier. To see this apartment *dans son plus beau jour*, it should be viewed in the glass over the chimney-piece. The range of apartments from the saloon to the ball-room, when the doors are open, formed one of the grandest spectacles that ever was beheld."

In the *Gentleman's Magazine*, for the very same month and year —March, 1784—is an account of another festival, in which another great gentleman of English extraction is represented as taking a principal share :—

"According to order, H.E. the Commander-in-Chief was admitted to a public audience of Congress; and, being seated, the President, after a pause, informed him that the United States assembled were ready to receive his communications. Whereupon he arose, and spoke as follows :—

"'Mr. President,—The great events on which my resignation depended having at length taken place, I present myself before Congress to surrender into their hands the trust committed to me, and to claim the indulgence of retiring from the service of my country.

"'Happy in the confirmation of our independence and sovereignty, I resign the appointment I accepted with diffidence; which, however, was superseded by a confidence in the rectitude of our cause, the support of the supreme power of the nation, and the patronage of

Heaven. I close this last act of my official life, by commending the interests of our dearest country to the protection of Almighty God, and those who have the superintendence of them to His holy keeping. Having finished the work assigned me, I retire from the great theatre of action ; and, bidding an affectionate farewell to this august body, under whose orders I have so long acted, I here offer my commission and take my leave of the employments of my public life.' To which the President replied :—

"' Sir, having defended the standard of liberty in the New World, having taught a lesson useful to those who inflict and those who feel oppression, you retire with the blessings of your fellow-citizens ; though the glory of your virtues will not terminate with your military command, but will descend to remotest ages.' "

Which was the most splendid spectacle ever witnessed ;—the opening feast of Prince George in London, or the resignation of Washington ? Which is the noble character for after ages to admire ; —yon fribble dancing in lace and spangles, or yonder hero who sheathes his sword after a life of spotless honour, a purity unreproached, a courage indomitable, and a consummate victory ? Which of these is the true gentleman ? What is it to be a gentleman ? Is it to have lofty aims, to lead a pure life, to keep your honour virgin ; to have the esteem of your fellow-citizens, and the love of your fireside ; to bear good fortune meekly ; to suffer evil with constancy ; and through evil or good to maintain truth always ? Show me the happy man whose life exhibits these qualities, and him we will salute as gentleman, whatever his rank may be ; show me the prince who possesses them, and he may be sure of our love and loyalty. The heart of Britain still beats kindly for George III.,—not because he was wise and just, but because he was pure in life, honest in intent, and because according to his lights he worshipped heaven. I think we acknowledge in the inheritrix of his sceptre, a wiser rule, and a life as honourable and pure ; and I am sure the future painter of our manners will pay a willing allegiance to that good life, and be loyal to the memory of that unsullied virtue.

THE END OF "THE FOUR GEORGES."

THE ENGLISH HUMOURISTS

OF THE

EIGHTEENTH CENTURY

PRIOR, GAY, AND POPE.

ATTHEW PRIOR was one of those famous and lucky wits of the auspicious reign of Queen Anne, whose name it behoves us not to pass over. Mat was a world-philosopher of no small genius, good nature, and acumen.* He loved, he drank, he sang. He describes himself, in one of his lyrics, "in a little Dutch chaise on a Saturday night; on his left hand his Horace, and a friend on his right," going out of town from the Hague to pass that evening, and the ensuing Sunday boozing at a Spielhaus with his companions, perhaps bobbing for perch in a Dutch canal and noting down, in a strain and with a grace not unworthy of his Epicurean master, the charms of his idleness, his retreat, and his Batavian Chloe. A vintner's son in Whitehall, and a

* Gay calls him—"Dear Prior . . . . beloved by every muse."—*Mr. Pope's Welcome from Greece.*

Swift and Prior were very intimate, and he is frequently mentioned in the "Journal to Stella." "Mr. Prior," says Swift, "walks to make himself fat, and I to keep myself down. . . . . We often walk round the park together."

In Swift's works there is a curious tract called "Remarks on the Characters of the Court of Queen Anne" [Scott's edition, vol. xii.] The "Remarks" are not by the Dean; but at the end of each is an addition in distinguished pupil of Busby of the Rod, Prior attracted some notice by writing verses at St. John's College, Cambridge, and, coming up to town, aided Montague * in an attack on the noble old English lion John Dryden ; in ridicule of whose work, " The Hind and the Panther," he brought out that remarkable and famous burlesque, " The Town and Country Mouse." Aren't you all acquainted with it ? Have you not all got it by heart ? What ! have you never heard of it ? See what fame is made of ! The wonderful part of the satire was, that, as a natural consequence of " The Town and Country Mouse," Matthew Prior was made Secretary of Embassy at the Hague ! I believe it is dancing, rather than singing, which distinguishes the young English diplomatists of the present day ; and have seen them in various parts perform that part of their duty very finely. In Prior's time it appears

italics from his hand, and these are always characteristic. Thus, to the Duke of Marlborough, he adds, " *Detestably covetous*," &c. Prior is thus noticed—

"MATTHEW PRIOR, Esq., Commissioner of Trade.

" On the Queen's accession to the throne, he was continued in his office ; is very well at court with the ministry, and is an entire creature of my Lord Jersey's, whom he supports by his advice ; is one of the best poets in England, but very facetious in conversation. A thin, hollow-looked man, turned of forty years old. *This is near the truth.*"

" Yet counting as far as to fifty his years,
    His virtues and vices were as other men's are.
High hopes he conceived and he smothered great fears,
    In a life party-coloured—half pleasure, half care.

" Not to business a drudge, nor to faction a slave,
    He strove to make interest and freedom agree ;
In public employments industrious and grave,
    And alone with his friends, Lord, how merry was he !

" Now in equipage stately, now humble on foot,
    Both fortunes he tried, but to neither would trust ;
And whirled in the round as the wheel turned about,
    He found riches had wings, and knew man was but dust."
                    PRIOR'S *Poems.* [*For my own monument.*]

* " They joined to produce a parody, entitled the ' Town and Country Mouse,' part of which Mr. Bayes is supposed to gratify his old friends, Smart and Johnson, by repeating to them. The piece is therefore founded upon the twice-told jest of the ' Rehearsal.' . . . There is nothing new or original in the idea. . . . In this piece, Prior, though the younger man, seems to have had by far the largest share."—SCOTT'S *Dryden*, vol. i. p. 330.

a different accomplishment led to preferment. Could you write a copy of Alcaics? that was the question. Could you turn out a neat epigram or two? Could you compose "The Town and Country Mouse?" It is manifest that, by the possession of this faculty, the most difficult treaties, the laws of foreign nations, and the interests of our own, are easily understood. Prior rose in the diplomatic service, and said good things, that proved his sense and his spirit. When the apartments at Versailles were shown to him, with the victories of Louis XIV. painted on the walls, and Prior was asked whether the palace of the King of England had any such decorations, "The monuments of my master's actions," Mat said, of William, whom he cordially revered, "are to be seen everywhere except in his own house." Bravo, Mat! Prior rose to be full ambassador at Paris,* where he somehow was cheated out of his ambassadorial plate ; and in an heroic poem, addressed by him to her late lamented Majesty, Queen Anne, Mat makes some magnificent allusions to these dishes and spoons, of which Fate had deprived him. All that he wants, he says, is her Majesty's picture ; without that he can't be happy.

> " Thee, gracious Anne, thee present I adore :
> Thee, Queen of Peace, if Time and Fate have power
> Higher to raise the glories of thy reign,
> In words sublimer and a nobler strain
> May future bards the mighty theme rehearse.
> Here, Stator Jove, and Phœbus, king of verse,
> The votive tablet I suspend."

With that word the poem stops abruptly. The votive tablet is suspended for ever, like Mahomet's coffin. News came that the Queen was dead. Stator Jove, and Phœbus, king of verse, were left there, hovering to this day, over the votive tablet. The picture was

---

* "He was to have been in the same commission with the Duke of Shrewsbury, but that that nobleman," says Johnson, "refused to be associated with one so meanly born. Prior therefore continued to act without a title till the Duke's return next year to England, and then he assumed the style and dignity of ambassador."

He had been thinking of slights of this sort when he wrote his Epitaph :—

> " Nobles and heralds, by your leave,
> Here lies what once was Matthew Prior,
> The son of Adam and of Eve ;
> Can Bourbon or Nassau claim higher ?"

But, in this case, the old prejudice got the better of the old joke.

never got, any more than the spoons and dishes : the inspiration ceased, the verses were not wanted—the ambassador wasn't wanted. Poor Mat was recalled from his embassy, suffered disgrace along with his patrons, lived under a sort of cloud ever after, and disappeared in Essex. When deprived of all his pensions and emoluments, the hearty and generous Oxford pensioned him. They played for gallant stakes—the bold men of those days—and lived and gave splendidly.

Johnson quotes from Spence a legend, that Prior, after spending an evening with Harley, St. John, Pope, and Swift, would go off and smoke a pipe with a couple of friends of his, a soldier and his wife, in Long Acre. Those who have not read his late Excellency's poems should be warned that they smack not a little of the conversation of his Long Acre friends. Johnson speaks slightingly of his lyrics ; but with due deference to the great Samuel, Prior's seem to me amongst the easiest, the richest, the most charmingly humourous of English lyrical poems.* Horace is always in his mind ; and his song, and his

---

* His epigrams have the genuine sparkle :

" THE REMEDY WORSE THAN THE DISEASE.

" I sent for Radcliff ; was so ill,
　　That other doctors gave me over :
He felt my pulse, prescribed his pill,
　　And I was likely to recover.

" But when the wit began to wheeze,
　　And wine had warmed the politician,
Cured yesterday of my disease,
　　I died last night of my physician."

" Yes, every poet is a fool ;
　　By demonstration Ned can show it ;
Happy could Ned's inverted rule
　　Prove every fool to be a poet."

" On his death-bed poor Lubin lies,
　　His spouse is in despair ;
With frequent sobs and mutual cries,
　　They both express their care.

" ' A different cause,' says Parson Sly,
　　' The same effect may give ;
Poor Lubin fears that he shall die,
　　His wife that he may live.' "

philosophy, his good sense, his happy easy turns and melody, his loves and his Epicureanism bear a great resemblance to that most delightful and accomplished master. In reading his works one is struck with their modern air, as well as by their happy similarity to the songs of the charming owner of the Sabine farm. In his verses addressed to Halifax, he says, writing of that endless theme to poets, the vanity of human wishes—

> " So whilst in fevered dreams we sink,
>   And waking, taste what we desire,
>   The real draught but feeds the fire,
> The dream is better than the drink.

> " Our hopes like towering falcons aim
>   At objects in an airy height :
>   To stand aloof and view the flight,
> Is all the pleasure of the game."

Would not you fancy that a poet of our own days was singing? and in the verses of Chloe weeping and reproaching him for his inconstancy, where he says—

> " The God of us versemen, you know, child, the Sun,
>   How, after his journeys, he sets up his rest.
> If at morning o'er earth 'tis his fancy to run,
>   At night he declines on his Thetis's breast.

> " So, when I am wearied with wandering all day,
>   To thee, my delight, in the evening I come :
> No matter what beauties I saw in my way ;
>   They were but my visits, but thou art my home !

> " Then finish, dear Chloe, this pastoral war,
>   And let us like Horace and Lydia agree :
> For thou art a girl as much brighter than her,
>   As he was a poet sublimer than me."

If Prior read Horace, did not Thomas Moore study Prior? Love and pleasure find singers in all days. Roses are always blowing and fading—to-day as in that pretty time when Prior sang of them, and of Chloe lamenting their decay—

> " She sighed, she smiled, and to the flowers
>   Pointing, the lovely moralist said :
> See, friend, in some few fleeting hours,
>   See yonder what a change is made !

" Ah me ! the blooming pride of May
    And that of Beauty are but one :
At morn both flourish, bright and gay,
    Both fade at evening, pale and gone.

" At dawn poor Stella danced and sung,
    The amorous youth around her bowed :
At night her fatal knell was rung ;
    I saw, and kissed her in her shroud.

" Such as she is who died to-day,
    Such I, alas, may be to-morrow :
Go, Damon, bid thy Muse display
    The justice of thy Chloe's sorrow."

Damon's knell was rung in 1721.   May his turf lie lightly on him !
Deus sit propitius huic potatori, as Walter de Mapes sang.*   Perhaps

* PRIOR TO SIR THOMAS HANMER.

" DEAR SIR,—   " *Aug.* 4, 1709.

   "FRIENDSHIP may live, I grant you, without being fed and cherished
by correspondence ; but with that additional benefit I am of opinion it will
look more cheerful and thrive better : for in this case, as in love, though a
man is sure of his own constancy, yet his happiness depends a good deal upon
the sentiments of another, and while you and Chloe are alive, 'tis not enough
that I love you both, except I am sure you both love me again ; and as one of
her scrawls fortifies my mind more against affliction than all Epictetus, with
Simplicius's comments into the bargain, so your single letter gave me more
real pleasure than all the works of Plato. . . . . I must return my
answer to your very kind question concerning my health.   The Bath waters
have done a good deal towards the recovery of it, and the great specific, *Cape
caballum*, will, I think, confirm it.   Upon this head I must tell you that my
mare Betty grows blind, and may one day, by breaking my neck, perfect my
cure : if at Rixham fair any pretty nagg that is between thirteen and fourteen
hands presented himself, and you would be pleased to purchase him for me,
one of your servants might ride him to Euston, and I might receive him there.
This, sir, is just as such a thing happens.   If you hear, too, of a Welch
widow, with a good jointure, that has her *goings* and is not very skittish, pray,
be pleased to cast your eye on her for me too.   You see, sir, the great trust I
repose in your skill and honour, when I dare put two such commissions in your
hand. . . . ."—*The Hanmer Correspondence*, p. 120.

" FROM MR. PRIOR.

" MY DEAR LORD AND FRIEND,—   " *Paris*, 1st—12th *May*, 1714.

   "MATTHEW never had so great occasion to write a word to Henry as
now : it is noised here that I am soon to return.   The question that I wish I

Samuel Johnson, who spoke slightingly of Prior's verses, enjoyed them more than he was willing to own. The old moralist had studied

could answer to the many that ask, and to our friend Colbert de Torcy (to whom I made your compliments in the manner you commanded) is, what is done for me ; and to what I am recalled ? It may look like a bagatelle, what is to become of a philosopher like me ? but it is not such : what is to become of a person who had the honour to be chosen, and sent hither as intrusted, in the midst of a war, with what the Queen designed should make the peace ; returning with the Lord Bolingbroke, one of the greatest men in England, and one of the finest heads in Europe (as they say here, if true or not, *n'importe*) ; having been left by him in the greatest character (that of Her Majesty's Plenipotentiary), exercising that power conjointly with the Duke of Shrewsbury, and solely after his departure ; having here received more distinguished honour than any Minister, except an Ambassador, ever did, and some which were never given to any but who had that character ; having had all the success that could be expected ; having (God be thanked !) spared no pains, at a time when at home the peace is voted safe and honourable—at a time when the Earl of Oxford is Lord Treasurer and Lord Bolingbroke First Secretary of State ? This unfortunate person, I say, neglected, forgot, unnamed to anything that may speak the Queen satisfied with his services, or his friends concerned as to his fortune.

"Mr. de Torcy put me quite out of countenance, the other day, by a pity that wounded me deeper than ever did the cruelty of the late Lord Godolphin. He said he would write to Robin and Harry about me. God forbid, my lord, that I should need any foreign intercession, or owe the least to any Frenchman living, besides the decency of behaviour and the returns of common civility : some say I am to go to Baden, others that I am to be added to the Commissioners for settling the commerce. In all cases I am ready, but in the meantime, *dic aliquid de tribus capellis.* Neither of these two are, I presume, honours or rewards, neither of them (let me say to my dear Lord Bolingbroke, and let him not be angry with me,) are what Drift may aspire to, and what Mr. Whitworth, who was his fellow-clerk, has or may possess. I am far from desiring to lessen the great merit of the gentleman I named, for I heartily esteem and love him ; but in this trade of ours, my lord, in which you are the general, as in that of the soldiery, there is a certain right acquired by time and long service. You would do anything for your Queen's service, but you would not be contented to descend, and be degraded to a charge, no way proportioned to that of Secretary of State, any more than Mr. Ross, though he would charge a party with a halbard in his hand, would be content all his life after to be Serjeant. Was my Lord Dartmouth, from Secretary, returned again to be Commissioner of Trade, or from Secretary of War, would Frank Gwyn think himself kindly used to be returned again to be Commissioner ? In short, my lord, you have put me above myself, and if I am to return to myself, I shall return to something very discontented and uneasy. I am sure, my lord, you them as well as Mr. Thomas Moore, and defended them and showed that he remembered them very well too, on an occasion when their morality was called in question by that noted puritan, James Boswell, Esq., of Auchinleck.*

In the great society of the wits, John Gay deserved to be a favourite, and to have a good place.† In his set all were fond of him.

will make the best use you can of this hint for my good. If I am to have anything, it will certainly be for Her Majesty's service, and the credit of my friends in the Ministry, that it be done before I am recalled from home, lest the world may think either that I have merited to be disgraced, or that ye dare not stand by me. If nothing is to be done, *fiat voluntas Dei.* I have writ to Lord Treasurer upon this subject, and having implored your kind intercession, I promise you it is the last remonstrance of this kind that I will ever make. Adieu, my lord; all honour, health, and pleasure to you.

" Yours ever, MATT."

" P.S.—Lady Jersey is just gone from me. We drank your healths together in usquebaugh after our tea : we are the greatest friends alive. Once more adieu. There is no such thing as the 'Book of Travels' you mentioned ; if there be, let friend Tilson send us more particular account of them, for neither I nor Jacob Tonson can find them. Pray send Barton back to me, I hope with some comfortable tidings."—*Bolingbroke's Letters.*

* " I asked whether Prior's poems were to be printed entire ; Johnson said they were. I mentioned Lord Hales' censure of Prior in his preface to a collection of sacred poems, by various hands, published by him at Edinburgh a great many years ago, where he mentions ' these impure tales, which will be the eternal opprobrium of their ingenious author.' JOHNSON : ' Sir, Lord Hales has forgot. There is nothing in Prior that will excite to lewdness. If Lord Hales thinks there is, he must be more combustible than other people.' I instanced the tale of ' Paulo Purganti and his wife.' JOHNSON : ' Sir, there is nothing there but that his wife wanted to be kissed, when poor Paulo was out of pocket. No, sir, Prior is a lady's book. No lady is ashamed to have it standing in her library."—BOSWELL'S *Life of Johnson.*

† Gay was of an old Devonshire family, but his pecuniary prospects not being great, was placed in his youth in the house of a silk-mercer in London. He was born in 1688—Pope's year, and in 1712 the Duchess of Monmouth made him her secretary. Next year he published his " Rural Sports," which he dedicated to Pope, and so made an acquaintance, which became a memorable friendship.

" Gay," says Pope, " was quite a natural man,—wholly withourt art or design, and spoke just what he thought and as he thought it. He dangled for twenty years about a court, and at last was offered to be made usher to the young princesses. Secretary Craggs made Gay a present of stock in the South Sea year ; and he was once worth 20,000*l.*, but lost it all again. He got

His success offended nobody. He missed a fortune once or twice. He was talked of for Court favour, and hoped to win it ; but the Court favour jilted him. Craggs gave him some South Sea Stock ; and at one time Gay had very nearly made his fortune. But Fortune shook her swift wings and jilted him too : and so his friends, instead of being angry with him, and jealous of him, were kind and fond of honest Gay. In the portraits of the literary worthies of the early part of the last century, Gay's face is the pleasantest perhaps of all. It appears adorned with neither periwig nor nightcap (the full dress and *negligée* of learning, without which the painters of those days scarcely ever pourtrayed wits), and he laughs at you over his shoulder with an honest boyish glee—an artless sweet humour. He was so kind, so gentle, so jocular, so delightfully brisk at times, so dismally wobegone at others, such a natural good creature, that the Giants loved him. The great Swift was gentle and sportive with him,* as the enormous Brobdingnag maids of honour were with little Gulliver. He could frisk and fondle round Pope,† and sport, and bark, and caper, without offending the most thin-skinned of poets and men ;

about 400*l.* by the first ' Beggar's Opera,' and 1,100*l.* or 1,200*l.* by the second. He was negligent and a bad manager. Latterly, the Duke of Queensberry took his money into his keeping, and let him only have what was necessary out of it, and, as he lived with them, he could not have occasion for much. He died worth upwards of 3,000*l.*"—POPE. *Spence's Anecdotes.*

* "Mr. Gay is, in all regards, as honest and sincere a man as ever I knew."—SWIFT, *To Lady Betty Germaine,* Jan. 1733.

> † " Of manners gentle, of affections mild ;
>   In wit a man ; simplicity, a child ;
>   With native humour temp'ring virtuous rage,
>   Form'd to delight at once and lash the age ;
>   Above temptation in a low estate,
>   And uncorrupted e'en among the great :
>   A safe companion, and an easy friend,
>   Unblamed through life, lamented in thy end.
>   These are thy honours ; not that here thy bust
>   Is mixed with heroes, or with kings thy dust ;
>   But that the worthy and the good shall say,
>   Striking their pensive bosoms, ' *Here* lies Gay.' "
>   POPE'S *Epitaph on Gay.*

> " A hare who, in a civil way,
>   Complied with everything, like Gay."
>   *Fables,* " *The Hare and many Friends.*"

and when he was jilted in that little Court affair of which we have
spoken, his warm-hearted patrons the Duke and Duchess of Queensberry * (the " Kitty, beautiful and young," of Prior,) pleaded his

* " I can give you no account of Gay," says Pope, curiously, " since he
was raffled for, and won back by his Duchess."—*Works*, *Roscoe's Ed.*, vol. ix.
p. 392.

Here is the letter Pope wrote to him when the death of Queen Anne
brought back Lord Clarendon from Hanover, and lost him the Secretaryship
of that nobleman, of which he had had but a short tenure.

Gay's Court prospects were never happy from this time.—His dedication of
the "Shepherd's Week" to Bolingbroke, Swift used to call the "original sin"
which had hurt him with the house of Hanover :—

"DEAR MR. GAY,—   "*Sept.* 23, 1714.

" WELCOME to your native soil ! welcome to your friends ! thrice
welcome to me ! whether returned in glory, blest with court interest, the love
and familiarity of the great, and filled with agreeable hopes ; or melancholy
with dejection, contemplative of the changes of fortune, and doubtful for the
future ; whether returned a triumphant Whig or a desponding Tory, equally
all hail ! equally beloved and welcome to me ! If happy, I am to partake in
your elevation ; if unhappy, you have still a warm corner in my heart, and a
retreat at Binfield in the worst of times at your service. If you are a Tory, or
thought so by any man, I know it can proceed from nothing but your gratitude to a few people who endeavoured to serve you, and whose politics were
never your concern. If you are a Whig, as I rather hope, and as I think your
principles and mine (as brother poets) had ever a bias to the side of liberty, I
know you will be an honest man and an inoffensive one. Upon the whole, I
know you are incapable of being so much of either party as to be good for nothing. Therefore, once more, whatever you are or in whatever state you are,
all hail !

" One or two of your own friends complained they had heard nothing from
you since the Queen's death ; I told them no man living loved Mr. Gay better
than I, yet I had not once written to him in all his voyage. This I thought
a convincing proof how truly one may be a friend to another without telling
him so every month. But they had reasons, too, themselves to allege in your
excuse, as men who really value one another will never want such as make
their friends and themselves easy. The late universal concern in public affairs
threw us all into a hurry of spirits : even I, who am more a philosopher than
to expect anything from any reign, was borne away with the current, and full
of the expectation of the successor. During your journeys, I knew not
whither to aim a letter after you ; that was a sort of shooting flying : add to
this the demand Homer had upon me, to write fifty verses a day, besides
learned notes, all which are at a conclusion for this year. Rejoice with me,
O my friend ! that my labour is over ; come and make merry with me in
much feasting. We will feed among the lilies (by the lilies I mean the ladies).

cause with indignation, and quitted the Court in a huff, carrying off with them into their retirement their kind gentle protégé. With these kind lordly folks, a real Duke and Duchess, as delightful as those who harboured Don Quixote, and loved that dear old Sancho, Gay lived, and was lapped in cotton, and had his plate of chicken, and his saucer of cream, and frisked, and barked, and wheezed, and grew fat, and so ended.* He became very melancholy and lazy, sadly plethoric, and only occasionally diverting in his latter days. But everybody loved him, and the remembrance of his pretty little tricks ; and the raging old Dean of St. Patrick's, chafing in his banishment, was afraid to open the letter which Pope wrote him announcing the sad news of the death of Gay.†

Are not the Rosalindas of Britain as charming as the Blousalindas of the Hague ? or have the two great Pastoral poets of our nation renounced love at the same time ? for Philips, immortal Philips, hath deserted, yea, and in a rustic manner kicked his Rosalind. Dr. Parnell and I have been inseparable ever since you went. We are now at the Bath, where (if you are not, as I heartily hope, better engaged) your coming would be the greatest pleasure to us in the world. Talk not of expenses : Homer shall support his children. I beg a line from you, directed to the Post-house in Bath. Poor Parnell is in an ill state of health.

"Pardon me if I add a word of advice in the poetical way. Write something on the King, or Prince, or Princess. On whatsoever foot you may be with the court, this can do no harm. I shall never know where to end, and am confounded in the many things I have to say to you, though they all amount but to this, that I am, entirely, as ever,

"Your," &c.

Gay took the advice "in the poetical way," and published "An Epistle to a Lady, occasioned by the arrival of her Royal Highness the Princess of Wales." But though this brought him access to Court, and the attendance of the Prince and Princess at his farce of the "What d'ye call it ?" it did not bring him a place. On the accession of George II., he was offered the situation of Gentleman Usher to the Princess Louisa (her Highness being then two years old) ; but "by this offer," says Johnson, "he thought himself insulted."

* "Gay was a great eater.—As the French philosopher used to prove his existence by *Cogito, ergo sum*, the greatest proof of Gay's existence is, *Edit, ergo est*."—CONGREVE, *in a Letter to Pope. Spence's Anecdotes.*

† Swift endorsed the letter—"On my dear friend Mr. Gay's death ; received Dec. 15, but not read till the 20th, by an impulse foreboding some misfortune."

"It was by Swift's interest that Gay was made known to Lord Bolingbroke, and obtained his patronage."— SCOTT's *Swift*, vol. i. p. 156. [Pope

Swift's letters to him are beautiful ; and having no purpose but kindness in writing to him, no party aim to advocate, or slight or anger to wreak, every word the Dean says to his favourite is natural, trustworthy, and kindly.   His admiration for Gay's parts and honesty, and his laughter at his weaknesses, were alike just and genuine.   He paints his character in wonderful pleasant traits of jocular satire.   " I writ lately to Mr. Pope," Swift says, writing to Gay : " I wish you had a little villakin in his neighbourhood ; but you are yet too volatile, and any lady with a coach and six horses would carry you to Japan." " If your ramble," says Swift, in another letter, " was on horseback, I am glad of it, on account of your health ; but I know your arts of patching up a journey between stage-coaches and friends' coaches—for you are as arrant a cockney as any hosier in Cheapside.   I have often had it in my head to put it into yours, that you ought to have some great work in scheme, which may take up seven years to finish, besides two or three under-ones that may add another thousand pounds to your stock.   And then I shall be in less pain about you.   I know you can find dinners, but you love twelvepenny coaches too well, without considering that the interest of a whole thousand pounds brings you but half-a-crown a day."   And then Swift goes off from Gay to pay some grand compliments to her Grace the Duchess of Queensberry, in whose sunshine Mr. Gay was basking, and in whose radiance the Dean would have liked to warm himself too.

But we have Gay here before us, in these letters—lazy, kindly, uncommonly idle ; rather slovenly, I'm afraid ; for ever eating and saying good things ; a little round French abbé of a man, sleek, soft-handed, and soft-hearted.

Our object in these lectures is rather to describe the men than their works ; or to deal with the latter only in as far as they seem to illustrate the character of their writers.   Mr. Gay's " Fables," which were written to benefit that amiable Prince, the Duke of Cumberland,

Pope wrote on the occasion of Gay's death, to Swift, thus :—

" [*Dec.* 5, 1732.]
" . . . . One of the nearest and longest ties I have ever had is broken all on a sudden by the unexpected death of poor Mr. Gay. An inflammatory fever hurried him out of this life in three days. . . . . He asked of you a few hours before when in acute torment by the inflammation in his bowels and breast. . . . . His sisters, we suppose, will be his heirs, who are two widows. . . . . Good God ! how often are we to die before we go quite off this stage ? In every friend we lose a part of ourselves, and the best part.   God keep those we have left ! few are worth praying for, and one's self the least of all."

the warrior of Dettingen and Culloden, I have not, I own, been
able to peruse since a period of very early youth ; and it must be

confessed that they did not effect much benefit upon the illustrious young Prince, whose manners they were intended to mollify, and whose natural ferocity our gentle-hearted Satirist perhaps proposed to restrain. But the six pastorals called the " Shepherd's Week," and the burlesque poem of " Trivia," any man fond of lazy literature will find delightful at the present day, and must read from beginning to end with pleasure. They are to poetry what charming little Dresden china figures are to sculpture : graceful, minikin, fantastic ; with a certain beauty always accompanying them. The pretty little personages of the pastoral, with gold clocks to their stockings, and fresh satin ribbons to their crooks and waistcoats and bodices, dance their loves to a minuet-tune played on a bird-organ, approach the charmer, or rush from the false one daintily on their red-heeled tip-toes, and die of despair or rapture, with the most pathetic little grins and ogles ; or repose, simpering at each other, under an arbour of pea-green crockery ; or piping to pretty flocks that have just been washed with the best Naples in a stream of Bergamot. Gay's gay plan seems to me far pleasanter than that of Phillips—his rival and Pope's—a serious and dreary idyllic cockney ; not that Gay's " Bumkinets " and " Hobnelias " are a whit more natural than the would-be serious characters of the other posture-master ; but the quality of this true humourist was to laugh and make laugh, though always with a secret kindness and tenderness, to perform the drollest little antics and capers, but always with a certain grace, and to sweet music—as you may have seen a Savoyard boy abroad, with a hurdy-gurdy and a monkey, turning over head and heels, or clattering and pirouetting in a pair of wooden shoes, yet always with a look of love and appeal in his bright eyes, and a smile that asks and wins affection and protection. Happy they who have that sweet gift of nature ! It was this which made the great folks and Court ladies free and friendly with John Gay—which made Pope and Arbuthnot love him—which melted the savage heart of Swift when he thought of him—and drove away, for a moment or two, the dark frenzies which obscured the lonely tyrant's brain, as he heard Gay's voice with its simple melody and artless ringing laughter.

What used to be said about Rubini, *qu'il avait des larmes dans la voix,* may be said of Gay,* and of one other humourist of whom we

---

* " Gay, like Goldsmith, had a musical talent. ' He could play on the flute,' says Malone, ' and was, therefore, enabled to adapt so happily some of the airs in the " Beggar's Opera." ' "—*Notes to Spence.*

shall have to speak. In almost every ballad of his, however slight,*

* " 'Twas when the seas were roaring
    With hollow blasts of wind,
  A damsel lay deploring
    All on a rock reclined.
  Wide o'er the foaming billows
    She cast a wistful look ;
  Her head was crown'd with willows
    That trembled o'er the brook.

" ' Twelve months are gone and over,
    And nine long tedious days ;
  Why didst thou, venturous lover—
    Why didst thou trust the seas ?
  Cease, cease, thou cruel Ocean,
    And let my lover rest ;
  Ah ! what's thy troubled motion
    To that within my breast ?

" ' The merchant, robb'd of pleasure,
    Sees tempests in despair ;
  But what's the loss of treasure
    To losing of my dear ?
  Should you some coast be laid on,
    Where gold and diamonds grow,
  You'd find a richer maiden,
    But none that loves you so.

" ' How can they say that Nature
    Has nothing made in vain ;
  Why, then, beneath the water
    Should hideous rocks remain ?
  No eyes the rocks discover
    That lurk beneath the deep,
  To wreck the wandering lover,
    And leave the maid to weep ? '

" All melancholy lying,
    Thus wailed she for her dear ;
  Repay'd each blast with sighing,
    Each billow with a tear ;
  When o'er the white wave stooping,
    His floating corpse she spy'd ;
  Then like a lily drooping,
    She bow'd her head, and died."
        —*A Ballad from the " What d'ye call it ?"*
                    ["What

in the " Beggar's Opera " * and in its wearisome continuation (where the verses are to the full as pretty as in the first piece, however), there is a peculiar, hinted, pathetic sweetness and melody. It charms and melts you. It's indefinable, but it exists; and is the property of John Gay's and Oliver Goldsmith's best verse, as fragrance is of a violet, or freshness of a rose.

Let me read a piece from one of his letters, which is so famous that most people here are no doubt familiar with it, but so delightful that it is always pleasant to hear :—

"I have just passed part of this summer at an old romantic seat of my Lord Harcourt's which he lent me. It overlooks a common field, where, under the shade of a haycock, sat two lovers—as constant as ever were found in romance—beneath a spreading beech. The name of the one (let it sound as it will) was John Hewet ; of the other Sarah Drew. John was a well-set man, about five and twenty ; Sarah a brown woman of eighteen. John had for several months borne the labour of the day in the same field with Sarah ; when she milked, it was his morning and evening charge to bring the cows to her pail. Their love was the talk, but not the scandal, of the whole neighbourhood, for all they aimed at was the blameless possession of each other in marriage. It was but this very morning that he had obtained her parents'

"What can be prettier than Gay's ballad, or, rather, Swift's, Arbuthnot's, Pope's and Gay's, in the 'What d'ye call it ?' ''Twas when the seas were roaring ?' I have been well informed that they all contributed."—*Cowper to Unwin,* 1783.

* "Dr. Swift had been observing once to Mr. Gay, what an odd pretty sort of thing a Newgate Pastoral might make. Gay was inclined to try at such a thing for some time, but afterwards thought it would be better to write a comedy on the same plan. This was what gave rise to the 'Beggar's Opera.' He began on it, and when he first mentioned it to Swift, the Doctor did not much like the project. As he carried it on, he showed what he wrote to both of us ; and we now and then gave a correction, or a word or two of advice ; but it was wholly of his own writing. When it was done, neither of us thought it would succeed. We showed it to Congreve, who, after reading it over, said, 'It would either take greatly, or be damned confoundedly.' We were all at the first night of it, in great uncertainty of the event, till we were very much encouraged by overhearing the Duke of Argyle, who sat in the next box to us, say, 'It will do—it must do !—I see it in the eyes of them !' This was a good while before the first act was over, and so gave us ease soon ; for the Duke [besides his own good taste] has a more particular knack than any one now living in discovering the taste of the public. He was quite right in this as usual ; the good nature of the audience appeared stronger and stronger every act, and ended in a clamour of applause."—POPE. *Spence's Anecdotes.*

consent, and it was but till the next week that they were to wait to be happy. Perhaps this very day, in the intervals of their work, they were talking of their wedding-clothes ; and John was now matching several kinds of poppies and field-flowers to her complexion, to make her a present of knots for the day. While they were thus employed (it was on the last of July) a terrible storm of thunder and lightning arose, that drove the labourers to what shelter the trees or hedges afforded. Sarah, frightened and out of breath, sunk on a haycock ; and John (who never separated from her), sat by her side, having raked two or three heaps together, to secure her. Immediately there was heard so loud a crack, as if heaven had burst asunder. The labourers, all solicitous for each other's safety, called to one another : those that were nearest our lovers, hearing no answer, stepped to the place where they lay : they first saw a little smoke, and after, this faithful pair—John, with one arm about his Sarah's neck, and the other held over her face, as if to screen her from the lightning. They were struck dead, and already grown stiff and cold in this tender posture. There was no mark or discolouring on their bodies—only that Sarah's eyebrow was a little singed, and a small spot between her breasts. They were buried the next day in one grave."

And the proof that this description is delightful and beautiful is, that the great Mr. Pope admired it so much that he thought proper to steal it and to send it off to a certain lady and wit, with whom he pretended to be in love in those days—my Lord Duke of Kingston's daughter, and married to Mr. Wortley Montagu, then his Majesty's Ambassador at Constantinople.

We are now come to the greatest name on our list—the highest among the poets, the highest among the English wits and humourists with whom we have to rank him. If the author of the " Dunciad " be not a humourist, if the poet of the "Rape of the Lock" be not a wit, who deserves to be called so ? Besides that brilliant genius and immense fame, for both of which we should respect him, men of letters should admire him as being the greatest literary *artist* that England has seen. He polished, he refined, he thought ; he took thoughts from other works to adorn and complete his own ; borrowing an idea or a cadence from another poet as he would a figure or a simile from a flower, or a river, stream, or any object which struck him in his walk, or contemplation of Nature. He began to imitate at an early age ; *

* " Waller, Spenser, and Dryden were Mr. Pope's great favourites, in the order they are named, in his first reading, till he was about twelve years old."—POPE. *Spence's Anecdotes.*

" Mr. Pope's father (who was an honest merchant, and dealt in Hollands, wholesale) was no poet, but he used to set him to make English verses when very young. He was pretty difficult in being pleased ; and used often to send and taught himself to write by copying printed books. Then he passed into the hands of the priests, and from his first clerical master, who came to him when he was eight years old, he went to a school at Twyford, and another school at Hyde Park, at which places he unlearned all that he had got from his first instructor. At twelve years old, he went with his father into Windsor Forest, and there learned for a few months under a fourth priest. "And this was all the teaching I ever had," he said, "and God knows it extended a very little way."

When he had done with his priests he took to reading by himself, for which he had a very great eagerness and enthusiasm, especially for poetry. He learnt versification from Dryden, he said. In his youthful poem of "Alcander," he imitated every poet, Cowley, Milton, Spenser, Statius, Homer, Virgil. In a few years he had dipped into a great number of the English, French, Italian, Latin, and Greek poets. "This I did," he says, "without any design, except to amuse myself; and got the languages by hunting after the stories in the several poets I read, rather than read the books to get the languages. I followed everywhere as my fancy led me, and was like a boy gathering flowers in the fields and woods, just as they fell in his way. These five or six years I looked upon as the happiest in my life." Is not here a beautiful holiday picture? The forest and the fairy story-book—the boy spelling Ariosto or Virgil under the trees, battling with the Cid for the love of Chimène, or dreaming of Armida's garden—peace and sunshine round about—the kindest

---

him back to new turn them. 'These are not good rhimes;' for that was my husband's word for verses."—POPE'S MOTHER. *Spence.*

"I wrote things, I'm ashamed to say how soon. Part of an Epic Poem when about twelve. The scene of it lay at Rhodes and some of the neighbouring islands; and the poem opened under water with a description of the Court of Neptune."—POPE. *Ibid.*

"His perpetual application (after he set to study of himself) reduced him in four years' time to so bad a state of health, that, after trying physicians for a good while in vain, he resolved to give way to his distemper; and sat down calmly in a full expectation of death in a short time. Under this thought, he wrote letters to take a last farewell of some of his more particular friends, and, among the rest, one to the Abbé Southcote. The Abbé was extremely concerned, both for his very ill state of health and the resolution he said he had taken. He thought there might yet be hope, and went immediately to Dr. Radcliffe, with whom he was well acquainted, told him Mr. Pope's case, got full directions from him, and carried them down to Pope in Windsor Forest. The chief thing the Doctor ordered him was to apply less, and to ride every day. The following his advice soon restored him to his health."—POPE. *Spence.*

love and tenderness waiting for him at his quiet home yonder—and Genius throbbing in his young heart, and whispering to him, " You shall be great, you shall be famous ; you too shall love and sing ; you will sing her so nobly that some kind heart shall forget you are weak and ill-formed. Every poet had a love. Fate must give one to you too,"—and day by day he walks the forest, very likely looking out for that charmer. " They were the happiest days of his life," he says, when he was only dreaming of his fame : when he had gained that mistress she was no consoler.

That charmer made her appearance, it would seem, about the year 1705, when Pope was seventeen. Letters of his are extant, addressed to a certain Lady M——, whom the youth courted, and to whom he expressed his ardour in language, to say no worse of it, that is entirely pert, odious, and affected. He imitated love-compositions as he had been imitating love-poems just before—it was a sham mistress he courted, and a sham passion, expressed as became it. These unlucky letters found their way into print years afterwards, and were sold to the congenial Mr. Curll. If any of my hearers, as I hope they may, should take a fancy to look at Pope's correspondence, let them pass over that first part of it ; over, perhaps, almost all Pope's letters to women ; in which there is a tone of not pleasant gallantry, and, amidst a profusion of compliments and politenesses, a something which makes one distrust the little pert, prurient bard. There is very little indeed to say about his loves, and that little not edifying. He wrote flames and raptures and elaborate verse and prose for Lady Mary Wortley Montagu ; but that passion probably came to a climax in an impertinence and was extinguished by a box on the ear, or some such rebuff, and he began on a sudden to hate her with a fervour much more genuine than that of his love had been. It was a feeble puny grimace of love, and paltering with passion. After Mr. Pope had sent off one of his fine compositions to Lady Mary, he made a second draft from the rough copy, and favoured some other friend with it. He was so charmed with the letter of Gay's that I have just quoted, that he had copied that and amended it, and sent it to Lady Mary as his own. A gentleman who writes letters *à deux fins*, and after having poured out his heart to the beloved, serves up the same dish *réchauffé* to a friend, is not very much in earnest about his loves, however much he may be in his piques and vanities when his impertinence gets its due.

But, save that unlucky part of the " Pope Correspondence," I do

not know, in the range of our literature, volumes more delightful.*
You live in them in the finest company in the world.   A little stately,

* "Mr. Pope to the Rev. Mr. Broom, Pulham, Norfolk.
"Dear Sir,—.   "*Aug.* 29*th*, 1730.

"I INTENDED to write to you on this melancholy subject, the death of
Mr. Fenton, before yours came, but stayed to have informed myself and you
of the circumstances of it.   All I hear is, that he felt a gradual decay, though
so early in life, and was declining for five or six months.   It was not, as I
apprehended, the gout in his stomach, but, I believe, rather a complication first
of gross humours, as he was naturally corpulent, not discharging themselves,
as he used no sort of exercise.   No man better bore the approaches of his
dissolution (as I am told), or with less ostentation yielded up his being.   The
great modesty which you know was natural to him, and the great contempt he
had for all sorts of vanity and parade, never appeared more than in his last
moments : he had a conscious satisfaction (no doubt) in acting right, in feeling
himself honest, true, and unpretending to more than his own.   So he died as
he lived, with that secret, yet sufficient contentment.

"As to any papers left behind him, I dare say they can be but few ; for
this reason, he never wrote out of vanity, or thought much of the applause of
men.   I know an instance when he did his utmost to conceal his own merit
that way ; and if we join to this his natural love of ease, I fancy we must
expect little of this sort : at least, I have heard of none, except some few
further remarks on Waller (which his cautious integrity made him leave an
order to be given to Mr. Tonson), and perhaps, though it is many years since
I saw it, a translation of the first book of 'Oppian.'   He had begun a tragedy
of 'Dion,' but made small progress in it.

"As to his other affairs, he died poor but honest, leaving no debts or
legacies, except of a few pounds to Mr. Trumbull and my lady, in token of
respect, gratefulness, and mutual esteem.

"I shall with pleasure take upon me to draw this amiable, quiet, deserving,
unpretending, Christian, and philosophical character in his epitaph.   There
truth may be spoken in a few words ; as for flourish, and oratory, and poetry,
I leave them to younger and more lively writers, such as love writing for
writing's sake, and would rather show their own fine parts than report the
valuable ones of any other man.   So the elegy I renounce.

"I condole with you from my heart on the loss of so worthy a man, and a
friend to us both. . . . . .

"Adieu ; let us love his memory and profit by his example.   Am very
sincerely, dear sir,   "Your affectionate and real servant."

"To the Earl of Burlington.
"My Lord,   "*August*, 1714.

"IF your mare could speak she would give you an account of what
extraordinary company she had on the road, which, since she cannot do,
I will.   [" It was

perhaps; a little *apprêté* and conscious that they are speaking to whole generations who are listening; but in the tone of their voices

"It was the enterprising Mr. Lintot, the redoubtable rival of Mr. Tonson, who, mounted on a stone-horse, overtook me in Windsor Forest. He said he heard I designed for Oxford, the seat of the Muses, and would, as my bookseller, by all means accompany me thither.

"I asked him where he got his horse? He answered he got it of his publisher; 'for that rogue, my printer' said he, 'disappointed me. I hoped to put him in good humour by a treat at the tavern of a brown fricassée of rabbits, which cost ten shillings, with two quarts of wine, besides my conversation. I thought myself cock-sure of his horse, which he readily promised me, but said that Mr. Tonson had just such another design of going to Cambridge, expecting there the copy of a new kind of Horace from Dr. ——; and if Mr. Tonson went, he was pre-engaged to attend him, being to have the printing of the said copy. So, in short, I borrowed this stone-horse of my publisher, which he had of Mr. Oldmixon for a debt. He lent me, too, the pretty boy you see after me. He was a smutty dog yesterday, and cost me more than two hours to wash the ink off his face; but the devil is a fair-conditioned devil, and very forward in his catechism. If you have any more bags he shall carry them.'

"I thought Mr. Lintot's civility not to be neglected, so gave the boy a small bag containing three shirts and an Elzevir Virgil, and, mounting in an instant, proceeded on the road, with my man before, my courteous stationer beside, and the aforesaid devil behind.

"Mr. Lintot began in this manner: 'Now, damn them! What if they should put it into the newspaper how you and I went together to Oxford? What would I care? If I should go down into Sussex they would say I was gone to the Speaker; but what of that? If my son were but big enough to go on with the business, by G—d, I would keep as good company as old Jacob.'

"Hereupon, I inquired of his son. 'The lad' says he, 'has fine parts, but is somewhat sickly, much as you are. I spare for nothing in his education at Westminster. Pray, don't you think Westminster to be the best school in England? Most of the late Ministry came out of it; so did many of this Ministry. I hope the boy will make his fortune.'

"'Don't you design to let him pass a year at Oxford?' 'To what purpose?' said he. 'The Universities do but make pedants, and I intend to breed him a man of business.'

"As Mr. Lintot was talking I observed he sat uneasy on his saddle, for which I expressed some solicitude. 'Nothing' says he. 'I can bear it well enough; but, since we have the day before us, methinks it would be very pleasant for you to rest awhile under the woods.' When we were alighted, 'See, here, what a mighty pretty Horace I have in my pocket? What, if you amused yourself in turning an ode till we mount again? Lord! if you

—pitched, as no doubt they are, beyond the mere conversation key
—in the expression of their thoughts, their various views and natures,

pleased, what a clever miscellany might you make at leisure hours?' 'Perhaps I may,' said I, 'if we ride on : the motion is an aid to my fancy; a round trot very much awakens my spirits ; then jog on apace, and I'll think as hard as I can.'

"Silence ensued for a full hour ; after which Mr. Lintot lugged the reins, stopped short, and broke out, 'Well, sir, how far have you gone?' I answered, seven miles. 'Z—ds, sir,' said Lintot, 'I thought you had done seven stanzas. Oldsworth, in a ramble round Wimbledon Hill, would translate a whole ode in half this time. I'll say that for Oldsworth [though I lost by his Timothy's], he translates an ode of Horace the quickest of any man in England. I remember Dr. King would write verses in a tavern, three hours after he could not speak : and there is Sir Richard, in that rumbling old chariot of his, between Fleet Ditch and St. Giles's Pound, shall make you half a Job.'

"'Pray, Mr. Lintot,' said I, 'now you talk of translators, what is your method of managing them?' 'Sir,' replied he, 'these are the saddest pack of rogues in the world : in a hungry fit, they'll swear they understand all the languages in the universe. I have known one of them take down a Greek book upon my counter and cry, "Ah, this is Hebrew, and must read it from the latter end." By G—d, I can never be sure in these fellows, for I neither understand Greek, Latin, French, nor Italian myself. But this is my way : I agree with them for ten shillings per sheet, with a proviso that I will have their doings corrected with whom I please ; so by one or the other they are led at last to the true sense of an author ; my judgment giving the negative to all my translators.' 'Then how are you sure these correctors may not impose upon you?' 'Why, I get any civil gentleman (especially any Scotchman) that comes into my shop, to read the original to me in English ; by this I know whether my first translator be deficient, and whether my corrector merits his money or not.

"'I'll tell you what happened to me last month. I bargained with S——— for a new version of "Lucretius," to publish against Tonson's, agreeing to pay the author so many shillings at his producing so many lines. He made a great progress in a very short time, and I gave it to the corrector to compare with the Latin ; but he went directly to Creech's translation, and found it the same, word for word, all but the first page. Now, what d'ye think I did? I arrested the translator for a cheat ; nay, and I stopped the corrector's pay, too, upon the proof that he had made use of Creech instead of the original.'

"'Pray tell me next how you deal with the critics?' 'Sir,' said he, 'nothing more easy. I can silence the most formidable of them : the rich ones for a sheet apiece of the blotted manuscript, which cost me nothing ; they'll go about with it to their acquaintance, and pretend they had it from the author, who submitted it to their correction : this has given some of them such an air, that in time they come to be consulted with and dedicated to as the

there is something generous, and cheering, and ennobling. You are
in the society of men who have filled the greatest parts in the world's

tip-top critics of the town.—As for the poor critics, I'll give you one instance
of my management, by which you may guess the rest : A lean man, that looked
like a very good scholar, came to me t'other day ; he turned over your Homer,
shook his head, shrugged up his shoulders, and pish'd at every line of it.
" One would wonder," says he, " at the strange presumption of some men ;
Homer is no such easy task as every stripling, every versifier "——he was
going on when my wife called to dinner. " Sir," said I, " will you please to
eat a piece of beef with me ? " " Mr. Lintot," said he, " I am very sorry you
should be at the expense of this great book : I am really concerned on your
account." " Sir, I am much obliged to you : if you can dine upon a piece of
beef, together with a slice of pudding——?"—" Mr. Lintot, I do not say but
Mr. Pope, if he would condescend to advise with men of learning——"—" Sir,
the pudding is upon the table, if you please to go in." My critic complies ;
he comes to a taste of your poetry, and tells me in the same breath that the
book is commendable, and the pudding excellent.

" ' Now, sir,' continued Mr. Lintot, ' in return for the frankness I have
shown, pray tell me, is it the opinion of your friends at court that my Lord
Lansdowne will be brought to the bar or not ? ' I told him I heard he would
not, and I hoped it, my lord being one I had particular obligations to.—' That
may be,' replied Mr. Lintot ; ' but by G—— if he is not, I shall lose the printing
of a very good trial.'

" These, my lord, are a few traits with which you discern the genius of
Mr. Lintot, which I have chosen for the subject of a letter. I dropped
him as soon as I got to Oxford, and paid a visit to my Lord Carleton, at
Middleton. . . .   " I am," &c.

"DR. SWIFT TO MR. POPE.

" *Sept.* 29, 1725.

" I am now returning to the noble scene of Dublin—into the *grand monde*
—for fear of burying my parts ; to signalise myself among curates and vicars,
and correct all corruptions crept in relating to the weight of bread-and-butter
through those dominions where I govern. I have employed my time (besides
ditching) in finishing, correcting, amending, and transcribing my ' Travels '
[Gulliver's], in four parts complete, newly augmented, and intended for the
press when the world shall deserve them, or rather, when a printer shall be
found brave enough to venture his ears. I like the scheme of our meeting
after distresses and dispersions ; but the chief end I propose to myself in all
my labours is to vex the world rather than divert it ; and if I could compass
that design without hurting my own person or fortune, I would be the most
indefatigable writer you have ever seen, without reading. I am exceedingly
pleased that you have done with translations ; Lord Treasurer Oxford often
lamented that a rascally world should lay you under a necessity of mis-

story—you are with St. John the statesman ; Peterborough the conqueror ; Swift, the greatest wit of all times ; Gay, the kindliest

employing your genius for so long a time ; but since you will now be so much better employed, when you think of the world, give it one lash the more at my request.   I have ever hated all nations, professions, and communities ; and all my love is towards individuals—for instance, I hate the tribe of lawyers, but I love Councillor Such-a-one and Judge Such-a-one : it is so with physicians (I will not speak of my own trade), soldiers, English, Scotch, French, and the rest.   But principally I hate and detest that animal called man—although I heartily love John, Peter, Thomas, and so forth.

" . . . . I have got materials towards a treatise proving the falsity of that definition *animal rationale*, and to show it should be only *rationis capax*. . . . . . The matter is so clear that it will admit of no dispute—nay, I will hold a hundred pounds that you and I agree in the point. . . . . .

"Mr. Lewis sent me an account of Dr. Arbuthnot's illness, which is a very sensible affliction to me, who, by living so long out of the world, have lost that hardness of heart contracted by years and general conversation.   I am daily losing friends, and neither seeking nor getting others.   Oh ! if the world had but a dozen of Arbuthnots in it, I would burn my ' Travels !' "

"Mr. Pope to Dr. Swift.

" *October* 15, 1725.

"I am wonderfully pleased with the suddenness of your kind answer.   It makes me hope you are coming towards us, and that you incline more and more to your old friends. . . . . Here is one [Lord Bolingbroke] who was once a powerful planet, but has now (after long experience of all that comes of shining) learned to be content with returning to his first point without the thought or ambition of shining at all.   Here is another [Edward, Earl of Oxford], who thinks one of the greatest glories of his father was to have distinguished and loved you, and who loves you hereditarily.   Here is Arbuthnot, recovered from the jaws of death, and more pleased with the hope of seeing you again than of reviewing a world, every part of which he has long despised but what is made up of a few men like yourself. . . . .

"Our friend Gay is used as the friends of Tories are by Whigs—and generally by Tories too.   Because he had humour, he was supposed to have dealt with Dr. Swift, in like manner as when any one had learning formerly, he was thought to have dealt with the devil. . . . . .

"Lord Bolingbroke had not the least harm by his fall ; I wish he had received no more by his other fall.   But Lord Bolingbroke is the most improved mind since you saw him, that ever was improved without shifting into a new body, or being *paullo minus ab angelis*.   I have often imagined to myself, that if ever all of us meet again, after so many varieties and changes, after so much of the old world and of the old man in each of us has been altered, that scarce a single thought of the one, any more than a single atom of the other, remains laugher—it is a privilege to sit in that company. Delightful and generous banquet! with a little faith and a little fancy any one of us here may enjoy it, and conjure up those great figures out of the past, and listen to their wit and wisdom. Mind that there is always a certain *cachet* about great men—they may be as mean on many points as you or I, but they carry their great air—they speak of common life more largely and generously than common men do—they regard the world with a manlier countenance, and see its real features more fairly than the timid shufflers who only dare to look up at life through blinkers, or to have an opinion when there is a crowd to back it. He who reads these noble records of a past age, salutes and reverences the great spirits who adorn it. You may go home now and talk with St. John; you may take a volume from your library and listen to Swift and Pope.

Might I give counsel to any young hearer, I would say to him, Try to frequent the company of your betters. In books and life that is the most wholesome society; learn to admire rightly; the great pleasure of life is that. Note what the great men admired; they admired great things: narrow spirits admire basely, and worship meanly. I know nothing in any story more gallant and cheering than the love and friendship which this company of famous men bore towards one another. There never has been a society of men more friendly, as there never was one more illustrious. Who dares quarrel with Mr. Pope, great and famous himself, for liking the society of men great and famous? and for liking them for the qualities which made them so? A mere pretty fellow from White's could not have written the "Patriot King," and would very likely have despised little Mr. Pope, the decrepit Papist, whom the great St. John held to be one of the best and greatest of men: a mere nobleman of the Court could no more have won Barcelona, than he could have written Peterborough's letters to Pope,* which are as

just the same; I have fancied, I say, that we should meet like the righteous in the millennium, quite in peace, divested of all our former passions, smiling at our past follies, and content to enjoy the kingdom of the just in tranquillity.

*　　　*　　　*　　　*　　　*　　　*

"I designed to have left the following page for Dr. Arbuthnot to fill, but he is so touched with the period in yours to me, concerning him, that he intends to answer it by a whole letter.　　*　　*　　*"

* Of the Earl of Peterborough, Walpole says:—"He was one of those men of careless wit and negligent grace, who scatter a thousand *bon-mots* and

witty as Congreve : a mere Irish Dean could not have written "Gulliver ; " and all these men loved Pope, and Pope loved all these men. To name his friends is to name the best men of his time. Addison had a senate ; Pope reverenced his equals. He spoke of Swift with respect and admiration always. His admiration for Bolingbroke was so great, that when some one said of his friend, "There is something in that great man which looks as if he was placed here by mistake," "Yes," Pope answered, "and when the comet appeared to us a month or two ago, I had sometimes an imagination that it might possibly be come to carry him home as a coach comes to one's door for visitors." So these great spirits spoke of one another. Show me six of the dullest middle-aged gentlemen that ever dawdled round a club table so faithful and so friendly.

We have said before that the chief wits of this time, with the exception of Congreve, were what we should now call men's men.

idle verses, which we painful compilers gather and hoard, till the authors stare to find themselves authors. Such was this lord, of an advantageous figure and enterprising spirit ; as gallant as Amadis and as brave ; but a little more expeditious in his journeys : for he is said to have seen more kings and more postilions than any man in Europe. . . . He was a man, as his friend said, who would neither live nor die like any other mortal."

"FROM THE EARL OF PETERBOROUGH TO POPE.

"You must receive my letters with a just impartiality, and give grains of allowance for a gloomy or rainy day ; I sink grievously with the weather-glass, and am quite spiritless when oppressed with the thoughts of a birthday or a return.

"Dutiful affection was bringing me to town ; but undutiful laziness, and being much out of order, keep me in the country : however, if alive, I must make my appearance at the birthday. . . .

"You seem to think it vexatious that I shall allow you but one woman at a time either to praise or love. If I dispute with you upon this point, I doubt every jury will give a verdict against me. So, sir, with a Mahometan indulgence, I allow your pluralities, the favourite privilege of our church.

"I find you don't mend upon correction ; again I tell you you must not think of women in a reasonable way ; you know we always make goddesses of those we adore upon earth ; and do not all the good men tell us we must lay aside reason in what relates to the Deity ?

" . . . I should have been glad of anything of Swift's. Pray, when you write to him next, tell him I expect him with impatience, in a place as odd and as much out of the way as himself.   "Yours."

Peterborough married Mrs. Anastasia Robinson, the celebrated singer.

They spent many hours of the four-and-twenty, a fourth part of each day nearly, in clubs and coffee-houses, where they dined, drank, and smoked. Wit and news went by word of mouth ; a journal of 1710 contained the very smallest portion of one or the other. The chiefs spoke, the faithful *habitués* sat round ; strangers came to wonder and listen. Old Dryden had his head-quarters at "Will's," in Russell Street, at the corner of Bow Street : at which place Pope saw him when he was twelve years old. The company used to assemble on the first floor—what was called the dining-room floor in those days— and sat at various tables smoking their pipes. It is recorded that the beaux of the day thought it a great honour to be allowed to take a pinch out of Dryden's snuff-box. When Addison began to reign, he with a certain crafty propriety—a policy let us call it—which belonged to his nature, set up his court, and appointed the officers of his royal house. His palace was "Button's," opposite "Will's." * A quiet opposition, a silent assertion of empire, distinguished this great man. Addison's ministers were Budgell, Tickell, Phillips, Carey ; his master of the horse, honest Dick Steele, who was what Duroc was to Napoleon, or Hardy to Nelson ; the man who performed his master's bidding, and would have cheerfully died in his quarrel. Addison lived with these people for seven or eight hours every day. The male society passed over their punch-bowls and tobacco-pipes about as much time as ladies of that age spent over Spadille and Manille.

For a brief space, upon coming up to town, Pope formed part of King Joseph's court, and was his rather too eager and obsequi- ous humble servant.† Dick Steele, the editor of the *Tatler*, Mr.

---

* "Button had been a servant in the Countess of Warwick's family, who, under the patronage of Addison, kept a coffee-house on the south side of Russell Street, about two doors from Covent Garden. Here it was that the wits of that time used to assemble. It is said that when Addison had suffered any vexation from the Countess, he withdrew the company from Button's house.

"From the coffee-house he went again to a tavern, where he often sat late and drank too much wine."—DR. JOHNSON.

Will's coffee-house was on the west side of Bow Street, and "corner of Russell Street." See "Handbook of London."

† "My acquaintance with Mr. Addison commenced in 1712 : I liked him then as well as I liked any man, and was very fond of his conversation. It was very soon after that Mr. Addison advised me 'not to be content with the applause of half the nation.' He used to talk much and often to me, of moderation in parties : and used to blame his dear friend Steele for being too much of a party man. He encouraged me in my design of translating the

Addison's man, and his own man too—a person of no little figure in the world of letters, patronized the young poet, and set him a task or two. Young Mr. Pope did the tasks very quickly and smartly (he had been at the feet, quite as a boy, of Wycherley's * decrepit reputation, and propped up for a year that doting old wit) : he was anxious to be well with the men of letters, to get a footing and a recognition. He thought it an honour to be admitted into their company ; to have the

'Iliad,' which was begun that year, and finished in 1718."—POPE. *Spence's Anecdotes.*

"Addison had Budgell, and I think Phillips, in the house with him.—Gay they would call one of my *élèves.*—They were angry with me for keeping so much with Dr. Swift and some of the late Ministry."—POPE. *Spence's Anecdotes.*

* "To MR. BLOUNT.

"*Jan.* 21, 1715–16.

"I know of nothing that will be so interesting to you at present as some circumstances of the last act of that eminent comic poet and our friend, Wycherley. He had often told me, and I doubt not he did all his acquaintance, that he would marry as soon as his life was despaired of. Accordingly, a few days before his death, he underwent the ceremony, and joined together those two sacraments which wise men say we should be the last to receive ; for, if you observe, matrimony is placed after extreme unction in our catechism, as a kind of hint of the order of time in which they are to be taken. The old man then lay down, satisfied in the consciousness of having, by this one act, obliged a woman who (he was told) had merit, and shown an heroic resentment of the ill-usage of his next heir. Some hundred pounds which he had with the lady discharged his debts ; a jointure of 500*l.* a year made her a recompence ; and the nephew was left to comfort himself as well as he could with the miserable remains of a mortgaged estate. I saw our friend twice after this was done—less peevish in his sickness than he used to be in his health ; neither much afraid of dying, nor (which in him had been more likely) much ashamed of marrying. The evening before he expired, he called his young wife to the bedside, and earnestly entreated her not to deny him one request—the last he should make. Upon her assurances of consenting to it, he told her : 'My dear, it is only this—that you will never marry an old man again.' I cannot help remarking that sickness, which often destroys both wit and wisdom, yet seldom has power to remove that talent which we call humour. Mr. Wycherley showed his even in his last compliment ; though I think his request a little hard, for why should he bar her from doubling her jointure on the same easy terms?

"So trivial as these circumstances are, I should not be displeased myself to know such trifles when they concern or characterize any eminent person. The wisest and wittiest of men are seldom wiser or wittier than others in these sober moments ; at least, our friend ended much in the same character he had confidence of Mr. Addison's friend, Captain Steele. His eminent parts obtained for him the honour of heralding Addison's triumph of " Cato " with his admirable prologue, and heading the victorious procession as it were. Not content with this act of homage and admiration, he wanted to distinguish himself by assaulting Addison's enemies, and attacked John Dennis with a prose lampoon, which highly offended his lofty patron. Mr. Steele was instructed to write to Mr. Dennis, and inform him that Mr. Pope's pamphlet against him was written quite without Mr. Addison's approval.* Indeed, " The Narrative of Dr. Robert Norris on the Phrenzy of J. D." is a vulgar and mean satire, and such a blow as the magnificent Addison could never desire to see any partisan of his strike in any literary quarrel. Pope was closely allied with Swift when he wrote this pamphlet. It is so dirty that it has been printed in Swift's works, too. It bears the foul marks of the master hand. Swift admired and enjoyed with all his heart the prodigious genius of the young Papist lad out of Windsor Forest, who had never seen a university in his life, and came and conquered the Dons and the doctors with his wit. He applauded, and loved him, too, and protected him, and taught him mischief. I wish Addison could have loved him better. The best satire that ever has been penned would never have been written then ; and one of the best characters the world ever knew would have been without a flaw. But he who had so few equals could not bear one, and Pope was more than that. When Pope, trying for himself, and soaring on his immortal young wings, found that his, too, was a genius, which no pinion of that age could follow, he rose and left Addison's company, settling on his own eminence, and singing his own song.

It was not possible that Pope should remain a retainer of Mr. Addison ; nor likely that after escaping from his vassalage and assuming an independent crown, the sovereign whose allegiance he

---

lived in ; and Horace's rule for play may as well be applied to him as a playwright : —

> " ' Servetur ad imum
> Qualis ab incepto processerit et sibi constet.'
>
> " I am," &c.

* " Addison, who was no stranger to the world, probably saw the selfishness of Pope's friendship ; and resolving that he should have the consequences of his officiousness to himself, informed Dennis by Steele that he was sorry for the insult."—JOHNSON : *Life of Addison.*

quitted should view him amicably.* They did not do wrong to mislike each other. They but followed the impulse of nature, and the consequence of position. When Bernadotte became heir to a throne, the Prince Royal of Sweden was naturally Napoleon's enemy. "There are many passions and tempers of mankind," says Mr. Addison in the *Spectator*, speaking a couple of years before the little differences between him and Mr. Pope took place, "which naturally dispose us to depress and vilify the merit of one rising in the esteem of mankind. All those who made their entrance into the world with the same advantages, and were once looked on as his equals, are apt to think the fame of his merits a reflection on their own deserts. Those who were once his equals envy and defame him, because they now see him the superior ; and those who were once his superiors, because they look upon him as their equal." Did Mr. Addison, justly perhaps thinking that, as young Mr. Pope had not had the benefit of a university education, he couldn't know Greek, therefore he couldn't translate Homer, encourage his young friend Mr. Tickell, of Queen's, to translate that poet, and aid him with his own known scholarship and skill ? † It was natural that Mr. Addison should doubt of the learning of an amateur Grecian, should have a high opinion of Mr. Tickell, of Queen's, and should help that ingenious young man. It was natural, on the other hand, that Mr. Pope and Mr. Pope's friends should believe that this counter-translation, suddenly advertised and so long written, though Tickell's college friends had never heard of it—though, when Pope first wrote to Addison regarding his scheme, Mr. Addison knew nothing of the similar project of Tickell, of Queen's—it was natural that Mr. Pope

---

* "While I was heated with what I heard, I wrote a letter to Mr. Addison, to let him know 'that I was not unacquainted with this behaviour of his ; that if I was to speak of him severely in return for it, it should not be in such a dirty way ; that I should rather tell him himself fairly of his faults, and allow his good qualities ; and that it should be something in the following manner.' I then subjoined the first sketch of what has since been called my satire on Addison. He used me very civilly ever after ; and never did me any injustice, that I know of, from that time to his death, which was about three years after."—POPE. *Spence's Anecdotes.*

† "That Tickell should have been guilty of a villany seems to us highly improbable; that Addison should have been guilty of a villany seems to us highly improbable ; but that these two men should have conspired together to commit a villany, seems, to us, improbable in a tenfold degree."—MACAULAY.

and his friends, having interests, passions, and prejudices of their own, should believe that Tickell's translation was but an act of opposition against Pope, and that they should call Mr. Tickell's emulation Mr. Addison's envy—if envy it were.

> " And were there one whose fires
> True genius kindles and fair fame inspires,
> Blest with each talent and each art to please,
> And born to write, converse, and live with ease ;
> Should such a man, too fond to rule alone,
> Bear like the Turk no brother near the throne ;
> View him with scornful yet with jealous eyes,
> And hate, for arts that caused himself to rise ;
> Damn with faint praise, assent with civil leer,
> And without sneering, teach the rest to sneer ;
> Willing to wound, and yet afraid to strike,
> Just hint a fault, and hesitate dislike ;
> Alike reserved to blame as to commend,
> A timorous foe and a suspicious friend ;
> Dreading even fools, by flatterers besieged,
> And so obliging that he ne'er obliged :
> Like Cato give his little senate laws,
> And sit attentive to his own applause ;
> While wits and templars every sentence raise,
> And wonder with a foolish face of praise ;
> Who but must laugh if such a man there be,
> Who would not weep if Atticus were he?"

" I sent the verses to Mr. Addison," said Pope, " and he used me very civilly ever after." No wonder he did. It was shame very likely more than fear that silenced him. Johnson recounts an interview between Pope and Addison after their quarrel, in which Pope was angry, and Addison tried to be contemptuous and calm. Such a weapon as Pope's must have pierced any scorn. It flashes for ever, and quivers in Addison's memory. His great figure looks out on us from the past—stainless but for that—pale, calm, and beautiful : it bleeds from that black wound. He should be drawn, like St. Sebastian, with that arrow in his side. As he sent to Gay and asked his pardon, as he bade his stepson come and see his death, be sure he had forgiven Pope, when he made ready to show how a Christian could die.

Pope then formed part of the Addisonian court for a short time, and describes himself in his letters as sitting with that coterie until two o'clock in the morning over punch and burgundy amidst the fumes of tobacco. To use an expression of the present day, the

"pace" of those *viveurs* of the former age was awful.   Peterborough
lived into the very jaws of death ; Godolphin laboured all day and
gambled at night ; Bolingbroke,* writing to Swift, from Dawley, in
his retirement, dating his letter at six o'clock in the morning, and
rising, as he says, refreshed, serene, and calm, calls to mind the time
of his London life ; when about that hour he used to be going to
bed, surfeited with pleasure, and jaded with business ; his head often
full of schemes, and his heart as often full of anxiety.   It was too
hard, too coarse a life for the sensitive, sickly Pope.   He was the
only wit of the day, a friend writes to me, who wasn't fat.†   Swift was
fat ; Addison was fat ; Steele was fat ; Gay and Thomson were pre-
posterously fat—all that fuddling and punch-drinking, that club and
coffee-house boozing, shortened the lives and enlarged the waistcoats
of the men of that age.   Pope withdrew in a great measure from this
boisterous London company, and being put into an independence by
the gallant exertions of Swift ‡ and his private friends, and by the

* "LORD BOLINGBROKE TO THE THREE YAHOOS OF TWICKENHAM.

"*July* 23, 1726.

"JONATHAN, ALEXANDER, JOHN, MOST EXCELLENT TRIUMVIRS OF
PARNASSUS,—

"Though you are probably very indifferent where I am, or what I am
doing, yet I resolve to believe the contrary.   I persuade myself that you have
sent at least fifteen times within this fortnight to Dawley farm, and that you
are extremely mortified at my long silence.   To relieve you, therefore, from
this great anxiety of mind, I can do no less than write a few lines to you ; and
I please myself beforehand with the vast pleasure which this epistle must needs
give you.   That I may add to this pleasure, and give further proofs of my
beneficent temper, I will likewise inform you, that I shall be in your neighbourhood again, by the end of next week : by which time I hope that
Jonathan's imagination of business will be succeeded by some imagination
more becoming a professor of that divine science, *la bagatelle*.   Adieu.
Jonathan, Alexander, John, mirth be with you !"

† Prior must be excepted from this observation.   "He was lank and
lean."

‡ Swift exerted himself very much in promoting the " Iliad " subscription ;
and also introduced Pope to Harley and Bolingbroke.—Pope realised by the
" Iliad " upwards of 5,000*l.*, which he laid out partly in annuities, and partly
in the purchase of his famous villa.   Johnson remarks that "it would be hard
to find a man so well entitled to notice by his wit, that ever delighted so much
in talking of his money."

enthusiastic national admiration which justly rewarded his great
achievement of the "Iliad," purchased that famous villa of Twickenham

which his song and life celebrated ; duteously bringing his old parent
to live and die there, entertaining his friends there, and making

occasional visits to London in his little chariot, in which Atterbury compared him to " Homer in a nutshell."

"Mr. Dryden was not a genteel man," Pope quaintly said to Spence, speaking of the manner and habits of the famous old patriarch of " Will's." With regard to Pope's own manners, we have the best contemporary authority that they were singularly refined and polished. With his extraordinary sensibility, with his known tastes, with his delicate frame, with his power and dread of ridicule, Pope could have been no other than what we call a highly-bred person.* His closest friends, with the exception of Swift, were among the delights and ornaments of the polished society of their age. Garth,† the accomplished and benevolent, whom Steele has described so charmingly, of whom Codrington said that his character was " all beauty," and whom Pope himself called the best of Christians without knowing it; Arbuthnot,‡ one of the wisest, wittiest, most

* " His (Pope's) voice in common conversation was so naturally musical, that I remember honest Tom Southerne used always to call him ' the little nightingale.' "—ORRERY.

† Garth, whom Dryden calls "generous as his Muse," was a Yorkshire-man. He graduated at Cambridge, and was made M.D. in 1691. He soon distinguished himself in his profession, by his poem of the " Dispensary," and in society, and pronounced Dryden's funeral oration. He was a strict Whig, a notable member of the " Kit-Cat," and a friendly, convivial, able man. He was knighted by George I., with the Duke of Marlborough's sword. He died in 1718.

‡ " Arbuthnot was the son of an episcopal clergyman in Scotland, and belonged to an ancient and distinguished Scotch family. He was educated at Aberdeen ; and, coming up to London—according to a Scotch practice often enough alluded to—to make his fortune—first made himself known by ' An Examination of Dr. Woodward's Account of the Deluge.' He became physician successively to Prince George of Denmark and to Queen Anne. He is usually allowed to have been the most learned, as well as one of the most witty and humourous members of the Scriblerus Club. The opinion enter-tained of him by the humourists of the day is abundantly evidenced in their correspondence. When he found himself in his last illness, he wrote thus, from his retreat at Hampstead, to Swift :—

" 'MY DEAR AND WORTHY FRIEND,—   '*Hampstead, Oct.* 4, 1734.

" ' You have no reason to put me among the rest of your forgetful friends, for I wrote two long letters to you, to which I never received one word of answer. The first was about your health ; the last I sent a great while ago, by one De la Mar. I can assure you with great truth that none of your friends accomplished, gentlest of mankind ; Bolingbroke, the Alcibiades of his age ; the generous Oxford ; the magnificent, the witty, the

or acquaintance has a more warm heart towards you than myself. I am going out of this troublesome world, and you, among the rest of my friends, shall have my last prayers and good wishes.

" ' . . . I came out to this place so reduced by a dropsy and an asthma, that I could neither sleep, breathe, eat, nor move. I most earnestly desired and begged of God that he would take me. Contrary to my expectation, upon venturing to ride (which I had forborne for some years), I recovered my strength to a pretty considerable degree, slept, and had my stomach again. . . . What I did, I can assure you was not for life, but ease ; for I am at present in the case of a man that was almost in harbour, and then blown back to sea—who has a reasonable hope of going to a good place, and an absolute certainty of leaving a very bad one. Not that I have any particular disgust at the world ; for I have as great comfort in my own family and from the kindness of my friends as any man ; but the world, in the main, displeases me, and I have too true a presentiment of calamities that are to befall my country. However, if I should have the happiness to see you before I die, you will find that I enjoy the comforts of life with my usual cheerfulness. I cannot imagine why you are frightened from a journey to England : the reasons you assign are not sufficient—the journey I am sure would do you good. In general, I recommend riding, of which I have always had a good opinion, and can now confirm it from my own experience.

" ' My family give you their love and service. The great loss I sustained in one of them gave me my first shock, and the trouble I have with the rest to bring them to a right temper to bear the loss of a father who loves them, and whom they love, is really a most sensible affliction to me. I am afraid, my dear friend, we shall never see one another more in this world. I shall, to the last moment, preserve my love and esteem for you, being well assured you will never leave the paths of virtue and honour ; for all that is in this world is not worth the least deviation from the way. It will be great pleasure to me to hear from you sometimes ; for none are with more sincerity than I am, my dear friend, your most faithful friend and humble servant.' "

" Arbuthnot," Johnson says, " was a man of great comprehension, skilful in his profession, versed in the sciences, acquainted with ancient literature, and able to animate his mass of knowledge by a bright and active imagination ; a scholar with great brilliance of wit ; a wit who, in the crowd of life, retained and discovered a noble ardour of religious zeal. "

Dugald Stewart has testified to Arbuthnot's ability in a department of which he was particularly qualified to judge : " Let me add, that, in the list of philosophical reformers, the authors of ' Martinus Scriblerus ' ought not to be overlooked. Their happy ridicule of the scholastic logic and metaphysics is universally known ; but few are aware of the acuteness and sagacity displayed in their allusions to some of the most vulnerable passages in Locke's ' Essay.'

famous, and chivalrous Peterborough : these were the fast and
faithful friends of Pope, the most brilliant company of friends, let us
repeat, that the world has ever seen.   The favourite recreation of his
leisure hours was the society of painters, whose art he practised.   In
his correspondence are letters between him and Jervas, whose pupil
he loved to be—Richardson, a celebrated artist of his time, and who
painted for him a portrait of his old mother, and for whose picture he
asked and thanked Richardson in one of the most delightful letters
that ever was penned,*—and the wonderful Kneller, who bragged
more, spelt worse, and painted better than any artist of his day.†

It is affecting to note, through Pope's Correspondence, the marked
way in which his friends, the greatest, the most famous, and wittiest
men of the time—generals and statesmen, philosophers and divines—
all have a kind word and a kind thought for the good simple old
mother, whom Pope tended so affectionately.   Those men would have

In this part of the work it is commonly understood that Arbuthnot had the
principal share."—*See Preliminary Dissertation to Encyclopædia Britannica*,
note to p. 242, and also note B. B. B., p. 285.

* " To Mr. Richardson.

" *Twickenham, June* 10, 1733.

" As I know you and I mutually desire to see one another, I hoped that this
day our wishes would have met, and brought you hither.   And this for the
very reason, which possibly might hinder you coming, that my poor mother is
dead.   I thank God, her death was as easy as her life was innocent ; and as it
cost her not a groan, or even a sigh, there is yet upon her countenance such an
expression of tranquillity, nay, almost of pleasure, that it is even amiable to
behold it.   It would afford the finest image of a saint expired that ever painting drew ; and it would be the greatest obligation which even that obliging
art could ever bestow on a friend, if you could come and sketch it for me.   I
am sure, if there be no very prevalent obstacle, you will leave any common
business to do this ; and I hope to see you this evening, as late as you will, or
to-morrow morning as early, before this winter flower is faded.   I will defer
her interment till to-morrow night.   I know you love me, or I could not have
written this—I could not (at this time) have written at all.   Adieu !   May you
die as happily !   " Yours " &c.

† " Mr. Pope was with Sir Godfrey Kneller one day, when his nephew, a
Guinea trader, came in.   ' Nephew,' said Sir Godfrey, ' you have the honour
of seeing the two greatest men in the world.'—' I don't know how great you
may be,' said the Guinea man, ' but I don't like your looks : I have often
bought a man much better than both of you together, all muscles and bones,
for ten guineas.' "—Dr. Warburton.   *Spence's Anecdotes.*

scarcely valued her, but that they knew how much he loved her, and that they pleased him by thinking of her. If his early letters to women are affected and insincere, whenever he speaks about this one, it is with a childish tenderness and an almost sacred simplicity. In 1713, when young Mr. Pope had, by a series of the most astonishing victories and dazzling achievements, seized the crown of poetry, and the town was in an uproar of admiration, or hostility, for the young chief; when Pope was issuing his famous decrees for the translation of the "Iliad;" when Dennis and the lower critics were hooting and assailing him; when Addison and the gentlemen of his court were sneering with sickening hearts at the prodigious triumphs of the young conqueror; when Pope, in a fever of victory, and genius, and hope, and anger, was struggling through the crowd of shouting friends and furious detractors to his temple of Fame, his old mother writes from the country, "My deare," says she—"My deare, there's Mr. Blount, of Mapel Durom, dead the same day that Mr. Inglefield died. Your sister is well; but your brother is sick. My service to Mrs. Blount, and all that ask of me. I hope to hear from you, and that you are well, which is my daily prayer; and this with my blessing." The triumph marches by, and the car of the young conqueror, the hero of a hundred brilliant victories: the fond mother sits in the quiet cottage at home and says, "I send you my daily prayers, and I bless you, my deare."

In our estimate of Pope's character, let us always take into account that constant tenderness and fidelity of affection which pervaded and sanctified his life, and never forget that maternal benediction.* It accompanied him always: his life seems purified by those artless and heartfelt prayers. And he seems to have received and deserved the fond attachment of the other members of his family. It is not a little touching to read in Spence of the enthusiastic admiration with which his half-sister regarded him, and the simple anecdote by which she illustrates her love. "I think no man was ever so little fond of money." Mrs. Rackett says about her brother, "I think my brother when he was young read more books than

---

* Swift's mention of him as one

> "—— whose filial piety excels
> Whatever Grecian story tells,"

is well known. And a sneer of Walpole's may be put to a better use than he ever intended it for, *àpropos* of this subject.—He charitably sneers, in one of his letters, at Spence's "fondling an old mother—in imitation of Pope!"

any man in the world ; " and she falls to telling stories of his school-days, and the manner in which his master at Twyford ill-used him. " I don't think my brother knew what fear was," she continues ; and the accounts of Pope's friends bear out this character for courage. When he had exasperated the dunces, and threats of violence and personal assault were brought to him, the dauntless little champion never for one instant allowed fear to disturb him, or condescended to take any guard in his daily walks except occasion-ally his faithful dog to bear him company. " I had rather die at once," said the gallant little cripple, " than live in fear of those rascals."

As for his death, it was what the noble Arbuthnot asked and enjoyed for himself—a euthanasia—a beautiful end. A perfect benevolence, affection, serenity, hallowed the departure of that high soul. Even in the very hallucinations of his brain, and weaknesses of his delirium, there was something almost sacred. Spence describes him in his last days, looking up and with a rapt gaze as if something had suddenly passed before him. " He said to me, 'What's that?' pointing into the air with a very steady regard, and then looked down and said, with a smile of the greatest softness, '''Twas a vision ! '" He laughed scarcely ever, but his companions describe his countenance as often illuminated by a peculiar sweet smile.

" When," said Spence,* the kind anecdotist whom Johnson despised—" When I was telling Lord Bolingbroke that Mr. Pope, on every catching and recovery of his mind, was always saying something kindly of his present or absent friends; and that this was so surprising, as it seemed to me as if humanity had outlasted understanding, Lord Bolingbroke said, ' It has so,' and then added, ' I never in my life knew a man who had so tender a heart for his particular friends, or a more general friendship for mankind. I have known him these thirty years, and value myself more for that man's love than——' Here," Spence says, " St. John sunk his head and lost his voice in tears." The sob which finishes the epitaph is finer than words. It is the cloak

---

* Joseph Spence was the son of a clergyman, near Winchester. He was a short time at Eton, and afterwards became a Fellow of New College, Oxford, a clergyman, and professor of poetry. He was a friend of Thomson's, whose reputation he aided. He published an " Essay on the Odyssey " in 1726, which introduced him to Pope. Everybody liked him. His " Anec-dotes " were placed, while still in MS., at the service of Johnson and also of Malone. They were published by Mr. Singer in 1820.

thrown over the father's face in the famous Greek picture, which hides the grief and heightens it.

In Johnson's " Life of Pope " you will find described, with rather a malicious minuteness, some of the personal habits and infirmities of the great little Pope. His body was crooked, he was so short that it was necessary to raise his chair in order to place him on a level with other people at table.* He was sewed up in a buckram suit every morning and required a nurse like a child. His contemporaries reviled these misfortunes with a strange acrimony, and made his poor deformed person the butt for many a bolt of heavy wit. The facetious Mr. Dennis, in speaking of him, says, " If you take the first letter of Mr. Alexander Pope's Christian name, and the first and last letters of his surname, you have A. P. E." Pope catalogues, at the end of the " Dunciad," with a rueful precision, other pretty names, besides Ape, which Dennis called him. That great critic pronounced Mr. Pope a little ass, a fool, a coward, a Papist, and therefore a hater of Scripture, and so forth. It must be remembered that the pillory was a flourishing and popular institution in those days. Authors stood in it in the body sometimes : and dragged their enemies thither morally, hooted them with foul abuse and assailed them with garbage of the gutter. Poor Pope's figure was an easy one for those clumsy caricaturists to draw. Any stupid hand could draw a hunchback and write Pope underneath. They did. A libel was published against Pope, with such a frontispiece. This kind of rude jesting was an evidence not only of an ill nature, but a dull one. When a child makes a pun or a lout breaks out into a laugh, it is some very obvious combination of words, or discrepancy of objects, which provokes the infantine satirist, or tickles the boorish wag ; and many of Pope's revilers laughed, not so much because they were wicked, as because they knew no better.

Without the utmost sensibility, Pope could not have been the poet he was ; and through his life, however much he protested that he disregarded their abuse, the coarse ridicule of his opponents stung and

---

* He speaks of Arbuthnot's having helped him through "that long disease, my life." But not only was he so feeble as is implied in his use of the " buckram," but " it now appears," says Mr. Peter Cunningham, " from his unpublished letters, that, like Lord Hervey, he had recourse to ass's-milk for the preservation of his health." It is to his lordship's use of that simple beverage that he alludes when he says—

> " Let Sporus tremble !—A. What, that thing of silk,
> Sporus, that mere white-curd of ass's milk ? "

tore him. One of Cibber's pamphlets coming into Pope's hands, whilst Richardson the painter was with him, Pope turned round and said, "These things are my diversions;" and Richardson, sitting by whilst Pope perused the libel, said he saw his features "writhing with anguish." How little human nature changes! Can't one see that little figure? Can't one fancy one is reading Horace? Can't one fancy one is speaking of to-day?

The tastes and sensibilities of Pope, which led him to cultivate the society of persons of fine manners, or wit, or taste, or beauty, caused him to shrink equally from that shabby and boisterous crew which formed the rank and file of literature in his time : and he was as unjust to these men as they to him. The delicate little creature sickened at habits and company which were quite tolerable to robuster men : and in the famous feud between Pope and the Dunces, and without attributing any peculiar wrong to either, one can quite understand how the two parties should so hate each other. As I fancy, it was a sort of necessity that when Pope's triumph passed, Mr. Addison and his men should look rather contemptuously down on it from their balcony; so it was natural for Dennis and Tibbald, and Welsted and Cibber, and the worn and hungry pressmen in the crowd below, to howl at him and assail him. And Pope was more savage to Grub Street than Grub Street was to Pope. The thong with which he lashed them was dreadful; he fired upon that howling crew such shafts of flame and poison, he slew and wounded so fiercely, that in reading the "Dunciad" and the prose lampoons of Pope, one feels disposed to side against the ruthless little tyrant, at least to pity those wretched folks on whom he was so unmerciful. It was Pope, and Swift to aid him, who established among us the Grub Street tradition. He revels in base descriptions of poor men's want ; he gloats over poor Dennis's garret, and flannel-nightcap and red stockings; he gives instructions how to find Curll's authors, the historian at the tallow-chandler's under the blind arch in Petty France, the two translators in bed together, the poet in the cock-loft in Budge Row, whose landlady keeps the ladder. It was Pope, I fear, who contributed, more than any man who ever lived, to depreciate the literary calling. It was not an unprosperous one before that time, as we have seen; at least there were great prizes in the profession which had made Addison a Minister, and Prior an Ambassador, and Steele a Commissioner, and Swift all but a Bishop. The profession of letters was ruined by that libel of the "Dunciad." If authors were wretched and poor before, if some of them lived in haylofts, of which their landladies kept the ladders, at least nobody came to disturb them in their straw ; if three of them had but one coat between them, the two remained invisible in the garret, the third, at any rate, appeared decently at the coffee-house and paid his twopence like a gentleman. It was Pope that dragged into light all this poverty and meanness, and held up those wretched shifts and rags to public ridicule. It was Pope that has made generations of the reading world (delighted with the mischief, as who would not be that reads it ?) believe that author and wretch, author and rags, author and dirt, author and drink, gin, cowheel, tripe, poverty, duns, bailiffs, squalling children and clamorous landladies, were always associated together. The condition of authorship began to fall from the days of the " Dunciad :" and I believe in my heart that much of that obloquy which has since pursued our calling was occasioned by Pope's libels and wicked wit. Everybody read those. Everybody was familiarised with the idea of the poor devil, the author. The manner is so captivating that young authors practise it, and begin their career with satire. It is so easy to write, and so pleasant to read ! to fire a shot that makes a giant wince, perhaps ; and fancy one's self his conqueror. It is easy to shoot—but not as Pope did. The shafts of his satire rise sublimely : no poet's verse ever mounted higher than that wonderful flight with which the " Dunciad " concludes :—*

> "She comes, she comes ! the sable throne behold
> Of Night primeval and of Chaos old ;
> Before her, Fancy's gilded clouds decay,
> And all its varying rainbows die away ;
> Wit shoots in vain its momentary fires,
> The meteor drops, and in a flash expires.
> As, one by one, at dread Medea's strain
> The sick'ning stars fade off the ethereal plain ;
> As Argus' eyes, by Hermes' wand oppress'd,
> Closed, one by one, to everlasting rest ;—
> Thus, at her fell approach and secret might,
> Art after Art goes out, and all is night.
> See skulking Truth to her old cavern fled,
> Mountains of casuistry heaped o'er her head ;
> Philosophy, that leaned on Heaven before,
> Shrinks to her second cause and is no more.
> Religion, blushing, veils her sacred fires,
> And, unawares, Morality expires.

---

* " He (Johnson) repeated to us, in his forcible melodious manner, the concluding lines of the ' Dunciad.' "—BOSWELL.

> Nor public flame, nor private, dares to shine,
> Nor human spark is left, nor glimpse divine.
> Lo ! thy dread empire, Chaos, is restored,
> Light dies before thy uncreating word ;
> Thy hand, great Anarch, lets the curtain fall,
> And universal darkness buries all." *

In these astonishing lines Pope reaches, I think, to the very greatest height which his sublime art has attained, and shows himself the equal of all poets of all times. It is the brightest ardour, the loftiest assertion of truth, the most generous wisdom illustrated by the noblest poetic figure, and spoken in words the aptest, grandest, and most harmonious. It is heroic courage speaking : a splendid declaration of righteous wrath and war. It is the gage flung down, and the silver trumpet ringing defiance to falsehood and tyranny, deceit, dulness, superstition. It is Truth, the champion, shining and intrepid, and fronting the great world-tyrant with armies of slaves at his back. It is a wonderful and victorious single-combat, in that great battle, which has always been waging since society began.

In speaking of a work of consummate art one does not try to show what it actually is, for that were vain ; but what it is like, and what are the sensations produced in the mind of him who views it. And in considering Pope's admirable career, I am forced into similitudes drawn from other courage and greatness, and into comparing him with those who achieved triumphs in actual war. I think of the works of young Pope as I do of the actions of young Buonaparte or young Nelson. In their common life you will find frailties and mean-nesses, as great as the vices and follies of the meanest men. But in the presence of the great occasion, the great soul flashes out, and conquers transcendent. In thinking of the splendour of Pope's young victories, of his merit, unequalled as his renown, I hail and salute the achieving genius, and do homage to the pen of a hero.

---

* "Mr. Langton informed me that he once related to Johnson (on the authority of Spence), that Pope himself admired these lines so much that when he repeated them his voice faltered. ' And well it might, sir,' said Johnson, " for they are noble lines.' "—J. BOSWELL, junior.

HOGARTH, SMOLLETT, AND FIELDING.

I SUPPOSE, as long as novels last and authors aim at interesting their public, there must always be in the story a virtuous and gallant hero, a wicked monster his opposite, and a pretty girl who finds a champion; bravery and virtue conquer beauty; and vice, after seeming to triumph through a certain number of pages, is sure to be discomfited in the last volume, when justice overtakes him and honest folks come by their own. There never was perhaps a greatly popular story but this simple plot was carried through it: mere satiric wit is addressed to a class of readers and thinkers quite different to those simple souls who laugh and weep over the novel. I fancy very few ladies, indeed, for instance, could be brought to like "Gulliver" heartily, and (putting the coarseness and difference of manners out of the question) to relish the wonderful satire of "Jonathan Wild." In that strange apologue, the author takes for a hero the greatest rascal, coward, traitor, tyrant, hypocrite, that his wit and experience, both large in this matter, could enable him to devise or depict; he accompanies this villain through all the actions of his life, with a grinning deference and a wonderful mock respect: and doesn't leave him, till he is dangling at the gallows, when the satirist makes him a low bow and wishes the scoundrel good day.

It was not by satire of this sort, or by scorn and contempt, that

Hogarth achieved his vast popularity and acquired his reputation.*
His art is quite simple,† he speaks popular parables to interest simple

* Coleridge speaks of the "beautiful female faces" in Hogarth's pictures,
'in whom," he says, "the satirist never extinguished that love of beauty which
belonged to him as a poet."—*The Friend.*

† "I was pleased with the reply of a gentleman, who, being asked which
book he esteemed most in his library, answered 'Shakespeare :' being asked
which he esteemed next best, replied 'Hogarth.' His graphic representations
are indeed books : they have the teeming, fruitful, suggestive meaning of
words. Other pictures we look at—his prints we read. . . . .

"The quantity of thought which Hogarth crowds into every picture would
almost unvulgarise every subject which he might choose. . . . .

"I say not that all the ridiculous subjects of Hogarth have necessarily
something in them to make us like them ; some are indifferent to us, some in
their nature repulsive, and only made interesting by the wonderful skill and
truth to nature in the painter ; but I contend that there is in most of them that
sprinkling of the better nature, which, like holy water, chases away and dis-
perses the contagion of the bad. They have this in them, besides, that they
bring us acquainted with the every-day human face,—they give us skill to
detect those gradations of sense and virtue (which escape the careless or
fastidious observer) in the circumstances of the world about us ; and prevent
that disgust at common life, that *tædium quotidianarum formarum,* which an
unrestricted passion for ideal forms and beauties is in danger of producing. In
this, as in many other things, they are analogous to the best novels of Smollett
and Fielding."—CHARLES LAMB.

"It has been observed that Hogarth's pictures are exceedingly unlike any
other representations of the same kind of subjects—that they form a class, and
have a character peculiar to themselves. It may be worth while to consider
in what this general distinction consists.

"In the first place, they are, in the strictest sense, *historical* pictures ; and
if what Fielding says be true, that his novel of 'Tom Jones' ought to be
regarded as an epic prose-poem, because it contained a regular development
of fable, manners, character, and passion, the compositions of Hogarth will,
in like manner, be found to have a higher claim to the title of epic pictures
than many which have of late arrogated that denomination to themselves.
When we say that Hogarth treated his subject historically, we mean that his
works represent the manners and humours of mankind in action, and their
characters by varied expression. Everything in his pictures has life and motion
in it. Not only does the business of the scene never stand still, but every
feature and muscle is put into full play ; the exact feeling of the moment
is brought out, and carried to its utmost height, and then instantly seized
and stamped on the canvas for ever. The expression is always taken *en
passant,* in a state of progress or change, and, as it were, at the salient point.
. . . . His figures are not like the back-ground on which they are

hearts, and to inspire them with pleasure or pity or warning and terror. Not one of his tales but is as easy as " Goody Twoshoes ; " it is the moral of Tommy was a naughty boy and the master flogged him, and Jacky was a good boy and had plum-cake, which pervades the whole works of the homely and famous English moralist. And if the moral is written in rather too large letters after the fable, we must remember how simple the scholars and schoolmaster both were, and like neither the less because they are so artless and honest. " It was a maxim of Dr. Harrison's," Fielding says, in " Amelia,"—speaking of the benevolent divine and philosopher who represents the good principle in that novel—' that no man can descend below himself, in doing any act which may contribute to protect an innocent person, *or to bring a rogue to the gallows*." The moralists of that age had no compunction, you see ; they had not begun to be sceptical about the theory of punishment, and thought that the hanging of a thief was a spectacle for edification. Masters sent their apprentices, fathers took their children, to see Jack Sheppard or Jonathan Wild hanged, and it was as undoubting subscribers to this moral law, that Fielding wrote and Hogarth painted. Except in one instance, where, in the mad-house scene in the " Rake's Progress," the girl whom he has ruined is represented as still tending and weeping over him in his insanity, a glimpse of pity for his rogues never seems to enter honest Hogarth's mind. There's not the slightest doubt in the breast of the jolly Draco.

The famous set of pictures called " Marriage à la Mode," and which are now exhibited in the National Gallery in London, contains the most important and highly wrought of the Hogarth comedies. The care and method with which the moral grounds of these pictures are laid is as remarkable as the wit and skill of the observing and dexterous artist. He has to describe the negotiations for a marriage pending between the daughter of a rich citizen Alderman and young Lord Viscount Squanderfield, the dissipated son of a gouty old Earl. Pride and pomposity appear in every accessory surrounding the Earl.

painted : even the pictures on the wall have a peculiar look of their own. Again, with the rapidity, variety, and scope of history, Hogarth's heads have all the reality and correctness of portraits. He gives the extremes of character and expression, but he gives them with perfect truth and accuracy. This is, in fact, what distinguishes his compositions from all others of the same kind, that they are equally remote from caricature, and from mere still life. . . . . . His faces go to the very verge of caricature, and yet never (we believe in any single instance) go beyond it."—HAZLITT.

He sits in gold lace and velvet—as how should such an Earl wear anything but velvet and gold lace? His coronet is everywhere : on his footstool, on which reposes one gouty toe turned out ; on the sconces and looking-glasses ; on the dogs ; on his lordship's very crutches ; on his great chair of state and the great baldaquin behind him ; under which he sits pointing majestically to his pedigree, which shows that his race is sprung from the loins of William the Conqueror, and confronting the old Alderman from the City, who has mounted his sword for the occasion, and wears his Alderman's chain, and has brought a bag full of money, mortgage-deeds and thousand-pound notes, for the arrangement of the transaction pending between them. Whilst the steward (a Methodist—therefore a hypocrite and cheat : for Hogarth scorned a Papist and a Dissenter,) is negotiating between the old couple, their children sit together, united but apart. My lord is admiring his countenance in the glass, while his bride is twiddling her marriage ring on her pocket-handkerchief, and listening with rueful countenance to Counsellor Silvertongue, who has been drawing the settlements. The girl is pretty, but the painter, with a curious watchfulness, has taken care to give her a likeness to her father; as in the young Viscount's face you see a resemblance to the Earl, his noble sire. The sense of the coronet pervades the picture, as it is supposed to do the mind of its wearer. The pictures round the room are sly hints indicating the situation of the parties about to marry. A martyr is led to the fire ; Andromeda is offered to sacrifice ; Judith is going to slay Holofernes. There is the ancestor of the house (in the picture it is the Earl himself as a young man), with a comet over his head, indicating that the career of the family is to be brilliant and brief. In the second picture, the old lord must be dead, for Madam has now the Countess's coronet over her bed and toilet-glass, and sits listening to that dangerous Counsellor Silvertongue, whose portrait now actually hangs up in her room, whilst the counsellor takes his ease on the sofa by her side, evidently the familiar of the house, and the confidant of the mistress. My lord takes his pleasure elsewhere than at home, whither he returns jaded and tipsy from the " Rose," to find his wife yawning in her drawing-room, her whist-party over, and the daylight streaming in ; or he amuses himself with the very worst company abroad, whilst his wife sits at home listening to foreign singers, or wastes her money at auctions, or, worse still, seeks amusement at masquerades. The dismal end is known. My lord draws upon the counsellor, who kills him, and is apprehended whilst endeavouring to escape. My lady goes back perforce to the Alderman in the City, and faints upon reading Counsellor Silvertongue's dying speech at Tyburn, where the counsellor has been executed for sending his lordship out of the world. Moral:—Don't listen to evil silver-tongued counsellors : don't marry a man for his rank, or a woman for her money : don't frequent foolish auctions and masquerade balls unknown to your husband : don't have wicked companions abroad and neglect your wife, otherwise you will be run through the body, and ruin will ensue, and disgrace, and Tyburn. The people are all naughty, and Bogey carries them all off. In the "Rake's Progress," a loose life is ended by a similar sad catastrophe. It is the spendthrift coming into possession of the wealth of the paternal miser; the prodigal surrounded by flatterers, and wasting his substance on the very worst company; the bailiffs, the gambling-house, and Bedlam for an end. In the famous story of "Industry and Idleness," the moral is pointed in a manner similarly clear. Fair-haired Frank Goodchild smiles at his work, whilst naughty Tom Idle snores over his loom. Frank reads the edifying ballads of "Whittington" and the "London 'Prentice" whilst that reprobate Tom Idle prefers "Moll Flanders," and drinks hugely of beer. Frank goes to church of a Sunday, and warbles hymns from the gallery; while Tom lies on a tombstone outside playing at "halfpenny-under-the-hat" with street blackguards, and is deservedly caned by the beadle. Frank is made overseer of the business, whilst Tom is sent to sea. Frank is taken into partner-ship and marries his master's daughter, sends out broken victuals to the poor, and listens in his nightcap and gown, with the lovely Mrs. Goodchild by his side, to the nuptial music of the City bands and the marrow-bones and cleavers; whilst idle Tom, returned from sea, shudders in a garret lest the officers are coming to take him for picking pockets. The Worshipful Francis Goodchild, Esq., becomes Sheriff of London, and partakes of the most splendid dinners which money can purchase or Alderman devour; whilst poor Tom is taken up in a night-cellar, with that one-eyed and disreputable accomplice who first taught him to play chuck-farthing on a Sunday. What happens next? Tom is brought up before the justice of his country, in the person of Mr. Alderman Goodchild, who weeps as he recognises his old brother 'prentice, as Tom's one-eyed friend peaches on him, and the clerk makes out the poor rogue's ticket for Newgate. Then the end comes. Tom goes to Tyburn in a cart with a coffin in it; whilst the Right Honourable Francis Goodchild, Lord Mayor of London, proceeds to his Mansion House, in his gilt coach with four footmen and a sword-bearer, whilst the Companies of London march in the august procession, whilst the trainbands of the City fire their pieces and get drunk in his honour; and—O crowning delight and glory of all—whilst his Majesty the King looks out from his royal balcony, with his ribbon on his breast, and his Queen and his star by his side, at the corner house of St. Paul's Churchyard.

How the times have changed! The new Post Office now not disadvantageously occupies that spot where the scaffolding is in the picture, where the tipsy trainband-man is lurching against the post, with his wig over one eye, and the 'prentice-boy is trying to kiss the pretty girl in the gallery. Passed away 'prentice-boy and pretty girl! Passed away tipsy trainband-man with wig and bandolier! On the spot where Tom Idle (for whom I have an unaffected pity) made his exit from this wicked world, and where you see the hangman smoking his pipe as he reclines on the gibbet and views the hills of Harrow or Hampstead beyond, a splendid marble arch, a vast and modern city —clean, airy, painted drab, populous with nursery-maids and children, the abode of wealth and comfort—the elegant, the prosperous, the polite Tyburnia rises, the most respectable district in the habitable globe.

In that last plate of the London Apprentices, in which the apotheosis of the Right Honourable Francis Goodchild is drawn, a ragged fellow is represented in the corner of the simple, kindly piece, offering for sale a broadside, purporting to contain an account of the appearance of the ghost of Tom Idle, executed at Tyburn. Could Tom's ghost have made its appearance in 1847, and not in 1747, what changes would have been remarked by that astonished escaped criminal! Over that road which the hangman used to travel constantly, and the Oxford stage twice a week, go ten thousand carriages every day: over yonder road, by which Dick Turpin fled to Windsor, and Squire Western journeyed into town, when he came to take up his quarters at the "Hercules Pillars" on the outskirts of London, what a rush of civilization and order flows now! What armies of gentlemen with umbrellas march to banks, and chambers, and counting-houses! What regiments of nursery-maids and pretty infantry; what peaceful processions of policemen, what light broughams and what gay carriages, what swarms of busy apprentices and artificers, riding on omnibus-roofs, pass daily and hourly! Tom Idle's times are quite changed: many of the institutions gone into disuse which were admired in his day. There's more pity and kindness and a better chance for poor Tom's successors now than at that simpler period when Fielding hanged him and Hogarth drew him.

To the student of history, these admirable works must be invaluable, as they give us the most complete and truthful picture of the manners, and even the thoughts, of the past century. We look, and see pass before us the England of a hundred years ago—the peer in his drawing-room, the lady of fashion in her apartment, foreign singers surrounding her, and the chamber filled with gew-gaws in the mode of that day; the church, with its quaint florid architecture and singing congregation; the parson with his great wig, and the beadle with his cane: all these are represented before us, and we are sure of the truth of the portrait. We see how the Lord Mayor dines in state; how the prodigal drinks and sports at the bagnio; how the poor girl beats hemp in Bridewell; how the thief divides his booty and drinks his punch at the night-cellar, and how he finishes his career at the gibbet. We may depend upon the perfect accuracy of these strange and varied portraits of the bygone generation: we see one of Walpole's Members of Parliament chaired after his election, and the lieges celebrating the event, and drinking confusion to the Pretender: we see the grenadiers and trainbands of the City marching out to meet the enemy; and have before us, with sword and firelock, and "White Hanoverian Horse" embroidered on the cap, the very figures of the men who ran away with Johnny Cope, and who conquered at Culloden. The Yorkshire waggon rolls into the inn yard; the country parson, in his jack-boots, and his bands and short cassock, comes trotting into town, and we fancy it is Parson Adams, with his sermons in his pocket. The Salisbury fly sets forth from the old "Angel"—you see the passengers entering the great heavy vehicle, up the wooden steps, their hats tied down with handkerchiefs over their faces, and under their arms, sword, hanger, and case-bottle; the landlady—apoplectic with the liquors in her own bar—is tugging at the bell; the hunchbacked postilion—he may have ridden the leaders to Humphrey Clinker— is begging a gratuity; the miser is grumbling at the bill; Jack of the "Centurion" lies on the top of the clumsy vehicle, with a soldier by his side—it may be Smollett's Jack Hatchway—it has a likeness to Lismahago. You see the suburban fair and the strolling company of actors; the pretty milkmaid singing under the windows of the enraged French musician: it is such a girl as Steele charmingly described in the *Guardian*, a few years before this date, singing, under Mr. Ironside's window in Shire Lane, her pleasant carol of a May morning. You see noblemen and blacklegs bawling and betting in the Cockpit: you see Garrick as he was arrayed in "King Richard;" Macheath and Polly in the dresses which they wore when they charmed our ancestors, and when noblemen in blue ribbons sat on the stage and listened to their delightful music. You see the ragged French soldiery, in their white coats and cockades, at Calais Gate : they are of the regiment, very likely, which friend Roderick Random joined before he was rescued by his preserver Monsieur de Strap with whom he fought on the famous day of Dettingen. You see the judges on the bench ; the audience laughing in the pit ; the student in the Oxford theatre ; the citizen on his country walk ; you see Broughton the boxer, Sarah Malcolm the murderess, Simon Lovat the traitor, John Wilkes the demagogue, leering at you with that squint which has become historical, and that face which, ugly as it was, he said he could make as captivating to woman as the countenance of the handsomest beau in town. All these sights and people are with you. After looking in the "Rake's Progress" at Hogarth's picture of St. James's Palace Gate, you may people the street, but little altered within these hundred years, with the gilded carriages and thronging chairmen that bore the courtiers your ancestors to Queen Caroline's drawing-room more than a hundred years ago.

What manner of man * was he who executed these portraits—so

---

* Hogarth (whose family name was Hogart) was the grandson of a Westmoreland yeoman. His father came to London, and was an author and schoolmaster. William was born in 1698 (according to the most probable conjecture) in the parish of St. Martin, Ludgate. He was early apprenticed to an engraver of arms on plate. The following touches are from his "Anecdotes of Himself." (Edition of 1833.)—

"As I had naturally a good eye, and a fondness for drawing, shows of all sorts gave me uncommon pleasure when an infant ; and mimicry, common to all children, was remarkable in me. An early access to a neighbouring painter drew my attention from play ; and I was, at every possible opportunity, employed in making drawings. I picked up an acquaintance of the same turn, and soon learnt to draw the alphabet with great correctness. My exercises, when at school, were more remarkable for the ornaments which adorned them, than for the exercise itself. In the former, I soon found that blockheads with better memories could much surpass me ; but for the latter I was particularly distinguished. . . . .

"I thought it still more unlikely that by pursuing the common method, and copying *old* drawings, I could ever attain the power of making *new* designs, which was my first and greatest ambition. I therefore endeavoured to habituate myself to the exercise of a sort of technical memory ; and by repeating in my own mind the parts of which objects were composed, I could by degrees combine and put them down with my pencil. Thus, with all the drawbacks which resulted from the circumstances I have mentioned, I had one material advantage over my competitors, viz. the early habit I thus acquired various, so faithful, and so admirable? In the National Collection of Pictures most of us have seen the best and most carefully finished

of retaining in my mind's eye, without coldly copying it on the spot, whatever I intended to imitate.

"The instant I became master of my own time, I determined to qualify myself for engraving on copper. In this I readily got employment ; and frontispieces to books, such as prints to 'Hudibras,' in twelves, &c., soon brought me into the way. But the tribe of booksellers remained as my father had left them . . . which put me upon publishing on my own account. But here again I had to encounter a monopoly of printsellers, equally mean and destructive to the ingenious ; for the first plate I published, called ' The Taste of the Town,' in which the reigning follies were lashed, had no sooner begun to take a run, than I found copies of it in the print-shops, vending at half-price, while the original prints were returned to me again, and I was thus obliged to sell the plate for whatever these pirates pleased to give me, as there was no place of sale but at their shops. Owing to this, and other circumstances, by engraving, until I was near thirty, I could do little more than maintain myself ; *but even then, I was a punctual paymaster.*

" I then married, and——— "

[But William is going too fast here. He made a "stolen union," on March 23, 1729, with Jane, daughter of Sir James Thornhill, serjeant-painter. For some time Sir James kept his heart and his purse-strings close, but " soon after became both reconciled and generous to the young couple."—*Hogarth's Works,* by NICHOLS and STEEVENS, vol. i. p. 44.]

"—commenced painter of small Conversation Pieces, from twelve to fifteen inches high. This, being a novelty, succeeded for a few years."

[About this time Hogarth had summer lodgings at South Lambeth, and did all kinds of work, "embellishing" the "Spring Gardens" at "Vauxhall," and the like. In 1731, he published a satirical plate against Pope, founded on the well-known imputation against him of his having satirised the Duke of Chandos, under the name of *Timon,* in his poem on "Taste." The plate represented a view of Burlington House, with Pope whitewashing it, and bespattering the Duke of Chandos's coach. Pope made no retort, and has never mentioned Hogarth.]

" Before I had done anything of much consequence in this walk, I entertained some hopes of succeeding in what the puffers in books call *The Great Style of History Painting;* so that without having had a stroke of this *grand* business before, I quitted small portraits and familiar conversations, and with a smile at my own temerity, commenced history-painter, and on a great staircase at St. Bartholomew's Hospital, painted two Scripture stories, the ' Pool of Bethesda ' and the ' Good Samaritan,' with figures seven feet high. . . . . But as religion, the great promoter of this style in other countries, rejected it in England, I was unwilling to sink into a *portrait manufacturer ;* and still ambitious of being singular, dropped all expectations of advantage series of his comic paintings, and the portrait of his own honest face, of which the bright blue eyes shine out from the canvas and give you

from that source, and returned to the pursuit of my former dealings with the public at large.

"As to portrait-painting, the chief branch of the art by which a painter can procure himself a tolerable livelihood, and the only one by which a lover of money can get a fortune, a man of very moderate talents may have great success in it, as the artifice and address of a mercer is infinitely more useful than the abilities of a painter. By the manner in which the present race of professors in England conduct it, that also becomes still life."

*   *   *   *   *

"By this inundation of folly and puff" (*he has been speaking of the success of Vanloo, who came over here in* 1737), "I must confess I was much disgusted, and determined to try if by any means I could stem the torrent, and, *by opposing, end it*. I laughed at the pretensions of these quacks in colouring, ridiculed their productions as feeble and contemptible, and asserted that it required neither taste nor talents to excel their most popular performances. This interference excited much enmity, because, as my opponents told me, my studies were in another way. 'You talk,' added they, 'with ineffable contempt of portrait-painting ; if it is so easy a task, why do not you convince the world, by painting a portrait yourself?' Provoked at this language, I, one day at the Academy in St. Martin's Lane, put the following question : 'Supposing any man, at this time, were to paint a portrait as well as Vandyke, would it be seen or acknowledged, and could the artist enjoy the benefit or acquire the reputation due to his performance?'

"They asked me in reply, If I could paint one as well? and I frankly answered, I believed I could. . . . .

"Of the mighty talents said to be requisite for portrait painting I had not the most exalted opinion."

Let us now hear him on the question of the Academy :—

"To pester the three great estates of the empire, about twenty or thirty students drawing after a man or a horse, appears, as must be acknowledged, foolish enough : but the real motive is, that a few bustling characters, who have access to people of rank, think they can thus get a superiority over their brethren, be appointed to places, and have salaries, as in France, for telling a lad when a leg or an arm is too long or too short. . . . .

"France, ever aping the magnificence of other nations, has in its turn assumed a foppish kind of splendour sufficient to dazzle the eyes of the neighbouring states, and draw vast sums of money from this country. . . . .

"To return to our Royal Academy : I am told that one of their leading objects will be, sending young men abroad to study the antique statues, for such kind of studies may sometimes improve an exalted genius, but they will not create it ; and whatever has been the cause, this same travelling to Italy has, in several instances that I have seen, seduced the student from nature, and led an idea of that keen and brave look with which William Hogarth regarded the world. No man was ever less of a hero ; you see him before you, and can fancy what he was—a jovial, honest London

him to paint marble figures, in which he has availed himself of the great works of antiquity, as a coward does when he puts on the armour of an Alexander ; for, with similar pretensions and similar vanity, the painter supposes he shall be adored as a second Raphael Urbino."

We must now hear him on his " Sigismunda : "—

" As the most violent and virulent abuse thrown on ' Sigismunda ' was from a set of miscreants, with whom I am proud of having been ever at war—I mean the expounders of the mysteries of old pictures—I have been sometimes told they were beneath my notice. This is true of them individually ; but as they have access to people of rank, who seem as happy in being cheated as these *merchants* are in cheating them, they have a power of doing much mischief to a modern artist. However mean the vendor of poisons, the mineral is destructive :—to me its operation was troublesome enough. Ill nature spreads so fast that now was the time for every little dog in the profession to bark ! "

Next comes a characteristic account of his controversy with Wilkes and Churchill.

"The stagnation rendered it necessary that I should do some *timed thing*, to recover my lost time, and stop a gap in my income. This drew forth my print of ' The Times,' a subject which tended to the restoration of peace and unanimity, and put the opposers of these humane objects in a light which gave great offence to those who were trying to foment disaffection in the minds of the populace. One of the most notorious of them, till now my friend and flatterer, attacked me in the *North Briton*, in so infamous and malign a style, that he himself, when pushed even by his best friends, was driven to so poor an excuse as to say he was drunk when he wrote it. . . .

"This renowned patriot's portrait, drawn like as I could as to features, and marked with some indications of his mind, fully answered my purpose. The ridiculous was apparent to every eye ! A Brutus ! A saviour of his country with such an aspect—was so arrant a farce, that though it gave rise to much laughter in the lookers-on, galled both him and his adherents to the bone. . . .

" Churchill, Wilkes's toad-echo, put the *North Briton* into verse, in an Epistle to Hogarth ; but as the abuse was precisely the same, except a little poetical heightening, which goes for nothing, it made no impression. . . . However, having an old plate by me, with some parts ready, such as the background and a dog, I began to consider how I could turn so much work laid aside to some account, and so patched up a print of Master Churchill in the character of a Bear. The pleasure and pecuniary advantage which I derived from these two engravings, together with occasionally riding on horseback, restored me to as much health as can be expected at my time of life."

citizen, stout and sturdy ; a hearty, plain-spoken man,* loving his
laugh, his friend, his glass, his roast-beef of Old England, and having
a proper *bourgeois* scorn for French frogs, for mounseers, and wooden
shoes in general, for foreign fiddlers, foreign singers, and, above all,
for foreign painters, whom he held in the most amusing contempt.

It must have been great fun to hear him rage against Correggio
and the Caracci ; to watch him thump the table and snap his fingers,
and say, " Historical painters be hanged ! here's the man that will
paint against any of them for a hundred pounds. Correggio's
' Sigismunda !' Look at Bill Hogarth's ' Sigismunda ;' look at my
altar-piece at St. Mary Redcliffe, Bristol ; look at my ' Paul before
Felix,' and see whether I'm not as good as the best of them.' †

* " It happened in the early part of Hogarth's life, that a nobleman who
was uncommonly ugly and deformed came to sit to him for his picture. It
was executed with a skill that did honour to the artist's abilities; but the
likeness was rigidly observed, without even the necessary attention to compliment or flattery. The peer, disgusted at this counterpart of himself, never
once thought of paying for a reflection that would only disgust him with his
deformities. Some time was suffered to elapse before the artist applied for his
money ; but afterwards many applications were made by him (who had then
no need of a banker) for payment, without success. The painter, however, at
last hit upon an expedient. . . .   It was couched in the following card :—

" ' Mr. Hogarth's dutiful respects to Lord ——. Finding that he does not
mean to have the picture which was drawn for him, is informed again of Mr.
Hogarth's necessity for the money. If, therefore, his Lordship does not send
for it, in three days it will be disposed of, with the addition of a tail, and
some other little appendages, to Mr. Hare, the famous wild-beast man : Mr.
Hogarth having given that gentleman a conditional promise of it, for an
exhibition-picture, on his Lordship's refusal.'

" This intimation had the desired effect."—*Works*, by NICHOLS and
STEEVENS, vol. i. p. 25.

† " Garrick himself was not more ductile to flattery. A word in favour of
' Sigismunda ' might have commanded a proof-print or forced an original print
out of our artist's hands. . . .

" The following authenticated story of our artist (furnished by the late Mr.
Belchior, F.R.S., a surgeon of eminence) will also serve to show how much
more easy it is to detect ill-placed or hyperbolical adulation respecting others,
than when applied to ourselves. Hogarth, being at dinner with the great
Cheselden and some other company, was told that Mr. John Freke, surgeon of
St. Bartholomew's Hospital, a few evenings before at Dick's Coffee-House,
had asserted that Greene was as eminent in composition as Handel. ' That
fellow Freke,' replied Hogarth, ' is always shooting his bolt absurdly, one
way or another. Handel is a giant in music ; Greene only a light Florimel

Posterity has not quite confirmed honest Hogarth's opinion about his talents for the sublime. Although Swift could not see the difference between tweedle-dee and tweedle-dum, posterity has not shared the Dean's contempt for Handel ; the world has discovered a difference between tweedle-dee and tweedle-dum, and given a hearty applause and admiration to Hogarth, too, but not exactly as a painter of scriptural subjects, or as a rival of Correggio. It does not take away from one's liking for the man, or from the moral of his story, or the humour of it—from one's admiration for the prodigious merit of his performances, to remember that he persisted to the last in believing that the world was in a conspiracy against him with respect to his talents as an historical painter, and that a set of miscreants, as he called them, were employed to run his genius down. They say it was Liston's firm belief, that he was a great and neglected tragic actor ; they say that every one of us believes in his heart, or would like to have others believe, that he is something which he is not. One of the most notorious of the "miscreants," Hogarth says, was Wilkes, who assailed him in the *North Briton ;* the other was Churchill, who put the *North Briton* attack into heroic verse, and published his "Epistle to Hogarth." Hogarth replied by that caricature of Wilkes, in which the patriot still figures before us, with his Satanic grin and squint, and by a caricature of Churchill, in which he is represented as a bear with a staff, on which, lie the first, lie the second—lie the tenth, are engraved in unmistakable letters. There is very little mistake about honest Hogarth's satire : if he has to paint a man with his throat cut, he draws him with his head almost off ; and he tried to do the same for his enemies in this little controversy. "Having an old plate by me," says he, "with some parts ready, such as the background, and a dog, I began to consider how I could turn so much work laid aside to some account, and so patched up a print of Master Churchill, in the character of a bear ; the pleasure and pecuniary advantage which I derived from these two engravings, together with occasionally riding on horseback, restored me to as much health as I can expect at my time of life."

And so he concludes his queer little book of Anecdotes : "I have gone through the circumstances of a life which till lately passed pretty

kind of a composer.' 'Ay,' says our artist's informant, 'but at the same time Mr. Freke declared you were as good a portrait-painter as Vandyke.' ' *There* he was right,' adds Hogarth, 'and so, by G——, I am, give me my time and let me choose my subject.' "—*Works*, by NICHOLS and STEEVENS, vol. i. pp. 236, 237.

much to my own satisfaction, and I hope in no respect injurious to
any other man.   This I may safely assert, that I have done my best to

make those about me tolerably happy, and my greatest enemy cannot
say I ever did an intentional injury.   What may follow, God knows." *

* Of Hogarth's kindliness of disposition, the story of his rescue of the

A queer account still exists of a holiday jaunt taken by Hogarth and four friends of his, who set out like the redoubted Mr. Pickwick and his companions, but just a hundred years before those heroes; and made an excursion to Gravesend, Rochester, Sheerness, and adjacent places.* One of the gentlemen noted down the proceedings of the journey, for which Hogarth and a brother artist made drawings. The book is chiefly curious at this moment from showing the citizen life of those days, and the rough jolly style of merriment, not of the five companions merely, but of thousands of jolly fellows of their time. Hogarth and his friends, quitting the "Bedford Arms," Covent Garden, with a song, took water to Billingsgate, exchanging compliments with the bargemen as they went down the river. At Billingsgate Hogarth made a "caracatura" of a facetious porter, called the Duke of Puddledock, who agreeably entertained the party with the humours of the place. Hence they took a Gravesend boat for themselves; had straw to lie upon, and a tilt over their heads, they say, and went down the river at night, sleeping and singing jolly choruses.

They arrived at Gravesend at six, when they washed their faces and hands, and had their wigs powdered. Then they sallied forth for Rochester on foot, and drank by the way three pots of ale. At one o'clock they went to dinner with excellent port, and a quantity more beer, and afterwards Hogarth and Scott played at hopscotch in the town hall. It would appear that they slept most of them in one room, and the chronicler of the party describes them all as waking at seven o'clock, and telling each other their dreams. You have rough sketches by Hogarth of the incidents of this holiday excursion. The sturdy little painter is seen sprawling over a plank to a boat at Gravesend; the whole company are represented in one design, in a fisherman's room, where they had all passed the night. One gentleman in a nightcap is shaving himself; another is being shaved by the fisherman; a third, with a handkerchief over his bald plate, is taking his breakfast; and Hogarth is sketching the whole scene.

They describe at night how they returned to their quarters, drank to their friends, as usual, emptied several cans of good flip, all singing merrily.

It is a jolly party of tradesmen engaged at high jinks. These were

drummer girl from the ruffian at Southwark Fair is an illustration : and in this case virtue was not its own reward, since her pretty face afterwards served him for a model in many a picture.

* He made this excursion in 1732, his companions being John Thornhill (son of Sir James), Scott the landscape-painter, Tothall, and Forrest.

the manners and pleasures of Hogarth, of his time very likely, of men not very refined, but honest and merry. It is a brave London citizen, with John Bull habits, prejudices, and pleasures.*

Of SMOLLETT'S associates and manner of life the author of the admirable "Humphrey Clinker" has given us an interesting account in that most amusing of novels.†

---

* Doctor Johnson made four lines once, on the death of poor Hogarth, which were equally true and pleasing ; I know not why Garrick's were preferred to them :—

> " ' The hand of him here torpid lies,
>   That drew th' essential forms of grace ;
>   Here, closed in death, th' attentive eyes,
>   That saw the manners in the face.'

"Mr. Hogarth, among the variety of kindnesses shown to me when I was too young to have a proper sense of them, was used to be very earnest that I should obtain the acquaintance, and if possible the friendship, of Dr. Johnson ; whose conversation was, to the talk of other men, like Titian's painting compared to Hudson's, he said : ' but don't you tell people now that I say so,' continued he : ' for the connoisseurs and I are at war, you know ; and because I hate *them*, they think I hate *Titian*—and let them !' . . . Of Dr. Johnson, when my father and he were talking about him one day, ' That man' says Hogarth, ' is not contented with believing the Bible ; but he fairly resolves, I think, to believe nothing *but* the Bible. Johnson,' added he, ' though so wise a fellow, is more like King David than King Solomon, for he says in his haste, *All men are liars.*' "—MRS. PIOZZI.

Hogarth died on the 26th of October, 1764. The day before his death, he was removed from his villa at Chiswick to Leicester Fields, "in a very weak condition, yet remarkably cheerful." He had just received an agreeable letter from Franklin. He lies buried at Chiswick.

† "TO SIR WATKIN PHILLIPS, BART., OF JESUS COLLEGE, OXON.

"DEAR PHILLIPS,—In my last, I mentioned my having spent an evening with a society of authors, who seemed to be jealous and afraid of one another. My uncle was not at all surprised to hear me say I was disappointed in their conversation. ' A man may be very entertaining and instructive upon paper,' said he, ' and exceedingly dull in common discourse. I have observed, that those who shine most in private company are but secondary stars in the constellation of genius. A small stock of ideas is more easily managed, and sooner displayed, than a great quantity crowded together. There is very seldom anything extraordinary in the appearance and address of a good writer ; whereas a dull author generally distinguishes himself by some oddity or

I have no doubt that this picture by Smollett is as faithful a one as any from the pencil of his kindred humourist, Hogarth.

extravagance. For this reason I fancy that an assembly of grubs must be very diverting.'

"My curiosity being excited by this hint, I consulted my friend Dick Ivy, who undertook to gratify it the very next day, which was Sunday last. He carried me to dine with S——, whom you and I have long known by his writings. He lives in the skirts of the town; and every Sunday his house is open to all unfortunate brothers of the quill, whom he treats with beef, pudding, and potatoes, port, punch, and Calvert's entire butt beer. He has fixed upon the first day of the week for the exercise of his hospitality, because some of his guests could not enjoy it on any other, for reasons that I need not explain. I was civilly received in a plain, yet decent habitation, which opened backwards into a very pleasant garden, kept in excellent order; and, indeed, I saw none of the outward signs of authorship either in the house or the landlord, who is one of those few writers of the age that stand upon their own foundation, without patronage, and above dependence. If there was nothing characteristic in the entertainer, the company made ample amends for his want of singularity.

"At two in the afternoon, I found myself one of ten messmates seated at table; and I question if the whole kingdom could produce such another assemblage of originals. Among their peculiarities, I do not mention those of dress, which may be purely accidental. What struck me were oddities originally produced by affectation, and afterwards confirmed by habit. One of them wore spectacles at dinner, and another his hat flapped; though (as Ivy told me) the first was noted for having a seaman's eye when a bailiff was in the wind; and the other was never known to labour under any weakness or defect of vision, except about five years ago, when he was complimented with a couple of black eyes by a player, with whom he had quarrelled in his drink. A third wore a laced stocking, and made use of crutches, because, once in his life, he had been laid up with a broken leg, though no man could leap over a stick with more agility. A fourth had contracted such an antipathy to the country, that he insisted upon sitting with his back towards the window that looked into the garden; and when a dish of cauliflower was set upon the table, he snuffed up volatile salts to keep him from fainting; yet this delicate person was the son of a cottager, born under a hedge, and had many years run wild among asses on a common. A fifth affected distraction: when spoke to, he always answered from the purpose. Sometimes he suddenly started up, and rapped out a dreadful oath; sometimes he burst out a laughing; then he folded his arms, and sighed; and then he hissed like fifty serpents.

"At first, I really thought he was mad; and, as he sat near me, began to be under some apprehensions for my own safety; when our landlord, perceiving me alarmed, assured me aloud that I had nothing to fear. 'The gentleman,' said he, 'is trying to act a part for which he is by no means qualified:

We have before us, and painted by his own hand, Tobias Smollett, the manly, kindly, honest, and irascible ; worn and battered, but still

if he had all the inclination in the world, it is not in his power to be mad ; his spirits are too flat to be kindled into phrenzy.' 'Tis no bad p-p-puff, how-owever,' observed a person in a tarnished laced coat : ' aff-ffected m-madness w-ill p-pass for w-wit w-with nine-nineteen out of t-twenty.' ' And affected stuttering for humour,' replied our landlord ; ' though, God knows ! there is no affinity between them.' It seems this wag, after having made some abortive attempts in plain speaking, had recourse to this defect, by means of which he frequently extorted the laugh of the company, without the least expense of genius ; and that imperfection, which he had at first counterfeited, was now become so habitual, that he could not lay it aside.

" A certain winking genius, who wore yellow gloves at dinner, had, on his first introduction, taken such offence at S——, because he looked and talked, and ate and drank, like any other man, that he spoke contemptuously of his understanding ever after, and never would repeat his visit, until he had exhibited the following proof of his caprice. Wat Wyvil, the poet, having made some unsuccessful advances towards an intimacy with S——, at last gave him to understand, by a third person, that he had written a poem in his praise, and a satire against his person : that if he would admit him to his house, the first should be immediately sent to press ; but that if he persisted in declining his friendship, he would publish the satire without delay. S—— replied, that he looked upon Wyvil's panegyric as, in effect, a species of infamy, and would resent it accordingly with a good cudgel ; but if he published the satire, he might deserve his compassion, and had nothing to fear from his revenge. Wyvil having considered the alternative, resolved to mortify S—— by printing the panegyric, for which he received a sound drubbing. Then he swore the peace against the aggressor, who, in order to avoid a prosecution at law, admitted him to his good graces. It was the singularity in S——'s conduct on this occasion, that reconciled him to the yellow-gloved philosopher, who owned he had some genius ; and from that period cultivated his acquaintance.

" Curious to know upon what subjects the several talents of my fellow-guests were employed, I applied to my communicative friend Dick Ivy, who gave me to understand that most of them were, or had been, understrappers, or journeymen, to more creditable authors, for whom they translated, collated, and compiled, in the business of bookmaking ; and that all of them had, at different times, laboured in the service of our landlord, thought they had now set up for themselves in various departments of literature. Not only their talents, but also their nations and dialects, were so various, that our conversation resembled the confusion of tongues at Babel. We had the Irish brogue, the Scotch accent, and foreign idiom, twanged off by the most discordant vociferation ; for as they all spoke together, no man had any chance to be heard, unless he could bawl louder than his fellows. It must be owned, brave and full of heart, after a long struggle against a hard fortune. His brain had been busied with a hundred different schemes ; he had

however, there was nothing pedantic in their discourse ; they carefully avoided all learned disquisitions, and endeavoured to be facetious : nor did their endeavours always miscarry ; some droll repartee passed, and much laughter was excited ; and if any individual lost his temper so far as to transgress the bounds of decorum, he was effectually checked by the master of the feast, who exerted a sort of paternal authority over this irritable tribe.

"The most learned philosopher of the whole collection, who had been expelled the university for atheism, has made great progress in a refutation of Lord Bolingbroke's metaphysical works, which is said to be equally ingenious and orthodox : but, in the meantime, he has been presented to the grand jury as a public nuisance for having blasphemed in an alehouse on the Lord's day. The Scotchman gives lectures on the pronunciation of the English language, which he is now publishing by subscription.

"The Irishman is a political writer, and goes by the name of My Lord Potatoe. He wrote a pamphlet in vindication of a Minister, hoping his zeal would be rewarded with some place or pension ; but finding himself neglected in that quarter, he whispered about that the pamphlet was written by the Minister himself, and he published an answer to his own production. In this he addressed the author under the title of 'your lordship,' with such solemnity, that the public swallowed the deceit, and bought up the whole impression. The wise politicians of the metropolis declared they were both masterly performances, and chuckled over the flimsy reveries of an ignorant garretteer, as the profound speculations of a veteran statesman, acquainted with all the secrets of the cabinet. The imposture was detected in the sequel, and our Hibernian pamphleteer retains no part of his assumed importance but the bare title of 'my lord,' and the upper part of the table at the potatoe - ordinary in Shoe Lane.

"Opposite to me sat a Piedmontese, who had obliged the public with a humourous satire, entitled 'The Balance of the English Poets ;' a performance which evinced the great modesty and taste of the author, and, in particular, his intimacy with the elegancies of the English language. The sage, who laboured under the ἀγροφοβία, or, 'horror of green fields,' had just finished a treatise on practical agriculture, though, in fact, he had never seen corn growing in his life, and was so ignorant of grain, that our entertainer, in the face of the whole company, made him own that a plate of hominy was the best rice-pudding he had ever eat.

"The stutterer had almost finished his travels through Europe and part of Asia, without ever budging beyond the liberties of the King's Bench, except in term-time with a tipstaff for his companion : and as for little Tim Cropdale, the most facetious member of the whole society, he had happily wound up the catastrophe of a virgin tragedy, from the exhibition of which he promised himself a large fund of profit and reputation. Tim had made shift to live been reviewer and historian, critic, medical writer, poet, pamphleteer. He had fought endless literary battles ; and braved and wielded for years the cudgels of controversy. It was a hard and savage fight in those days, and a niggard pay. He was oppressed by illness, age, narrow fortune ; but his spirit was still resolute, and his courage steady ; the battle over, he could do justice to the enemy with whom he had been so fiercely engaged, and give a not unfriendly grasp to the hand that had mauled him. He is like one of those Scotch cadets, of whom history gives us so many examples, and whom, with a national fidelity, the great Scotch novelist has painted so charmingly. Of gentle birth * and narrow means, going out from his northern

many years by writing novels, at the rate of five pounds a volume ; but that branch of business is now engrossed by female authors, who publish merely for the propagation of virtue, with so much ease, and spirit, and delicacy, and knowledge of the human heart, and all in the serene tranquillity of high life, that the reader is not only enchanted by their genius, but reformed by their morality.

" After dinner, we adjourned into the garden, where I observed Mr. S—— give a short separate audience to every individual in a small remote filbert-walk, from whence most of them dropped off one after another, without further ceremony."

Smollett's house was in Lawrence Lane, Chelsea, and is now destroyed. See *Handbook of London*, p. 115.

" The person of Smollett was eminently handsome, his features prepossessing, and, by the joint testimony of all his surviving friends, his conversation, in the highest degree, instructive and amusing. Of his disposition, those who have read his works (and who has not ?) may form a very accurate estimate ; for in each of them he has presented, and sometimes, under various points of view, the leading features of his own character without disguising the most unfavourable of them. . . . . . . When unseduced by his satirical propensities, he was kind, generous, and humane to others ; bold, upright, and independent in his own character ; stooped to no patron, sued for no favour, but honestly and honourably maintained himself on his literary labours. . . . . He was a doating father, and an affectionate husband ; and the warm zeal with which his memory was cherished by his surviving friends showed clearly the reliance which they placed upon his regard."—Sir WALTER SCOTT.

* Smollett of Bonhill, in Dumbartonshire. *Arms*, azure, a bend, or, between a lion rampant, ppr., holding in his paw a banner, argent, and a bugle-horn, also ppr. *Crest*, an oak-tree, ppr. *Motto, Viresco.*

Smollett's father, Archibald, was the fourth son of Sir James Smollett of Bonhill, a Scotch Judge and Member of Parliament, and one of the commissioners for framing the Union with England. Archibald married, without the home to win his fortune in the world, and to fight his way, armed with courage, hunger, and keen wits. His crest is a shattered oak-tree, with green leaves yet springing from it. On his ancient coat-of-arms there is a lion and a horn ; this shield of his was battered and dinted in a hundred fights and brawls,* through which the stout

old gentleman's consent, and died early, leaving his children dependent on their grandfather. Tobias, the second son, was born in 1721, in the old house of Dalquharn in the valley of Leven ; and all his life loved and admired that valley and Loch Lomond beyond all the valleys and lakes in Europe. He learned the "rudiments" at Dumbarton Grammar School, and studied at Glasgow.

But when he was only ten, his grandfather died, and left him without provision (figuring as the old judge in "Roderick Random" in consequence, according to Sir Walter). Tobias, armed with the "Regicide, a Tragedy"—a provision precisely similar to that with which Doctor Johnson had started, just before—came up to London. The "Regicide" came to no good, though at first patronized by Lord Lyttelton ("one of those little fellows who are some-times called great men," Smollett says) ; and Smollett embarked as "surgeon's mate" on board a line-of-battle ship, and served in the Carthagena expedition, in 1741. He left the service in the West Indies, and after residing some time in Jamaica, returned to England in 1746.

He was now unsuccessful as a physician, to begin with ; published the satires, "Advice" and "Reproof," without any luck ; and (1747) married the "beautiful and accomplished Miss Lascelles."

In 1748 he brought out his "Roderick Random," which at once made a "hit." The subsequent events of his life may be presented, chronologically, in a bird's-eye view :—

1750. Made a tour to Paris, where he chiefly wrote "Peregrine Pickle."
1751. Published "Peregrine Pickle."
1753. Published "Adventures of Ferdinand Count Fathom."
1755. Published version of "Don Quixote."
1756. Began the "Critical Review."
1758. Published his "History of England."
1763—1766. Travelling in France and Italy ; published his "Travels."
1769. Published "Adventures of an Atom."
1770. Set out for Italy ; died at Leghorn 21st of Oct., 1771, in the fifty-first year of his age.

* A good specimen of the old "slashing" style of writing is presented by the paragraph on Admiral Knowles, which subjected Smollett to prosecution and imprisonment. The admiral's defence on the occasion of the failure of the Rochfort expedition came to be examined before the tribunal of the "Critical Review."

"He is," said our author, "an admiral without conduct, an engineer

Scotchman bore it courageously. You see somehow that he is a gentleman, through all his battling and struggling, his poverty, his hard-fought successes, and his defeats. His novels are recollections of his own adventures ; his characters drawn, as I should think, from personages with whom he became acquainted in his own career of life. Strange companions he must have had ; queer acquaintances he made in the Glasgow College—in the country apothecary's shop ; in the gun-room of the man-of-war where he served as surgeon ; and in the hard life on shore, where the sturdy adventurer struggled for

without knowledge, an officer without resolution, and a man without veracity ! "

Three months' imprisonment in the King's Bench avenged this stinging paragraph.

But the " Critical " was to Smollett a perpetual fountain of " hot water." Among less important controversies may be mentioned that with Grainger, the translator of " Tibullus."   Grainger replied in a pamphlet ; and in the next number of the " Review " we find him threatened with " castigation," as an " owl that has broken from his mew ! "

In Doctor Moore's biography of him is a pleasant anecdote. After publishing the " Don Quixote," he returned to Scotland to pay a visit to his mother : —

" On Smollett's arrival, he was introduced to his mother with the connivance of Mrs. Telfer (her daughter), as a gentleman from the West Indies, who was intimately acquainted with her son. The better to support his assumed character, he endeavoured to preserve a serious countenance, approaching to a frown ; but while his mother's eyes were riveted on his countenance, he could not refrain from smiling : she immediately sprung from her chair, and throwing her arms round his neck, exclaimed, ' Ah, my son ! my son ! I have found you at last ! '

" She afterwards told him, that if he had kept his austere looks and continued to *gloom*, he might have escaped detection some time longer, but ' your old roguish smile,' added she, ' betrayed you at once.' "

" Shortly after the publication of ' The Adventures of an Atom,' disease again attacked Smollett with redoubled violence. Attempts being vainly made to obtain for him the office of Consul in some part of the Mediterranean, he was compelled to seek a warmer climate, without better means of provision than his own precarious finances could afford. The kindness of his distinguished friend and countryman, Dr. Armstrong (then abroad), procured for Dr. and Mrs. Smollett a house at Monte Nero, a village situated on the side of a mountain overlooking the sea, in the neighbourhood of Leghorn, a romantic and salutary abode, where he prepared for the press, the last, and like music ' sweetest in the close,' the most pleasing of his compositions, ' The Expedition of Humphrey Clinker.' This delightful work was published in 1771."—Sir WALTER SCOTT.

fortune. He did not invent much, as I fancy, but had the keenest perceptive faculty, and described what he saw with wonderful relish and delightful broad humour. I think Uncle Bowling, in "Roderick Random," is as good a character as Squire Western himself; and Mr. Morgan, the Welsh apothecary, is as pleasant as Doctor Caius. What man who has made his inestimable acquaintance—what novel-reader who loves Don Quixote and Major Dalgetty—will refuse his most cordial acknowledgments to the admirable Lieutenant Lismahago? The novel of "Humphrey Clinker" is, I do think, the most laughable story that has ever been written since the goodly art of novel-writing began. Winifred Jenkins and Tabitha Bramble must keep Englishmen on the grin for ages yet to come; and in their letters and the story of their loves there is a perpetual fount of sparkling laughter, as inexhaustible as Bladud's well.

FIELDING, too, has described, though with a greater hand, the characters and scenes which he knew and saw. He had more than ordinary opportunities for becoming acquainted with life. His family and education, first—his fortunes and misfortunes afterwards, brought him into the society of every rank and condition of man. He is himself the hero of his books: he is wild Tom Jones, he is wild Captain Booth; less wild, I am glad to think, than his predecessor: at least heartily conscious of demerit, and anxious to amend.

When Fielding first came upon the town in 1727, the recollection of the great wits was still fresh in the coffee-houses and assemblies, and the judges there declared that young Harry Fielding had more spirits and wit than Congreve or any of his brilliant successors. His figure was tall and stalwart; his face handsome, manly, and noble-looking; to the very last days of his life he retained a grandeur of air, and although worn down by disease, his aspect and presence imposed respect upon the people round about him.

A dispute took place between Mr. Fielding and the captain* of the

---

* The dispute with the captain arose from the wish of that functionary to intrude on his right to his cabin, for which he had paid thirty pounds. After recounting the circumstances of the apology, he characteristically adds :—

"And here, that I may not be thought the sly trumpeter of my own praises, I do utterly disclaim all praise on the occasion. Neither did the greatness of my mind dictate, nor the force of my Christianity exact this forgiveness. To speak truth, I forgave him from a motive which would make men much more forgiving, if they were much wiser than they are : because it was convenient for me so to do."

ship in which he was making his last voyage, and Fielding relates how the man finally went down on his knees, and begged his passenger's pardon. He was living up to the last days of his life, and his spirit never gave in. His vital power must have been immensely strong. Lady Mary Wortley Montagu * prettily characterizes Fielding and this capacity for happiness which he possessed, in a little notice of his death when she compares him to Steele, who was as improvident and as happy as he was, and says that both should have gone on living for ever. One can fancy the eagerness and gusto with which a man of Fielding's frame, with his vast health and robust appetite, his ardent spirits, his joyful humour, and his keen and healthy relish for life, must have seized and drunk that cup of pleasure which the town offered to him. Can any of my hearers remember the youthful feats of a college breakfast— the meats devoured and the cups quaffed in that Homeric feast? I can call to mind some of the heroes of those youthful banquets, and fancy young Fielding from Leyden rushing upon the feast, with his great laugh, and immense healthy young appetite, eager and vigorous to enjoy. The young man's wit and manners made him friends everywhere : he lived with the grand Man's society of those days ; he was courted by peers and men of wealth and fashion. As he had a paternal allowance from his father, General Fielding, which, to use Henry's own phrase, any man might

---

* Lady Mary was his second-cousin—their respective grandfathers being sons of George Fielding, Earl of Desmond, son of William, Earl of Denbigh.

In a letter dated just a week before his death, she says—

" H. Fielding has given a true picture of himself and his first wife in the characters of *Mr.* and *Mrs. Booth*, some compliments to his own figure excepted ; and I am persuaded, several of the incidents he mentions are real matters of fact. I wonder he does not perceive *Tom Jones* and *Mr. Booth* are sorry scoundrels. . . . . Fielding has really a fund of true humour, and was to be pitied at his first entrance into the world, having no choice, as he said himself, but to be a hackney writer or a hackney coachman. His genius deserved a better fate ; but I cannot help blaming that continued indiscretion, to give it the softest name, that has run through his life, and I am afraid still remains. . . . . Since I was born no original has appeared excepting Congreve, and Fielding, who would, I believe, have approached nearer to his excellences, if not forced by his necessities to publish without correction, and throw many productions into the world he would have thrown into the fire, if meat could have been got without money, or money without scribbling. . . . . I am sorry not to see any more of Peregrine Pickle's performances ; I wish you would tell me his name."—*Letters and Works* (Lord WHARNCLIFFE's Ed.), vol. iii. pp. 93, 94.

pay who would ; as he liked good wine, good clothes, and good
company, which are all expensive articles to purchase, Harry
Fielding began to run into debt, and borrow money in that easy
manner in which Captain Booth borrows money in the novel : was in
nowise particular in accepting a few pieces from the purses of his
rich friends, and bore down upon more than one of them, as Walpole
tells us only too truly, for a dinner or a guinea. To supply himself
with the latter, he began to write theatrical pieces, having already,
no doubt, a considerable acquaintance amongst the Oldfields and
Bracegirdles behind the scenes. He laughed at these pieces and
scorned them. When the audience upon one occasion began to hiss
a scene which he was too lazy to correct, and regarding which, when
Garrick remonstrated with him, he said that the public was too stupid
to find out the badness of his work : when the audience began to hiss,
Fielding said with characteristic coolness—"They have found it out,
have they?" He did not prepare his novels in this way, and with a
very different care and interest laid the foundations and built up the
edifices of his future fame.

Time and shower have very little damaged those. The fashion
and ornaments are, perhaps, of the architecture of that age ; but the
buildings remain strong and lofty, and of admirable proportions—
masterpieces of genius and monuments of workmanlike skill.

I cannot offer or hope to make a hero of Harry Fielding. Why
hide his faults? Why conceal his weaknesses in a cloud of peri-
phrases? Why not show him, like him as he is, not robed in a
marble toga, and draped and polished in an heroic attitude, but with
inked ruffles, and claret-stains on his tarnished laced coat, and on
his manly face the marks of good-fellowship, of illness, of kindness,
of care and wine. Stained as you see him, and worn by care and
dissipation, that man retains some of the most precious and splendid
human qualities and endowments. He has an admirable natural love
of truth, the keenest instinctive antipathy to hypocrisy, the happiest
satirical gift of laughing it to scorn. His wit is wonderfully wise and
detective ; it flashes upon a rogue and lightens up a rascal like a
policeman's lantern. He is one of the manliest and kindliest of
human beings : in the midst of all his imperfections, he respects
female innocence and infantine tenderness as you would suppose
such a great-hearted, courageous soul would respect and care for
them. He could not be so brave, generous, truth-telling as he is, were
he not infinitely merciful, pitiful, and tender. He will give any man
his purse—he can't help kindness and profusion. He may have low

tastes, but not a mean mind ; he admires with all his heart good and virtuous men, stoops to no flattery, bears no rancour, disdains all disloyal arts, does his public duty uprightly, is fondly loved by his family, and dies at his work.*

If that theory be—and I have no doubt it is—the right and safe one, that human nature is always pleased with the spectacle of innocence rescued by fidelity, purity, and courage ; I suppose that of the heroes of Fielding's three novels, we should like honest Joseph Andrews the best, and Captain Booth the second, and Tom Jones the third.†

Joseph Andrews, though he wears Lady Booby's cast-off livery, is, I think, to the full as polite as Tom Jones in his fustian-suit, or Captain Booth in regimentals. He has, like those heroes, large calves, broad shoulders, a high courage, and a handsome face. The accounts of Joseph's bravery and good qualities ; his voice, too musical to halloo to the dogs ; his bravery in riding races for the gentlemen of the county, and his constancy in refusing bribes and temptation, have something affecting in their *naïveté* and freshness, and prepossess one in favour of that handsome young hero. The rustic bloom of Fanny, and the delightful simplicity of Parson Adams, are described with a friendliness which wins the reader of their story ; we part from them with more regret than from Booth and Jones.

Fielding, no doubt, began to write this novel in ridicule of " Pamela," for which work one can understand the hearty contempt and antipathy which such an athletic and boisterous genius as Fielding's must have entertained. He couldn't do otherwise than laugh at the puny cockney bookseller, pouring out endless volumes of sentimental twaddle, and hold him up to scorn as a mollcoddle and a milksop. *His* genius had been nursed on sack posset, and

---

* He sailed for Lisbon, from Gravesend, on Sunday morning, June 30th, 1754 ; and began " The Journal of a Voyage " during the passage. He died at Lisbon, in the beginning of October of the same year. He lies buried there, in the English Protestant churchyard, near the Estrella Church, with this inscription over him :—

" HENRICUS FIELDING.
LUGET BRITANNIA GREMIO NON DATUM
FOVERE NATUM."

† Fielding himself is said by Doctor Warton to have preferred " Joseph Andrews " to his other writings.

not on dishes of tea. *His* muse had sung the loudest in tavern choruses, had seen the daylight streaming in over thousands of emptied bowls, and reeled home to chambers on the shoulders of the watchman. Richardson's goddess was attended by old maids and dowagers, and fed on muffins and bohea. " Milksop ! " roars Harry Fielding, clattering at the timid shop-shutters. "Wretch ! Monster ! Mohock ! " shrieks the sentimental author of " Pamela ; "* and all the ladies of his court cackle out an affrighted chorus. Fielding proposes to write a book in ridicule of the author, whom he disliked and utterly scorned and laughed at ; but he is himself of so generous, jovial, and kindly a turn that he begins to like the characters which he invents, can't help making them manly and pleasant as well as ridiculous, and before he has done with them all, loves them heartily every one.

Richardson's sickening antipathy for Harry Fielding is quite as natural as the other's laughter and contempt at the sentimentalist. I have not learned that these likings and dislikings have ceased in the present day : and every author must lay his account not only to misrepresentation, but to honest enmity among critics, and to being hated and abused for good as well as for bad reasons. Richardson disliked Fielding's works quite honestly : Walpole quite honestly spoke of them as vulgar and stupid. Their squeamish stomachs sickened at the rough fare and the rough guests assembled at Fielding's jolly revel. Indeed the cloth might have been cleaner : and the dinner and the company were scarce such as suited a dandy. The kind and wise old Johnson would not sit down with him.† But a greater scholar than Johnson could afford to admire that astonishing

---

* " Richardson," says worthy Mrs. Barbauld, in her Memoir of him, pre-fixed to his Correspondence, "was exceedingly hurt at this ' Joseph An-drews '), the more so as they had been on good terms, and he was very intimate with Fielding's two sisters. He never appears cordially to have forgiven it (perhaps it was not in human nature he should), and he always speaks in his letters with a great deal of asperity of ' Tom Jones,' more indeed than was quite graceful in a rival author. No doubt he himself thought his indignation was solely excited by the loose morality of the work and of its author, but he could tolerate Cibber."

† It must always be borne in mind, that besides that the Doctor couldn't be expected to like Fielding's wild life (to say nothing of the fact that they were of opposite sides in politics), Richardson was one of his earliest and kindest friends. Yet Johnson too (as Boswell tells us) read "Amelia" through without stopping.

genius of Harry Fielding : and we all know the lofty panegyric which
Gibbon wrote of him, and which remains a towering monument to
the great novelist's memory. " Our immortal Fielding," Gibbon
writes, "was of the younger branch of the Earls of Denbigh, who
drew their origin from the Counts of Hapsburgh. The successors of
Charles V. may disdain their brethren of England, but the romance
of ' Tom Jones,' that exquisite picture of humour and manners, will
outlive the palace of the Escurial and the Imperial Eagle of Austria."

There can be no gainsaying the sentence of this great judge. To
have your name mentioned by Gibbon, is like having it written
on the dome of St. Peter's. Pilgrims from all the world admire and
behold it.

As a picture of manners, the novel of " Tom Jones " is indeed
exquisite : as a work of construction, quite a wonder : the by-play of
wisdom ; the power of observation; the multiplied felicitous turns
and thoughts ; the varied character of the great Comic Epic : keep
the reader in a perpetual admiration and curiosity.* But against
Mr. Thomas Jones himself we have a right to put in a protest, and
quarrel with the esteem the author evidently has for that character.
Charles Lamb says finely of Jones, that a single hearty laugh from
him "clears the air "—but then it is in a certain state of the atmo-
sphere. It might clear the air when such personages as Blifil or Lady
Bellaston poison it. But I fear very much that (except until the very
last scene of the story), when Mr. Jones enters Sophia's drawing-room,
the pure air there is rather tainted with the young gentleman's tobacco-
pipe and punch. I can't say that I think Mr. Jones a virtuous

* " Manners change from generation to generation, and with manners
morals appear to change—actually change with some, but appear to change
with all but the abandoned. A young man of the present day who should act
as Tom Jones is supposed to act at Upton, with Lady Bellaston, &c. would
not be a Tom Jones ; and a Tom Jones of the present day, without perhaps
being in the ground a better man, would have perished rather than submit to
be kept by a harridan of fortune. Therefore, this novel is, and indeed
pretends to be, no example of conduct. But, notwithstanding all this, I do
loathe the cant which can recommend ' Pamela ' and ' Clarissa Harlowe ' as
strictly moral, although they poison the imagination of the young with continued doses of *tinct. lyttæ*, while 'Tom Jones ' is prohibited as loose. I do not
speak of young women ; but a young man whose heart or feelings can be in-
jured, or even his passions excited by this novel, is already thoroughly corrupt. There is a cheerful, sunshiny, breezy spirit, that prevails everywhere,
strongly contrasted with the close, hot, day-dreamy continuity of Richardson."—
COLERIDGE : *Literary Remains*, vol. ii. p. 374.

character ; I can't say but that I think Fielding's evident liking and admiration for Mr. Jones shows that the great humourist's moral sense was blunted by his life, and that here, in Art and Ethics, there is a great error. If it is right to have a hero whom we may admire, let us at least take care that he is admirable : if, as is the plan of some authors (a plan decidedly against their interests, be it said), it is propounded that there exists in life no such being, and therefore that in novels, the picture of life, there should appear no such character ; then Mr. Thomas Jones becomes an admissible person, and we examine his defects and good qualities, as we do those of Parson Thwackum, or Miss Seagrim. But a hero with a flawed reputation ; a hero spunging for a guinea ; a hero who can't pay his landlady, and is obliged to let his honour out to hire, is absurd, and his claim to heroic rank untenable. I protest against Mr. Thomas Jones holding such rank at all. I protest even against his being considered a more than ordinary young fellow, ruddy-cheeked, broad-shouldered, and fond of wine and pleasure. He would not rob a church, but that is all ; and a pretty long argument may be debated, as to which of these old types, the spendthrift, the hypocrite, Jones and Blifil, Charles and Joseph Surface,—is the worst member of society and the most deserving of censure. The prodigal Captain Booth is a better man than his predecessor Mr. Jones, in so far as he thinks much more humbly of himself than Jones did : goes down on his knees, and owns his weaknesses, and cries out, "Not for my sake, but for the sake of my pure and sweet and beautiful wife Amelia, I pray you, O critical reader, to forgive me." That stern moralist regards him from the bench (the judge's practice out of court is not here the question), and says, "Captain Booth, it is perfectly true that your life has been disreputable, and that on many occasions you have shown yourself to be no better than a scamp—you have been tippling at the tavern, when the kindest and sweetest lady in the world has cooked your little supper of boiled mutton and awaited you all the night ; you have spoilt the little dish of boiled mutton thereby, and caused pangs and pains to Amelia's tender heart.* You have got into debt without the means of paying

---

* "Nor was she (Lady Mary Wortley Montagu) a stranger to that beloved first wife, whose picture he drew in his 'Amelia,' when, as she said, even the glowing language he knew how to employ, did not do more than justice to the amiable qualities of the original, or to her beauty, although this had suffered a little from the accident related in the novel—a frightful overturn, which destroyed the gristle of her nose. He loved her passionately, and she returned his affection. . . . ["His

it. You have gambled the money with which you ought to have paid your rent. You have spent in drink or in worse amusements the sums which your poor wife has raised upon her little home treasures, her own ornaments, and the toys of her children. But, you rascal! you own humbly that you are no better than you should be; you never for one moment pretend that you are anything but a miserable weak-minded rogue. You do in your heart adore that angelic woman, your wife, and for her sake, sirrah, you shall have your discharge. Lucky for you and for others like you, that in spite of your failings and imperfections, pure hearts pity and love you. For your wife's sake you are permitted to go hence without a remand; and I beg you, by the way, to carry to that angelical lady the expression of the cordial respect and admiration of this court." Amelia pleads for her husband, Will Booth: Amelia pleads for her reckless kindly old father, Harry Fielding. To have invented that character, is not only a triumph of art, but it is a good action. They say it was in his own home that Fielding knew her and loved her: and from his own wife that he drew the most charming character in English fiction. Fiction! why fiction? why not history? I know Amelia just as well as Lady Mary Wortley Montagu. I believe in Colonel Bath almost as much as in Colonel Gardiner or the Duke of Cumberland. I admire the author of "Amelia," and thank the kind master who introduced me to that

" His biographers seem to have been shy of disclosing that, after the death of this charming woman, he married her maid. And yet the act was not so discreditable to his character as it may sound. The maid had few personal charms, but was an excellent creature, devotedly attached to her mistress, and almost broken-hearted for her loss. In the first agonies of his own grief, which approached to frenzy, he found no relief but from weeping along with her; nor solace when a degree calmer, but in talking to her of the angel they mutually regretted. This made her his habitual confidential associate, and in process of time he began to think he could not give his children a tenderer mother, or secure for himself a more faithful housekeeper and nurse. At least, this was what he told his friends; and it is certain that her conduct as his wife confirmed it, and fully justified his good opinion."—*Letters and Works of Lady Mary Wortley Montagu.* Edited by Lord WHARNCLIFFE. *Introductory Anecdotes,* vol. i. pp. 80, 81.

Fielding's first wife was Miss Craddock, a young lady from Salisbury, with a fortune of 1,500*l.*, whom he married in 1736. About the same time he succeeded, himself, to an estate of 200*l.* per annum, and on the joint amount he lived for some time as a splendid country gentleman in Dorsetshire. Three years brought him to the end of his fortune; when he returned to London, and became a student of law.

sweet and delightful companion and friend. "Amelia" perhaps is not a better story than "Tom Jones," but it has the better ethics; the prodigal repents at least, before forgiveness,—whereas that odious broad-backed Mr. Jones carries off his beauty with scarce an interval of remorse for his manifold errors and short-comings ; and is not half punished enough before the great prize of fortune and love falls to his share. I am angry with Jones. Too much of the plum-cake and rewards of life fall to that boisterous, swaggering young scapegrace. Sophia actually surrenders without a proper sense of decorum ; the fond, foolish, palpitating little creature !—"Indeed, Mr. Jones," she says,—" it rests with you to appoint the day." I suppose Sophia is drawn from life as well as Amelia ; and many a young fellow, no better than Mr. Thomas Jones, has carried by a *coup de main* the heart of many a kind girl who was a great deal too good for him.

What a wonderful art ! What an admirable gift of nature was it by which the author of these tales was endowed, and which enabled him to fix our interest, to waken our sympathy, to seize upon our credulity, so that we believe in his people—speculate gravely upon their faults or their excellences, prefer this one or that, deplore Jones's fondness for drink and play, Booth's fondness for play and drink, and the unfortunate position of the wives of both gentlemen—love and admire those ladies with all our hearts, and talk about them as faithfully as if we had breakfasted with them this morning in their actual drawing-rooms, or should meet them this afternoon in the Park ! What a genius ! what a vigour ! what a bright-eyed intelligence and observation ! what a wholesome hatred for meanness and knavery ! what a vast sympathy ! what a cheerfulness ! what a manly relish of life ! what a love of human kind ! what a poet is here !—watching, meditating, brooding, creating ! What multitudes of truths has that man left behind him ! What generations he has taught to laugh wisely and fairly ! What scholars he has formed and accustomed to the exercise of thoughtful humour and the manly play of wit ! What a courage he had ! What a dauntless and constant cheerfulness of intellect, that burned bright and steady through all the storms of his life, and never deserted its last wreck ! It is wonderful to think of the pains and misery which the man suffered ; the pressure of want, illness, remorse which he endured ! and that the writer was neither malignant nor melancholy, his view of truth never warped, and his generous human kindness never surrendered.*

* In the *Gentleman's Magazine* for 1786, an anecdote is related of Harry Fielding, "in whom," says the correspondent, "good-nature and

In the quarrel mentioned before, which happened on Fielding's
last voyage to Lisbon, and when the stout captain of the ship fell

philanthropy in their extreme degree were known to be the prominent features."
It seems that " some parochial taxes " for his house in Beaufort Buildings had
long been demanded by the collector.   " At last, Harry went off to Johnson,
and obtained by a process of literary mortgage the needful sum.   He was returning with it, when he met an old college chum whom he had not seen for
many years.   He asked the chum to dinner with him at a neighbouring
tavern ; and learning that he was in difficulties, emptied the contents of his
pocket into his.   On returning home he was informed that the collector had
been twice for the money.   ' Friendship has called for the money and had it,'
said Fielding ; ' let the collector call again.' "

It is elsewhere told of him, that being in company with the Earl of
Denbigh, his kinsman, and the conversation turning upon their relationship,
the Earl asked him how it was that he spelled his name " Fielding," and
not "Feilding," like the head of the house ?   " I cannot tell, my lord," said
he, "except it be that my branch of the family were the first that knew how
to spell."

In 1748, he was made Justice of the Peace for Westminster and Middlesex,
an office then paid by fees and very laborious, without being particularly re-
putable.   It may be seen from his own words, in the Introduction to the
"Voyage," what kind of work devolved upon him, and in what a state he was,
during these last years ; and still more clearly, how he comported himself
through all.

"Whilst I was preparing for my journey, and when I was almost fatigued
to death with several long examinations, relating to five different murders, all
committed within the space of a week, by different gangs of street-robbers, I
received a message from his Grace the Duke of Newcastle, by Mr. Carrington,
the King's messenger, to attend his Grace the next morning in Lincoln's Inn
Fields, upon some business of importance : but I excused myself from comply-
ing with the message, as, besides being lame, I was very ill with the great
fatigues I had lately undergone, added to my distemper.

"His Grace, however, sent Mr. Carrington the very next morning, with
another summons ; with which, though in the utmost distress, I immediately
complied ; but the Duke happening, unfortunately for me, to be then particularly engaged, after I had waited some time, sent a gentleman to discourse
with me on the best plan which could be invented for these murders and
robberies, which were every day committed in the streets ; upon which I promised to transmit my opinion in writing to his Grace, who, as the gentleman
informed me, intended to lay it before the Privy Council.

" Though this visit cost me a severe cold, I, notwithstanding, set myself
down to work, and in about four days sent the Duke as regular a plan as I
could form, with all the reasons and arguments I could bring to support it,
drawn out on several sheets of paper ; and soon received a message from the

down on his knees and asked the sick man's pardon—" I did not suffer," Fielding says, in his hearty, manly way, his eyes lighting up as it were with their old fire—" I did not suffer a brave man and an old man to remain a moment in that posture, but immediately forgave him." Indeed, I think, with his noble spirit and unconquerable generosity, Fielding reminds one of those brave men of whom one reads in stories of English shipwrecks and disasters—of the officer on the African shore, when disease had destroyed the crew, and he himself is seized by fever, who throws the lead with a death-stricken hand, takes the soundings, carries the ship out of the river or off the dangerous coast, and dies in the manly endeavour—of the wounded captain, when the vessel founders, who never loses his heart, who eyes the danger steadily, and has a cheery word for all, until the inevitable fate overwhelms him, and the gallant ship goes down. Such a brave and gentle heart, such an intrepid and courageous spirit, I love to recognize in the manly, the English Harry Fielding.

Duke, by Mr. Carrington, acquainting me that my plan was highly approved of, and that all the terms of it would be complied with.

" The principal and most material of these terms was the immediately depositing 600*l.* in my hands ; at which small charge I undertook to demolish the then reigning gangs, and to put the civil policy into such order, that no such gangs should ever be able for the future to form themselves into bodies, or at least to remain any time formidable to the public.

" I had delayed my Bath journey for some time, contrary to the repeated advice of my physical acquaintances and the ardent desire of my warmest friends, though my distemper was now turned to a deep jaundice ; in which case the Bath waters are generally reputed to be almost infallible. But I had the most eager desire to demolish this gang of villains and cut-throats. . . . .

" After some weeks the money was paid at the Treasury, and within a few days after 200*l.* of it had come into my hands, the whole gang of cut-throats was entirely dispersed. . . . . "

Further on, he says—

" I will confess that my private affairs at the beginning of the winter had but a gloomy aspect ; for I had not plundered the public or the poor of those sums which men, who are always ready to plunder both as much as they can, have been pleased to suspect me of taking ; on the contrary, by composing, instead of inflaming, the quarrels of porters and beggars (which I blush when I say hath not been universally practised), and by refusing to take a shilling from a man who most undoubtedly would not have had another left, I had reduced an income of about 500*l.* a year of the dirtiest money upon earth, to little more than 300*l.*, a considerable portion of which remained with my clerk."

STERNE AND GOLDSMITH.

OGER STERNE, Sterne's father, was the second son of a numerous race, descendants of Richard Sterne, Archbishop of York, in the reign of James II.; and children of Simon Sterne and Mary Jaques, his wife, heiress of Elvington, near York.* Roger was a lieutenant in Handyside's regiment, and engaged in Flanders in Queen Anne's wars. He married the daughter of a noted sutler—" N.B., he was in debt to him," his son writes, pursuing the paternal biography—and marched through the world with this companion ; she following the regiment and bringing many children to poor Roger Sterne. The captain was an irascible but kind and simple little man, Sterne says, and informs us that his sire was run through the body at Gibraltar, by a brother officer, in a duel which arose out of a dispute about a goose. Roger never entirely recovered from the effects of this rencontre, but died presently at Jamaica, whither he had followed the drum.

Laurence, his second child, was born at Clonmel, in Ireland, in 1713, and travelled, for the first ten years of his life, on his father's march, from barrack to transport, from Ireland to England.†

* He came of a Suffolk family—one of whom settled in Nottinghamshire. The famous " starling " was actually the family crest.

† " It was in this parish (of Animo, in Wicklow), during our stay, that I had that wonderful escape in falling through a mill-race, whilst the mill was

One relative of his mother's took her and her family under shelter for ten months at Mullingar : another collateral descendant of the Archbishop's housed them for a year at his castle near Carrickfergus. Larry Sterne was put to school at Halifax in England, finally was adopted by his kinsman of Elvington, and parted company with his father, the Captain who marched on his path of life till he met the fatal goose, which closed his career. The most picturesque and delightful parts of Laurence Sterne's writings, we owe to his recollections of the military life. Trim's montero cap, and Le Fevre's sword, and dear Uncle Toby's roquelaure, are doubtless reminiscences of the boy, who had lived with the followers of William and Marlborough, and had beat time with his little feet to the fifes of Ramillies in Dublin barrack-yard, or played with the torn flags and halberds of Malplaquet on the parade-ground at Clonmel.

Laurence remained at Halifax school till he was eighteen years old. His wit and cleverness appear to have acquired the respect of his master here ; for when the usher whipped Laurence for writing his name on the newly whitewashed school-room ceiling, the pedagogue in chief rebuked the understrapper, and said that the name should never be effaced, for Sterne was a boy of genius, and would come to preferment.

His cousin, the Squire of Elvington, sent Sterne to Jesus College, Cambridge, where he remained five years, and taking orders, got, through his uncle's interest, the living of Sutton and the prebendary of York. Through his wife's connections, he got the living of Stillington. He married her in 1741, having ardently courted the young lady for some years previously. It was not until the young lady fancied herself dying, that she made Sterne acquainted with the extent of her liking for him. One evening when he was sitting with her, with an almost broken heart to see her so ill (the Rev. Mr. Sterne's heart was a good deal broken in the course of his life), she said—" My dear Laurey, I never can be yours, for I verily believe I have not long to live ; but I have left you every shilling of my fortune ; " a generosity which overpowered Sterne. She recovered : and so they were married, and grew heartily tired of each other before many years were over. " Nescio quid est materia cum me," Sterne writes to one of his friends (in dog-Latin, and very sad dog-Latin too) ; " sed sum fatigatus et ægrotus de meâ uxore plus quam unquam : " which means, I am

going, and of being taken up unhurt ; the story is incredible, but known for truth in all that part of Ireland, where hundreds of the common people flocked to see me."—STERNE.

sorry to say, " I don't know what is the matter with me ; but I am more tired and sick of my wife than ever." *

This to be sure was five-and-twenty years after Laurey had been overcome by her generosity and she by Laurey's love. Then he wrote to her of the delights of marriage, saying, " We will be as merry and as innocent as our first parents in Paradise, before the arch fiend entered that indescribable scene. The kindest affections will have room to expand in our retirement : let the human tempest and hurricane rage at a distance, the desolation is beyond the horizon of peace. My L. has seen a polyanthus blow in December ?—Some friendly wall has sheltered it from the biting wind. No planetary influence shall reach us, but that which presides and cherishes the sweetest flowers. The gloomy family of care and distrust shall be banished from our dwelling, guarded by thy kind and tutelar deity. We will sing our choral songs of gratitude and rejoice to the end of our pilgrimage. Adieu, my L. Return to one who languishes for thy society !—As I take up my pen, my poor pulse quickens, my pale face glows, and tears are trickling down on my paper as I trace the word L."

And it is about this woman, with whom he finds no fault but that she bores him, that our philanthropist writes, "Sum fatigatus et ægrotus"—*Sum mortaliter in amore* with somebody else! That fine flower of love, that polyanthus over which Sterne snivelled so many tears, could not last for a quarter of a century !

Or rather it could not be expected that a gentleman with such a fountain at command should keep it to *arroser* one homely old lady, when a score of younger and prettier people might be refreshed from the same gushing source.† It was in December, 1767, that the Rev.

---

* " My wife returns to Toulouse, and proposes to pass the summer at Bagnères. I, on the contrary, go and visit my wife, the church, in York-shire. We all live the longer, at least the happier, for having things our own way ; this is my conjugal maxim. I own 'tis not the best of maxims, but I maintain 'tis not the worst."—STERNE'S *Letters :* 20th January, 1764.

† In a collection of "Seven Letters by Sterne and his Friends " (printed for private circulation in 1844), is a latter of M. Tollot, who was in France with Sterne and his family in 1764. Here is a paragraph :—

"Nous arrivâmes le lendemain à Montpellier, où nous trouvâmes notre ami Mr. Sterne, sa femme, sa fille, Mr. Huet, et quelques autres Anglaises. J'eus, je vous l'avoue, beaucoup de plaisir en revoyant le bon et agréable Tristram. . . . . Il avait été assez longtemps à Toulouse, où il se serait amusé sans sa femme, qui le poursuivit partout, et qui voulait être de tout.

Laurence Sterne, the famous Shandean, the charming Yorick, the delight of the fashionable world, the delicious divine, for whose sermons the whole polite world was subscribing,* the occupier of Rabelais's

Ces dispositions dans cette bonne dame lui ont fait passer d'assez mauvais momens ; il supporte tous ces désagrémens avec une patience d'ange."

About four months after this very characteristic letter, Sterne wrote to the same gentleman to whom Tollot had written ; and from his letter we may extract a companion paragraph :—

". . . . . . All which being premised, I have been for eight weeks smitten with the tenderest passion that ever tender wight underwent. I wish, dear cousin, thou could'st conceive (perhaps thou canst without my wishing it) how deliciously I cantered away with it the first month, two up, two down, always upon my *hanches*, along the streets from my hotel to hers, at first once—then twice, then three times a day, till at length I was within an ace of setting up my hobby-horse in her stable for good and all. I might as well, considering how the enemies of the Lord have blasphemed thereupon. The last three weeks we were every hour upon the doleful ditty of parting ; and thou may'st conceive, dear cousin, how it altered my gait and air : for I went and came like any louden'd carl, and did nothing but *jouer des sentimens* with her from sun-rising even to the setting of the same ; and now she is gone to the south of France ; and to finish the comédie, I fell ill, and broke a vessel in my lungs, and half bled to death. Voilà mon histoire ! "

Whether husband or wife had most of the "*patience d'ange*" may be uncertain ; but there can be no doubt which needed it most !

* " ' Tristram Shandy ' is still a greater object of admiration, the man as well as the book : one is invited to dinner, where he dines, a fortnight before. As to the volumes yet published, there is much good fun in them and humour sometimes hit and sometimes missed. Have you read his ' Sermons,' with his own comick figure, from a painting by Reynolds, at the head of them ? They are in the style I think most proper for the pulpit, and show a strong imagination and a sensible heart ; but you see him often tottering on the verge of laughter, and ready to throw his periwig in the face of the audience."—GRAY'S *Letters* : June 22nd, 1760.

" It having been observed that there was little hospitality in London— Johnson : ' Nay, sir, any man who has a name, or who has the power of pleasing, will be very generally invited in London. The man, Sterne, I have been told, has had engagements for three months.' Goldsmith : ' And a very dull fellow.' Johnson : ' Why, no, sir.' "—BOSWELL'S *Life of Johnson.*

" Her [Miss Monckton's] vivacity enchanted the sage, and they used to talk together with all imaginable ease. A singular instance happened one evening, when she insisted that some of Sterne's writings were very pathetic. Johnson bluntly denied it. ' I am sure,' said she, ' they have affected me.' ' Why,' said Johnson, smiling, and rolling himself about—' that is, because, dearest, you're a dunce.' When she some time afterwards mentioned this to

easy chair, only fresh stuffed and more elegant than when in possession
of the cynical old curate of Meudon,*—the more than rival of the

him, he said with equal truth and politeness, 'Madam, if I had thought so, I
certainly should not have said it.'"—*Ibid.*

* A passage or two from Sterne's " Sermons " may not be without interest
here. Is not the following, levelled against the cruelties of the Church of
Rome, stamped with the autograph of the author of the "Sentimental
Journey?"—

"To be convinced of this, go with me for a moment into the prisons of
the Inquisition—behold *religion* with mercy and justice chained down under
her feet,—there, sitting ghastly upon a black tribunal, propped up with racks,
and instruments of torment.—Hark!—what a piteous groan!—See the
melancholy wretch who uttered it, just brought forth to undergo the anguish
of a mock-trial, and endure the utmost pain that a studied system of *religious
cruelty* has been able to invent. Behold this helpless victim delivered up to
his tormentors. *His body so wasted with sorrow and long confinement, you'll
see every nerve and muscle as it suffers.*—Observe the last movement of that
horrid engine.—What convulsions it has thrown him into! Consider the
nature of the posture in which he now lies stretched.—What exquisite torture
he endures by it!—'Tis all nature can bear.—Good GOD! see how it keeps his
weary soul hanging upon his trembling lips, willing to take its leave, but not
suffered to depart. Behold the unhappy wretch led back to his cell,—dragg'd
out of it again to meet the flames—and the insults in his last agonies, which
this principle—this principle, that there can be religion without morality—has
prepared for him."—*Sermon 27th.*

The next extract is preached on a text to be found in Judges xix. vv. 1, 2,
3, concerning a "certain Levite:"—

"Such a one the Levite wanted to share his solitude and fill up that un-
comfortable blank in the heart in such a situation: for, notwithstanding all we
meet with in books, in many of which, no doubt, there are a good many handsome things said upon the sweets of retirement, &c. . . . . yet still 'it
is not good for man to be alone:' nor can all which the cold-hearted pedant
stuns our ears with upon the subject, ever give one answer of satisfaction to
the mind; in the midst of the loudest vauntings of philosophy, nature will
have her yearnings for society and friendship;—a good heart wants some
object to be kind to—and the best parts of our blood, and the purest of our
spirits, suffer most under the destitution.

"Let the torpid monk seek Heaven comfortless and alone. God speed
him! For my own part, I fear I should never so find the way : *let me be wise
and religious, but let me be* MAN; wherever thy Providence places me, or
whatever be the road I take to Thee, give me some companion in my journey,
be it only to remark to, 'How our shadows lengthen as our sun goes down;'—
to whom I may say, 'How fresh is the face of Nature; how sweet the flowers
of the field! how delicious are these fruits!'"—*Sermon 18th.*   [The

Dean of St. Patrick's, wrote the above-quoted respectable letter to his friend in London : and it was in April of the same year that he was pouring out his fond heart to Mrs. Elizabeth Draper, wife of " Daniel Draper, Esq., Councillor of Bombay, and, in 1775, chief of the factory of Surat—a gentleman very much respected in that quarter of the globe."

" I got thy letter last night, Eliza," Sterne writes, " on my return from Lord Bathurst's, where I dined "—(the letter has this merit in it, that it contains a pleasant reminiscence of better men than Sterne, and introduces us to a portrait of a kind old gentleman)—" I got thy letter last night, Eliza, on my return from Lord Bathurst's ; and where I was heard—as I talked of thee an hour without intermission—with so much pleasure and attention, that the good old Lord toasted your health three different times ; and now he is in his 85th year, says he hopes to live long enough to be introduced as a friend to my fair Indian disciple, and to see her eclipse all other Nabobesses as much in wealth as she does already in exterior and, what is far better " (for Sterne is nothing without his morality), " in interior merit. This nobleman is an old friend of mine. You know he was always the protector of men of wit and genius, and has had those of the last century, Addison, Steele, Pope, Swift, Prior, &c., always at his table. The manner in which his notice began of me was as singular as it was polite. He came up to me one day as I was at the Princess of Wales's court, and said, ' I want to know you, Mr. Sterne, but it is fit you also should know who it is that wishes this pleasure. You have heard of an old Lord Bathurst, of whom your Popes and Swifts have sung and spoken so much ? I have lived my life with geniuses of that cast ; but have survived them ; and, despairing ever to find their equals, it is some years since I have shut up my books and closed my accounts ; but you have kindled a desire in me of opening them once more before I die : which I now do : so go home and dine with me.' This nobleman, I say, is a prodigy, for he has all the wit and promptness of a man of thirty ; a disposition to be pleased, and a power to please others, beyond whatever I knew : added to which a man of learning, courtesy, and feeling.

" He heard me talk of thee, Eliza, with uncommon satisfaction—for there was only a third person, *and of sensibility*, with us : and a most

The first of these passages gives us another drawing of the famous "Captive." The second shows that the same reflection was suggested to the Rev. Laurence by a text in Judges as by the *fille-de-chambre*.

Sterne's Sermons were published as those of "Mr. Yorick."

sentimental afternoon till nine o'clock have we passed !* But thou,
Eliza, wert the star that conducted and enlivened the discourse ! And

* "I am glad that you are in love : 'twill cure you at least of the spleen,
which has a bad effect on both man and woman. I myself must ever have

when I talked not of thee, still didst thou fill my mind, and warm every thought I uttered, for I am not ashamed to acknowledge I greatly miss thee. Best of all good girls !—the sufferings I have sustained all night in consequence of thine, Eliza, are beyond the power of words. . . . And so thou hast fixed thy Bramin's portrait over thy writing-desk, and will consult it in all doubts and difficulties ?—Grateful and good girl ! Yorick smiles contentedly over all thou dost : his picture does not do justice to his own complacency. I am glad your ship-mates are friendly beings" (Eliza was at Deal, going back to the Councillor at Bombay, and indeed it was high time she should be off). "You could least dispense with what is contrary to your own nature, which is soft and gentle, Eliza ; it would civilize savages—though pity were it thou should'st be tainted with the office. Write to me, my child, thy delicious letters. Let them speak the easy carelessness of a heart that opens itself anyhow, everyhow. Such, Eliza, I write to thee !" (The artless rogue, of course he did !) "And so I should ever love thee, most artlessly, most affectionately, if Providence per-mitted thy residence in the same section of the globe : for I am all that honour and affection can make me ' THY BRAMIN.' "

The Bramin continues addressing Mrs. Draper until the departure of the "Earl of Chatham" Indiaman from Deal, on the 2nd of April, 1767. He is amiably anxious about the fresh paint for Eliza's cabin ; he is uncommonly solicitous about her companions on board : "I fear the best of your shipmates are only genteel by comparison with the contrasted crew with which thou beholdest them. So was—you know who—from the same fallacy which was put upon your judgment when—but I will not mortify you !"

"You know who" was, of course, Daniel Draper, Esq., of Bombay

some Dulcinea in my head ; it harmonises the soul ; and in these cases I first endeavour to make the lady believe so, or rather, I begin first to make myself believe that I am in love ; but I carry on my affairs quite in the French way, sentimentally : ' *L'amour*,' say they, ' *n'est rien sans sentiment*.' Now, not-withstanding they make such a pother about the *word*, they have no precise idea annexed to it. And so much for that same subject called love."—STERNE'S *Letters:* May 23, 1765.

"P.S.—My ' Sentimental Journey ' will please Mrs. J—— and my Lydia " [his daughter, afterwards Mrs. Medalle]—" I can answer for those two. It is a subject which works well, and suits the frame of mind I have been in for some time past. I told you my design in it was to teach us to love the world and our fellow-creatures better than we do—so it runs most upon those gentler passions and affections which aid so much to it."—*Letters* [1767].

—a gentleman very much respected in that quarter of the globe, and about whose probable health our worthy Bramin writes with delightful candour :—

"I honour you, Eliza, for keeping secret some things which, if explained, had been a panegyric on yourself. There is a dignity in venerable affliction which will not allow it to appeal to the world for pity or redress. Well have you supported that character, my amiable, my philosophic friend ! And, indeed, I begin to think you have as many virtues as my Uncle Toby's widow. Talking of widows—pray, Eliza, if ever you are such, do not think of giving yourself to some wealthy Nabob, because I design to marry you myself. My wife cannot live long, and I know not the woman I should like so well for her substitute as yourself. 'Tis true I am ninety-five in constitution, and you but twenty-five ; but what I want in youth, I will make up in wit and good-humour. Not Swift so loved his Stella, Scarron his Maintenon, or Waller his Saccharissa. Tell me, in answer to this, that you approve and honour the proposal."

Approve and honour the proposal ! The coward was writing gay letters to his friends this while, with sneering allusions to this poor foolish *Bramine*. Her ship was not out of the Downs and the charming Sterne was at the "Mount Coffee-house," with a sheet of gilt-edged paper before him, offering that precious treasure his heart to Lady P——, asking whether it gave her pleasure to see him unhappy? whether it added to her triumph that her eyes and lips had turned a man into a fool ?—quoting the Lord's Prayer, with a horrible baseness of blasphemy, as a proof that he had desired not to be led into temptation, and swearing himself the most tender and sincere fool in the world. It was from his home at Coxwould that he wrote the Latin Letter, which, I suppose, he was ashamed to put into English. I find in my copy of the Letters, that there is a note of I can't call it admiration, at Letter 112, which seems to announce that there was a No. 3 to whom the wretched worn-out old scamp was paying his addresses ;*

---

* "To Mrs. H——.

"*Coxwould*, Nov. 15, 1767.

"Now be a good dear woman, my H——, and execute those commissions well, and when I see you I will give you a kiss—there's for you ! But I have something else for you which I am fabricating at a great rate, and that is my 'Sentimental Journey,' which shall make you cry as much as it has affected me, or I will give up the business of sentimental writing. . . .

"I am yours, &c. &c.,

"T. SHANDY."

"To THE

and the year after, having come back to his lodgings in Bond Street, with his " Sentimental Journey " to launch upon the town, eager as ever for praise and pleasure—as vain, as wicked, as witty, as false as he had ever been—death at length seized the feeble wretch, and on the 18th of March, 1768, that " bale of cadaverous goods," as he calls his body, was consigned to Pluto.* In his last letter there is one sign of grace—the real affection with which he entreats a friend to be a guardian to his daughter Lydia. All his letters to her are artless, kind, affectionate, and *not* sentimental ; as a hundred pages in his writings are beautiful, and full, not of surprising humour merely, but of genuine love and kindness. A perilous trade, indeed, is that of a man who has

"To the Earl of ——

"*Coxwould*, Nov. 28, 1767.

" My Lord,—'Tis with the greatest pleasure I take my pen to thank your lordship for your letter of inquiry about Yorick : he was worn out, both his spirits and body, with the 'Sentimental Journey.' 'Tis true, then, an author must feel himself, or his reader will not ; but I have torn my whole frame into pieces by my feelings : I believe the brain stands as much in need of recruiting as the body. Therefore I shall set out for town the twentieth of next month, after having recruited myself a week at York. I might indeed solace myself with my wife (who is come from France) ; but, in fact, I have long been a sentimental being, whatever your lordship may think to the contrary."

* " In February, 1768, Laurence Sterne, his frame exhausted by long debilitating illness, expired at his lodgings in Bond Street, London. There was something in the manner of his death singularly resembling the particulars detailed by *Mrs. Quickly* as attending that of *Falstaff*, the compeer of *Yorick* for infinite jest, however unlike in other particulars. As he lay on his bed totally exhausted, he complained that his feet were cold, and requested the female attendant to chafe them. She did so, and it seemed to relieve him. He complained that the cold came up higher ; and whilst the assistant was in the act of chafing his ankles and legs, he expired without a groan. It was also remarkable that his death took place much in the manner which he himself had wished ; and that the last offices were rendered him, not in his own house, or by the hand of kindred affection, but in an inn, and by strangers.

"We are well acquainted with Sterne's features and personal appearance, to which he himself frequently alludes. He was tall and thin, with a hectic and consumptive appearance."—Sir Walter Scott.

" It is known that Sterne died in hired lodgings, and I have been told that his attendants robbed him even of his gold sleeve-buttons while he was expiring."—Dr. Ferriar.

"He died at No. 41 (now a cheesemonger's on the west side of Old Bond Street."—*Handbook of London.*

to bring his tears and laughter, his recollections, his personal griefs and joys, his private thoughts and feelings to market to write them on paper, and sell them for money. Does he exaggerate his grief, so as to get his reader's pity for a false sensibility? feign indignation, so as to establish a character for virtue; elaborate repartees, so that he may pass for a wit; steal from other authors, and put down the theft to the credit side of his own reputation for ingenuity and learning? feign originality? affect benevolence or misanthropy? appeal to the gallery gods with claptraps and vulgar baits to catch applause?

How much of the paint and emphasis is necessary for the fair business of the stage, and how much of the rant and rouge is put on for the vanity of the actor? His audience trusts him: can he trust himself? How much was deliberate calculation and imposture—how much was false sensibility—and how much true feeling? Where did the lie begin, and did he know where? and where did the truth end in the art and scheme of this man of genius, this actor, this quack? Some time since, I was in the company of a French actor who began after dinner, and at his own request, to sing French songs of the sort called *des chansons grivoises*, and which he performed admirably, and to the dissatisfaction of most persons present. Having finished these, he commenced a sentimental ballad — it was so charmingly sung, that it touched all persons present, and especially the singer himself, whose voice trembled, whose eyes filled with emotion, and who was snivelling and weeping quite genuine tears by the time his own ditty was over. I suppose Sterne had this artistical sensibility; he used to blubber perpetually in his study, and finding his tears infectious, and that they brought him a great popularity, he exercised the lucrative gift of weeping: he utilized it, and cried on every occasion. I own that I don't value or respect much the cheap dribble of those fountains. He fatigues me with his perpetual disquiet and his uneasy appeals to my risible or sentimental faculties. He is always looking in my face, watching his effect, uncertain whether I think him an impostor or not; posture-making, coaxing, and imploring me. " See what sensibility I have—own now that I'm very clever—do cry now, you can't resist this." The humour of Swift and Rabelais, whom he pretended to succeed, poured from them as naturally as song does from a bird; they lose no manly dignity with it, but laugh their hearty great laugh out of their broad chests as nature bade them. But this man—who can make you laugh, who can make you cry too—never lets his reader alone, or will permit his audience repose:

when you are quiet, he fancies he must rouse you, and turns over head
and heels, or sidles up and whispers a nasty story. The man is a
great jester, not a great humourist. He goes to work systematically
and of cold blood; paints his face, puts on his ruff and motley clothes,
and lays down his carpet and tumbles on it.

For instance, take the "Sentimental Journey," and see in the
writer the deliberate propensity to make points and seek applause.
He gets to "Dessein's Hotel," he wants a carriage to travel to Paris,
he goes to the inn-yard, and begins what the actor's call "business" at

once. There is that little carriage (the *désobligeante*). "Four months
had elapsed since it had finished its career of Europe in the corner
of Monsieur Dessein's coach-yard, and having sallied out thence but
a vamped-up business at first, though it had been twice taken to
pieces on Mont Cenis, it had not profited much by its adventures,
but by none so little as the standing so many months unpitied in the
corner of Monsieur Dessein's coach-yard. Much, indeed, was not to
be said for it—but something might—and when a few words will
rescue misery out of her distress, I hate the man who can be a churl
of them."

Le tour est fait! Paillasse has tumbled! Paillasse has jumped over the *desobligeante*, cleared it, hood and all, and bows to the noble company. Does anybody believe that this is a real Sentiment? that this luxury of generosity, this gallant rescue of Misery—out of an old cab, is genuine feeling? It is as genuine as the virtuous oratory of Joseph Surface when he begins, " The man who," &c. &c., and wishes to pass off for a saint with his credulous, good-humoured dupes.

Our friend purchases the carriage : after turning that notorious old monk to good account, and effecting (like a soft and good-natured Paillasse as he was, and very free with his money when he had it,) an exchange of snuff-boxes with the old Franciscan, jogs out of Calais ; sets down in immense figures on the credit side of his account the sous he gives away to the Montreuil beggars ; and, at Nampont, gets out of the chaise and whimpers over that famous dead donkey, for which any sentimentalist may cry who will. It is agreeably and skilfully done—that dead jackass : like M. de Soubise's cook on the campaign, Sterne dresses it, and serves it up quite tender and with a very piquante sauce. But tears and fine feelings, and a white pocket handkerchief, and a funeral sermon, and horses and feathers, and a procession of mutes, and a hearse with a dead donkey inside ! Psha, mountebank ! I'll not give thee one penny more for that trick, donkey and all !

This donkey had appeared once before with signal effect. In 1765, three years before the publication of the " Sentimental Journey," the seventh and eighth volumes of " Tristram Shandy " were given to the world, and the famous Lyons donkey makes his entry in those volumes (pp. 315, 316) :—

"'Twas by a poor ass, with a couple of large panniers at his back, who had just turned in to collect eleemosynary turnip-tops and cabbage-leaves, and stood dubious, with his two forefeet at the inside of the threshold, and with his two hinder feet towards the street, as not knowing very well whether he was to go in or no.

" Now 'tis an animal (be in what hurry I may) I cannot bear to strike : there is a patient endurance of suffering wrote so unaffectedly in his looks and carriage which pleads so mightily for him, that it always disarms me, and to that degree that I do not like to speak unkindly to him : on the contrary, meet him where I will, whether in town or country, in cart or under panniers, whether in liberty or bondage, I have ever something civil to say to him on my part ; and, as one word begets another (if he has as little to do as I), I generally

fall into conversation with him ; and surely never is my imagination
so busy as in framing responses from the etchings of his countenance ;
and where those carry me not deep enough, in flying from my own
heart into his, and seeing what is natural for an ass to think—as well
as a man, upon the occasion. In truth, it is the only creature of all
the classes of beings below me with whom I can do this. . . . With
an ass I can commune for ever.

"'Come, Honesty,' said I, seeing it was impracticable to pass
betwixt him and the gate, 'art thou for coming in or going out?'

" The ass twisted his head round to look up the street.

"'Well!' replied I, 'we'll wait a minute for thy driver.'

" He turned his head thoughtful about, and looked wistfully the
opposite way.

"'I understand thee perfectly,' answered I : 'if thou takest a
wrong step in this affair, he will cudgel thee to death. Well! a
minute is but a minute; and if it saves a fellow-creature a drubbing,
it shall not be set down as ill-spent.'

" He was eating the stem of an artichoke as this discourse went
on, and, in the little peevish contentions between hunger and un-
savouriness, had dropped it out of his mouth half-a-dozen times,
and had picked it up again. 'God help thee, Jack! said I, 'thou
hast a bitter breakfast on't—and many a bitter day's labour, and
many a bitter blow, I fear, for its wages! 'Tis all, all bitterness to
thee—whatever life is to others ! And now thy mouth, if one knew
the truth of it, is as bitter, I dare say, as soot' (for he had cast aside
the stem), 'and thou hast not a friend perhaps in all this world that
will give thee a macaroon.' In saying this, I pulled out a paper of
'em, which I had just bought, and gave him one ;—and, at this
moment that I am telling it, my heart smites me that there was more
of pleasantry in the conceit of seeing *how* an ass would eat a
macaroon, than of benevolence in giving him one, which presided in
the act.

" When the ass had eaten his macaroon, I pressed him to come
in. The poor beast was heavy loaded—his legs seemed to tremble
under him—he hung rather backwards, and, as I pulled at his halter,
it broke in my hand. He looked up pensive in my face : 'Don't
thrash me with it ; but if you will you may.' 'If I do,' said I, 'I'll
be d——.'"

A critic who refuses to see in this charming description wit,
humour, pathos, a kind nature speaking, and a real sentiment, must
be hard indeed to move and to please. A page or two farther we

come to a description not less beautiful—a landscape and figures, deliciously painted by one who had the keenest enjoyment and the most tremulous sensibility :—

" 'Twas in the road between Nismes and Lunel, where is the best Muscatto wine in all France : the sun was set, they had done their work : the nymphs had tied up their hair afresh, and the swains were preparing for a carousal. My mule made a dead point. ' 'Tis the pipe and tambourine,' said I—' I never will argue a point with one of your family as long as I live ;' so leaping off his back, and kicking off one boot into this ditch and t'other into that, ' I'll take a dance,' said I, ' so stay you here.'

" A sun-burnt daughter of labour rose up from the group to meet me as I advanced towards them ; her hair, which was of a dark chestnut approaching to a black, was tied up in a knot, all but a single tress.

" 'We want a cavalier,' said she, holding out both her hands, as if to offer them. ' And a cavalier you shall have,' said I, taking hold of both of them. ' We could not have done without you,' said she, letting go one hand, with self-taught politeness, and leading me up with the other.

" A lame youth, whom Apollo had recompensed with a pipe, and to which he had added a tambourine of his own accord, ran sweetly over the prelude, as he sat upon the bank. ' Tie me up this tress instantly,' said Nannette, putting a piece of string into my hand. It taught me to forget I was a stranger. The whole knot fell down—we had been seven years acquainted. The youth struck the note upon the tambourine, his pipe followed, and off we bounded.

" The sister of the youth—who had stolen her voice from heaven— sang alternately with her brother. 'Twas a Gascoigne roundelay : ' *Viva la joia, fidon la tristessa.*' The nymphs joined in unison, and their swains an octave below them.

" *Viva la joia* was in Nannette's lips, *viva la joia* in her eyes. A transient spark of amity shot across the space betwixt us. She looked amiable. Why could I not live and end my days thus ? ' Just Disposer of our joys and sorrows !' cried I, ' why could not a man sit down in the lap of content here, and dance, and sing, and say his prayers, and go to heaven with this nut-brown maid ?' Capriciously did she bend her head on one side, and dance up insidious. ' Then 'tis time to dance off,' quoth I."

And with this pretty dance and chorus, the volume artfully concludes. Even here one can't give the whole description. There is not a page in Sterne's writing but has something that were better away, a latent corruption—a hint, as of an impure presence.*

Some of that dreary *double entendre* may be attributed to freer times and manners than ours, but not all. The foul Satyr's eyes leer out of the leaves constantly : the last words the famous author wrote were bad and wicked—the last lines the poor stricken wretch penned were for pity and pardon. I think of these past writers and of one who lives amongst us now, and am grateful for the innocent laughter and the sweet and unsullied page which the author of "David Copperfield" gives to my children.

> " Jete sur cette boule,
> Laid, chétif et souffrant ;
> Etouffé dans la foule,
> Faute d'être assez grand :

---

* " With regard to Sterne, and the charge of licentiousness which presses so seriously upon his character as a writer, I would remark that there is a sort of knowingness, the wit of which depends, 1st, on the modesty it gives pain to ; or, 2ndly, on the innocence and innocent ignorance over which it triumphs ; or, 3rdly, on a certain oscillation in the individual's own mind between the remaining good and the encroaching evil of his nature—a sort of dallying with the devil—a fluxionary art of combining courage and cowardice, as when a man snuffs a candle with his fingers for the first time, or better still, perhaps, like that trembling daring with which a child touches a hot tea-urn, because it has been forbidden ; so that the mind has its own white and black angel ; the same or similar amusement as may be supposed to take place between an old debauchee and a prude—the feeling resentment, on the one hand, from a prudential anxiety to preserve appearances and have a character ; and, on the other, an inward sympathy with the enemy. We have only to suppose society innocent, and then nine-tenths of this sort of wit would be like a stone that falls in snow, making no sound, because exciting no resistance ; the remainder rests on its being an offence against the good manners of human nature itself.

" This source, unworthy as it is, may doubtless be combined with wit, drollery, fancy, and even humour ; and we have only to regret the misalliance ; but that the latter are quite distinct from the former, may be made evident by abstracting in our imagination the morality of the characters of Mr. Shandy, my Uncle Toby, and Trim, which are all antagonists to this spurious sort of wit, from the rest of ' Tristram Shandy,' and by supposing, instead of them, the presence of two or three callous debauchees. The result will be pure disgust. Sterne cannot be too severely censured for thus using the best dispositions of our nature as the panders and condiments for the basest."— COLERIDGE : *Literary Remains*, vol. i. pp. 141, 142.

" Une plainte touchante
De ma bouche sortit.
Le bon Dieu me dit : Chante,
Chante, pauvre petit !

" Chanter, ou je m'abuse,
Est ma tâche ici-bas.
Tous ceux qu'ainsi j'amuse,
Ne m'aimeront-ils pas ? "

In those charming lines of Béranger, one may fancy described the career, the sufferings, the genius, the gentle nature of GOLDSMITH, and the esteem in which we hold him. Who, of the millions whom he has amused, doesn't love him? To be the most beloved of English writers, what a title that is for a man`! * A wild youth, wayward, but full of tenderness and affection, quits the country village, where his boyhood has been passed in happy musing, in idle shelter, in fond longing to see the great world out of doors, and achieve name and fortune ; and after years of dire struggle, and neglect and poverty, his heart turning back as fondly to his native place as it had longed eagerly for change when sheltered there, he writes a book and a poem, full of the recollections and feelings of home : he paints the friends and scenes of his youth, and peoples Auburn and Wakefield with remembrances of Lissoy. Wander he must, but he carries away a home-relic with him, and dies with it on his breast. His nature is truant ; in repose it longs for change : as on the journey it looks back for friends and quiet. He passes to-day in building an air-castle for to-morrow, or in writing yesterday's elegy ; and he would fly away this hour, but that a cage and necessity keep him. What is the charm of his verse, of his style, and humour ? His sweet regrets, his delicate compassion, his soft smile, his tremulous sympathy, the weakness which he owns? Your love for him is half pity. You come hot and

---

* " He was a friend to virtue, and in his most playful pages never forgets what is due to it. A gentleness, delicacy, and purity of feeling distinguishes whatever he wrote, and bears a correspondence to the generosity of a disposition which knew no bounds but his last guinea. . . . .

" The admirable ease and grace of the narrative, as well as the pleasing truth with which the principal characters are designed, make the 'Vicar of Wakefield ' one of the most delicious morsels of fictitious composition on which the human mind was ever employed.

" . . . . We read the ' Vicar of Wakefield ' in youth and in age— we return to it again and again, and bless the memory of an author who contrives so well to reconcile us to human nature."—Sir WALTER SCOTT.

tired from the day's battle, and this sweet minstrel sings to you. Who could harm the kind vagrant harper? Whom did he ever hurt? He carries no weapon, save the harp on which he plays to you ; and with which he delights great and humble, young and old, the captains in the tents, or the soldiers round the fire, or the women and children in the villages, at whose porches he stops and sings his simple songs of love and beauty. With that sweet story of the " Vicar of Wakefield " * he

* " Now Herder came," says Goethe in his Autobiography, relating his first acquaintance with Goldsmith's masterpiece, " and together with his great knowledge brought many other aids, and the later publications besides. Among these he announced to us the ' Vicar of Wakefield ' as an excellent work, with the German translation of which he would make us acquainted by reading it aloud to us himself. . . . .

" A Protestant country clergyman is perhaps the most beautiful subject for a modern idyl ; he appears like Melchizedeck, as priest and king in one person. To the most innocent situation which can be imagined on earth, to that of a husbandman, he is, for the most part, united by similarity of occupation as well as by equality in family relationships ; he is a father, a master of a family, an agriculturist, and thus perfectly a member of the community. On this pure, beautiful earthly foundation rests his higher calling ; to him is it given to guide men through life, to take care of their spiritual education, to bless them at all the leading epochs of their existence, to instruct, to strengthen, to console them, and if consolation is not sufficient for the present, to call up and guarantee the hope of a happier future. Imagine such a man with pure human sentiments, strong enough not to deviate from them under any circumstances, and by this already elevated above the multitude of whom one cannot expect purity and firmness ; give him the learning necessary for his office, as well as a cheerful, equable activity, which is even passionate, as it neglects no moment to do good—and you will have him well endowed. But at the same time add the necessary limitation, so that he must not only pause in a small circle, but may also, perchance, pass over to a smaller ; grant him good-nature, placability, resolution, and everything else praiseworthy that springs from a decided character, and over all this a cheerful spirit of compliance, and a smiling toleration of his own failings and those of others, —then you will have put together pretty well the image of our excellent Wakefield.

" The delineation of this character on his course of life through joys and sorrows, the ever-increasing interest of the story, by the combination of the entirely natural with the strange and the singular, make this novel one of the best which has ever been written ; besides this, it has the great advantage that it is quite moral, nay, in a pure sense, Christian—represents the reward of a good-will and perseverance in the right, strengthens an unconditional confidence in God, and attests the final triumph of good over evil ; and all this without a trace of cant or pedantry. The author was preserved from both of has found entry into every castle and every hamlet in Europe. Not one of us, however busy or hard, but once or twice in our lives has passed an evening with him, and undergone the charm of his delightful music.

Goldsmith's father was no doubt the good Doctor Primrose, whom we all of us know.* Swift was yet alive, when the little Oliver was born

these by an elevation of mind that shows itself throughout in the form of irony, by which this little work must appear to us as wise as it is amiable. The author, Dr. Goldsmith, has, without question, a great insight into the moral world, into its strength and its infirmities ; but at the same time he can thankfully acknowledge that he is an Englishman, and reckon highly the advantages which his country and his nation afford him. The family, with the delineation of which he occupies himself, stands upon one of the last steps of citizen comfort, and yet comes in contact with the highest ; its narrow circle, which becomes still more contracted, touches upon the great world through the natural and civil course of things ; this little skiff floats on the agitated waves of English life, and in weal or woe it has to expect injury or help from the vast fleet which sails around it.

"I may suppose that my readers know this work, and have it in memory ; whoever hears it named for the first time here, as well as he who is induced to read it again, will thank me."—GOETHE : *Truth and Poetry ; from my own Life.* (English Translation, vol. i. pp. 378, 379.)

"He seems from infancy to have been compounded of two natures, one bright, the other blundering ; or to have had fairy gifts laid in his cradle by the 'good people' who haunted his birthplace, the old goblin mansion on the banks of the Inny.

"He carries with him the wayward elfin spirit, if we may so term it, throughout his career. His fairy gifts are of no avail at school, academy, or college : they unfit him for close study and practical science, and render him heedless of everything that does not address itself to his poetical imagination and genial and festive feelings ; they dispose him to break away from restraint, to stroll about hedges, green lanes, and haunted streams, to revel with jovial companions, or to rove the country like a gipsy in quest of odd adventures. . . . .

"Though his circumstances often compelled him to associate with the poor, they never could betray him into companionship with the depraved. His relish for humour, and for the study of character, as we have before observed, brought him often into convivial company of a vulgar kind ; but he discriminated between their vulgarity and their amusing qualities, or rather wrought from the whole store familiar features of life which form the staple of his most popular writings."—WASHINGTON IRVING.

* "The family of Goldsmith, Goldsmyth, or, as it was occasionally written, Gouldsmith, is of considerable standing in Ireland, and seems always

at Pallas, or Pallasmore, in the county of Longford, in Ireland. In 1730, two years after the child's birth, Charles Goldsmith removed his family to Lissoy, in the county Westmeath, that sweet "Auburn" which every person who hears me has seen in fancy. Here the kind parson * brought up his eight children; and loving all the world, as his son says, fancied all the world loved him. He had a crowd of poor dependants besides those hungry children. He kept an open table; round which sat flatterers and poor friends, who laughed at the honest rector's many jokes, and ate the produce of his seventy acres of farm. Those who have seen an Irish house in the present day can fancy that one of Lissoy. The old beggar still has his allotted corner by the kitchen turf; the maimed old soldier still gets his potatoes and buttermilk; the poor cottier still asks his honour's charity, and prays God bless his reverence for the sixpence; the ragged pensioner still takes his place by right and sufferance. There's still a crowd in the kitchen, and a crowd round the parlour table, profusion, confusion, kindness, poverty. If an Irishman comes to London to make his fortune, he has a half-dozen of Irish dependants who take a percentage of his earnings. The good Charles Goldsmith † left but little provision for his hungry race when death

to have held a respectable station in society. Its origin is English, supposed to be derived from that which was long settled at Crayford in Kent."—PRIOR's *Life of Goldsmith.*

Oliver's father, great-grandfather, and great-great-grandfather were clergymen; and two of them married clergymen's daughters.

> * "At church, with meek and unaffected grace,
> His looks adorn'd the venerable place;
> Truth from his lips prevail'd with double sway,
> And fools who came to scoff remain'd to pray.
> The service past, around the pious man,
> With steady zeal each honest rustic ran;
> E'en children follow'd with endearing wile,
> And pluck'd his gown to share the good man's smile.
> His ready smile a parent's warmth exprest,
> Their welfare pleased him, and their cares distrest;
> To them his heart, his love, his griefs were given,
> But all his serious thoughts had rest in Heaven.
> As some tall cliff that lifts its awful form,
> Swells from the vale, and midway leaves the storm,
> Though round its breast the rolling clouds are spread,
> Eternal sunshine settles on its head."—*The Deserted Village.*

† "In May this year (1768), he lost his brother, the Rev. Henry

summoned him : and one of his daughters being engaged to a Squire of rather superior dignity, Charles Goldsmith impoverished the rest of his family to provide the girl with a dowry.

The small-pox, which scourged all Europe at that time, and ravaged the roses off the cheeks of half the world, fell foul of poor little Oliver's face, when the child was eight years old, and left him scarred and disfigured for his life. An old woman in his father's village taught him his letters, and pronounced him a dunce : Paddy Byrne, the hedge-schoolmaster, took him in hand ; and from Paddy Byrne, he was transmitted to a clergyman at Elphin. When a child was sent to school in those days, the classic phrase was that he was placed under Mr. So-and-so's *ferule*. Poor little ancestors ! It is hard to think how ruthlessly you were birched ; and how much of needless whipping and tears our small forefathers had to undergo ! A relative—kind uncle Contarine——took the main charge of little Noll ; who went through his school-days righteously doing as little work as he could : robbing orchards, playing at ball, and making his pocket-money fly about whenever fortune sent it to him. Everybody knows the story of that famous " Mistake of a Night," when the young schoolboy, provided with a guinea and a nag, rode up to the " best house " in Ardagh, called for the landlord's company over a bottle of wine at supper, and for a hot cake for breakfast in the morning ; and found, when he asked for the bill, that the best house was Squire Featherstone's, and not the inn for which he mistook it.

Goldsmith, for whom he had been unable to obtain preferment in the church. . . .

". . . To the curacy of Kilkenny West, the moderate stipend of which, forty pounds a year, is sufficiently celebrated by his brother's lines. It has been stated that Mr. Goldsmith added a school, which, after having been held at more than one place in the vicinity, was finally fixed at Lissoy. Here his talents and industry gave it celebrity, and under his care the sons of many of the neighbouring gentry received their education. A fever breaking out among the boys about 1765, they dispersed for a time, but re-assembling at Athlone, he continued his scholastic labours there until the time of his death, which happened, like that of his brother, about the forty-fifth year of his age. He was a man of an excellent heart and an amiable disposition."—PRIOR'S *Goldsmith.*

> " Where'er I roam, whatever realms to see,
> My heart, untravell'd, fondly turns to thee :
> Still to my brother turns with ceaseless pain,
> And drags at each remove a lengthening chain."
> *—The Traveller.*

Who does not know every story about Goldsmith? That is a delightful and fantastic picture of the child dancing and capering about in the kitchen at home, when the old fiddler gibed at him for his ugliness, and called him Æsop; and little Noll made his repartee of "Heralds proclaim aloud this saying—See Æsop dancing and his monkey playing." One can fancy a queer pitiful look of humour and appeal upon that little scarred face—the funny little dancing figure, the funny little brogue. In his life, and his writings, which are the

honest expression of it, he is constantly bewailing that homely face and person; anon he surveys them in the glass ruefully; and presently assumes the most comical dignity. He likes to deck out his little person in splendour and fine colours. He presented himself to be examined for ordination in a pair of scarlet breeches, and said honestly that he did not like to go into the church, because he was fond of coloured clothes. When he tried to practise as a doctor, he got by hook or by crook a black velvet suit, and looked as big and grand as he could, and kept his hat over a patch on the old coat: in better days he bloomed out in plum-colour, in blue silk, and in new velvet. For some of those splendours the heirs and assignees of Mr. Filby, the tailor, have never been paid to this day : perhaps the kind tailor and his creditor have met and settled their little account in Hades.*

They showed until lately a window at Trinity College, Dublin, on which the name of O. Goldsmith was engraved with a diamond. Whose diamond was it ? Not the young sizar's, who made but a poor figure in that place of learning. He was idle, penniless, and fond of pleasure : † he learned his way early to the pawnbroker's shop. He wrote ballads, they say, for the street-singers, who paid him a crown for a poem : and his pleasure was to steal out at night and hear his verses sung. He was chastised by his tutor for giving a dance in his rooms, and took the box on the ear so much to heart, that he packed up his all, pawned his books and little property, and disappeared from college and family. He said he intended to go to America, but when his money was spent, the young prodigal came home ruefully, and the good folks there killed their calf—it was but a lean one—and welcomed him back.

After college he hung about his mother's house, and lived for some years the life of a buckeen—passed a month with this relation and that, a year with one patron, a great deal of time at the public-house.‡ Tired of this life, it was resolved that he should go to London, and study at the Temple ; but he got no farther on the road to London and the woolsack than Dublin, where he gambled away the fifty pounds given to him for his outfit, and whence he returned to the indefatigable forgiveness of home. Then he determined to be a

---

* " When Goldsmith died, half the unpaid bill he owed to Mr. William Filby (amounting in all to 79*l*.) was for clothes supplied to this nephew Hodson."—FORSTER'S *Goldsmith*, p. 520.

As this nephew Hodson ended his days (see the same page) " a prosperous Irish gentleman," it is not unreasonable to wish that he had cleared off Mr. Filby's bill.

† " Poor fellow ! He hardly knew an ass from a mule, nor a turkey from a goose, but when he saw it on the table."—CUMBERLAND'S *Memoirs*.

‡ " These youthful follies, like the fermentation of liquors, often disturb the mind only in order to its future refinement : a life spent in phlegmatic apathy resembles those liquors which never ferment, and are consequently always muddy."—GOLDSMITH : *Memoir of Voltaire*.

" He [Johnson] said ' Goldsmith was a plant that flowered late. There appeared nothing remarkable about him when he was young.' "—BOSWELL.

doctor, and uncle Contarine helped him to a couple of years at Edinburgh. Then from Edinburgh he felt that he ought to hear the famous professors of Leyden and Paris, and wrote most amusing pompous letters to his uncle about the great Farheim, Du Petit, and Duhamel du Monceau, whose lectures he proposed to follow. If uncle Contarine believed those letters—if Oliver's mother believed that story which the youth related of his going to Cork, with the purpose of embarking for America, of his having paid his passage-money, and having sent his kit on board ; of the anonymous captain sailing away with Oliver's valuable luggage, in a nameless ship, never to return ; if uncle Contarine and the mother at Ballymahon believed his stories, they must have been a very simple pair ; as it was a very simple rogue indeed who cheated them. When the lad, after failing in his clerical examination, after failing in his plan for studying the law, took leave of these projects and of his parents, and set out for Edinburgh, he saw mother, and uncle, and lazy Ballymahon, and green native turf, and sparkling river for the last time. He was never to look on old Ireland more, and only in fancy revisit her.

> "But me not destined such delights to share,
> My prime of life in wandering spent and care,
> Impelled, with steps unceasing, to pursue
> Some fleeting good that mocks me with the view ;
> That like the circle bounding earth and skies
> Allures from far, yet, as I follow, flies :
> My fortune leads to traverse realms alone,
> And find no spot of all the world my own."

I spoke in a former lecture of that high courage which enabled Fielding, in spite of disease, remorse, and poverty, always to retain a cheerful spirit and to keep his manly benevolence and love of truth intact, as if these treasures had been confided to him for the public benefit, and he was accountable to posterity for their honourable employ ; and a constancy equally happy and admirable I think was shown by Goldsmith, whose sweet and friendly nature bloomed kindly always in the midst of a life's storm, and rain, and bitter weather.* The poor fellow was never so friendless but he could

---

* "An 'inspired idiot,' Goldsmith, hangs strangely about him [Johnson]. . . . . Yet, on the whole, there is no evil in the 'gooseberry-fool,' but rather much good ; of a finer, if of a weaker sort than Johnson's ; and all the more genuine that he himself could never become *conscious* of it,—though unhappily never cease *attempting* to become so : the author of the genuine

befriend some one ; never so pinched and wretched but he could give of his crust, and speak his word of compassion. If he had but his flute left, he could give that, and make the children happy in the dreary London court. He could give the coals in that queer coal scuttle we read of to his poor neighbour : he could give away his blankets in college to the poor widow, and warm himself as he best might in the feathers : he could pawn his coat to save his landlord from gaol : when he was a school-usher he spent his earnings in treats for the boys, and the good-natured schoolmaster's wife said justly that she ought to keep Mr. Goldsmith's money as well as the young gentlemen's. When he met his pupils in later life, nothing would satisfy the Doctor but he must treat them still. " Have you seen the print of me after Sir Joshua Reynolds ? " he asked of one of his old pupils. " Not seen it ? not bought it ? Sure, Jack, if your picture had been published, I'd not have been without it half-an-hour." His purse and his heart were everybody's, and his friends' as much as his own. When he was at the height of his reputation, and the Earl of Northumberland, going as Lord Lieutenant to Ireland, asked if he could be of any service to Doctor Goldsmith, Goldsmith recommended his brother, and not himself, to the great man. " My patrons," he gallantly said, " are the booksellers, and I want no others."* Hard patrons they were, and hard work he did ; but he did not complain much : if in his early writings some bitter words escaped him, some allusions to

'Vicar of Wakefield,' nill he will he, must needs fly towards such a mass of genuine manhood."—CARLYLE'S *Essays* (2nd ed.), vol. iv. p. 91.

* "At present, the few poets of England no longer depend on the great for subsistence ; they have now no other patrons but the public, and the public, collectively considered, is a good and a generous master. It is indeed too frequently mistaken as to the merits of every candidate for favour ; but to make amends it is never mistaken long. A performance indeed may be forced for a time into reputation, but, destitute of real merit, it soon sinks ; time, the touchstone of what is truly valuable, will soon discover the fraud, and an author should never arrogate to himself any share of success till his works have been read at least ten years with satisfaction.

" A man of letters at present, whose works are valuable, is perfectly sensible of their value. Every polite member of the community, by buying what he writes, contributes to reward him. The ridicule, therefore, of living in a garret might have been wit in the last age, but continues such no longer, because no longer true. A writer of real merit now may easily be rich, if his heart be set only on fortune; and for those who have no merit, it is but fit. that such should remain in merited obscurity."—GOLDSMITH : *Citizen of the World*, Let. 84.

neglect and poverty, he withdrew these expressions when his works were republished, and better days seemed to oper for him ; and he did not care to complain that printer or publisher had overlooked his merit, or left him poor. The Court face was turned from honest Oliver, the Court patronized Beattie ; the fashion did not shine on him—fashion adored Sterne.* Fashion pronounced Kelly to be the great writer of comedy of his day. A little—not ill-humour, but plaintiveness—a little betrayal of wounded pride which he showed render him not the less amiable. The author of the " Vicar of Wakefield " had a right to protest when Newbery kept back the MS. for two years ; had a right to be a little peevish with Sterne ; a little angry when Colman's actors declined their parts in his delightful comedy, when the manager refused to have a scene painted for it, and pronounced its damnation before hearing. He had not the great public with him ; but he had the noble Johnson, and the admirable Reynolds, and the great Gibbon, and the great Burke, and the great Fox—friends and admirers illustrious indeed, as famous as those who, fifty years before, sat round Pope's table.

Nobody knows, and I dare say Goldsmith's buoyant temper kept no account of all the pains which he endured during the early period of his literary career. Should any man of letters in our day

---

* Goldsmith attacked Sterne obviously enough, censuring his indecency, and slighting his wit, and ridiculing his manner, in the 53rd letter in the " Citizen of the World."

"As in common conversation," says he, " the best way to make the audience laugh is by first laughing yourself ; so in writing, the properest manner is to show an attempt at humour, which will pass upon most for humour in reality. To effect this, readers must be treated with the most perfect familiarity ; in one page the author is to make them a low bow, and in the next to pull them by the nose ; he must talk in riddles, and then send them to bed in order to dream for the solution," &c.

Sterne's humourous *mot* on the subject of the gravest part of the charges, then, as now, made against him, may perhaps be quoted here, from the excellent, the respectable Sir Walter Scott :—

"Soon after 'Tristram' had appeared, Sterne asked a Yorkshire lady of fortune and condition, whether she had read his book. 'I have not, Mr. Sterne,' was the answer ; 'and to be plain with you, I am informed it is not proper for female perusal.' 'My dear good lady,' replied the author, 'do not be gulled by such stories ; the book is like your young heir there' (pointing to a child of three years old, who was rolling on the carpet in his white tunic) : 'he shows at times a good deal that is usually concealed, but it is all in perfect innocence.' "

have to bear up against such, heaven grant he may come out of the period of misfortune with such a pure kind heart as that which Goldsmith obstinately bore in his breast. The insults to which he had to submit are shocking to read of—slander, contumely, vulgar satire, brutal malignity perverting his commonest motives and actions ; he had his share of these, and one's anger is roused at reading of them, as it is at seeing a woman insulted or a child assaulted, at the notion that a creature so very gentle and weak, and full of love, should have had to suffer so. And he had worse than insult to undergo—to own to fault and deprecate the anger of ruffians. There is a letter of his extant to one Griffiths, a bookseller, in which poor Goldsmith is forced to confess that certain books sent by Griffiths are in the hands of a friend from whom Goldsmith had been forced to borrow money. "He was wild, sir," Johnson said, speaking of Goldsmith to Boswell, with his great, wise benevolence and noble mercifulness of heart— "Dr. Goldsmith was wild, sir; but he is so no more." Ah! if we pity the good and weak man who suffers undeservedly, let us deal very gently with him from whom misery extorts not only tears, but shame ; let us think humbly and charitably of the human nature that suffers so sadly and falls so low. Whose turn may it be to-morrow ? What weak heart, confident before trial, may not succumb under temptation invincible ? Cover the good man who has been vanquished—cover his face and pass on.

For the last half-dozen years of his life, Goldsmith was far removed from the pressure of any ignoble necessity : and in the receipt, indeed, of a pretty large income from the booksellers his patrons. Had he lived but a few years more, his public fame would have been as great as his private reputation, and he might have enjoyed alive a part of that esteem which his country has ever since paid to the vivid and versatile genius who has touched on almost every subject of literature, and touched nothing that he did not adorn. Except in rare instances, a man is known in our profession, and esteemed as a skilful workman, years before the lucky hit which trebles his usual gains, and stamps him a popular author. In the strength of his age, and the dawn of his reputation, having for backers and friends the most illustrious literary men of his time,* fame and

* "Goldsmith told us that he was now busy in writing a Natural History ; and that he might have full leisure for it, he had taken lodgings at a farmer's house, near to the six-mile stone in the Edgware Road, and had carried down his books in two returned postchaises. He said he believed the farmer's family thought him an odd character, similar to that in which the *Spectator*

prosperity might have been in store for Goldsmith, had fate so willed
it ; and, at forty-six, had not sudden disease carried him off. I say
prosperity rather than competence, for it is probable that no sum
could have put order into his affairs or sufficed for his irreclaimable
habits of dissipation. It must be remembered that he owed 2,000*l.*
when he died. "Was ever poet," Johnson asked, "so trusted
before ? " As has been the case with many another good fellow of
his nation, his life was tracked and his substance wasted by crowds of
hungry beggars and lazy dependants. If they came at a lucky time
(and be sure they knew his affairs better than he did himself, and
watched his pay-day), he gave them of his money : if they begged
on empty-purse days he gave them his promissory bills : or he treated
them to a tavern where he had credit ; or he obliged them with an
order upon honest Mr. Filby for coats, for which he paid as long as
he could earn, and until the shears of Filby were to cut for him no
more. Staggering under a load of debt and labour, tracked by
bailiffs and reproachful creditors, running from a hundred poor
dependants, whose appealing looks were perhaps the hardest of all
pains for him to bear, devising fevered plans for the morrow, new
histories, new comedies, all sorts of new literary schemes, flying from
all these into seclusion, and out of seclusion into pleasure—at last, at
five-and-forty, death seized him and closed his career.* I have been
many a time in the chambers in the Temple which were his, and
passed up the staircase, which Johnson and Burke, and Reynolds
trod to see their friend, their poet, their kind Goldsmith—the stair on
which the poor women sat weeping bitterly when they heard that the
greatest and most generous of all men was dead within the black oak

appeared to his landlady and her children ; he was *The Gentleman.* Mr.
Mickle, the translator of the ' Lusiad,' and I, went to visit him at this place a
few days afterwards. He was not at home ; but having a curiosity to see his
apartment, we went in, and found curious scraps of descriptions of animals
scrawled upon the wall with a blacklead pencil."—BOSWELL.

* "When Goldsmith was dying, Dr. Turton said to him, 'Your pulse is in
greater disorder than it should be, from the degree of fever which you have ;
is your mind at ease ? ' Goldsmith answered it was not."—DR. JOHNSON
(*in Boswell*).

"Chambers, you find, is gone far, and poor Goldsmith is gone much
further. He died of a fever, exasperated, as I believe, by the fear of distress.
He had raised money and squandered it, by every artifice of acquisition and
folly of expense. But let not his failings be remembered ; he was a very great
man."—DR. JOHNSON to *Boswell*, July 5th, 1774.

door.* Ah, it was a different lot from that for which the poor fellow sighed, when he wrote with heart yearning for home those most charming of all fond verses, in which he fancies he revisits Auburn—

> " Here, as I take my solitary rounds,
>   Amidst thy tangling walks and ruined grounds,
>   And, many a year elapsed, return to view
>   Where once the cottage stood, the hawthorn grew,
>   Remembrance wakes, with all her busy train,
>   Swells at my breast, and turns the past to pain.
>
> In all my wanderings round this world of care,
> In all my griefs—and God has given my share—
> I still had hopes my latest hours to crown,
> Amidst these humble bowers to lay me down ;
> To husband out life's taper at the close,
> And keep the flame from wasting by repose ;
> I still had hopes—for pride attends us still—
> Amidst the swains to show my book-learned skill,
> Around my fire an evening group to draw,
> And tell of all I felt and all I saw ;
> And, as a hare, whom hounds and horns pursue,
> Pants to the place from whence at first he flew—
> I still had hopes—my long vexations past,
> Here to return, and die at home at last.
>
> O blest retirement, friend to life's decline !
> Retreats from care that never must be mine—
> How blest is he who crowns, in shades like these,
> A youth of labour with an age of ease ;

---

* " When Burke was told [of Goldsmith's death] he burst into tears. Reynolds was in his painting-room when the messenger went to him ; but at once he laid his pencil aside, which in times of great family distress he had not been known to do, left his painting-room, and did not re-enter it that day. . . . .

" The staircase of Brick Court is said to have been filled with mourners, the reverse of domestic ; women without a home, without domesticity of any kind, with no friend but him they had come to weep for ; outcasts of that great, solitary, wicked city, to whom he had never forgotten to be kind and charitable. And he had domestic mourners, too. His coffin was reopened at the request of Miss Horneck and her sister (such was the regard he was known to have for them !) that a lock might be cut from his hair. It was in Mrs. Gwyn's possession when she died, after nearly seventy years."—FORSTER'S *Goldsmith.*

Who quits a world where strong temptations try,
And, since 'tis hard to combat, learns to fly !
For him no wretches born to work and weep
Explore the mine or tempt the dangerous deep ;
No surly porter stands in guilty state
To spurn imploring famine from the gate :
But on he moves to meet his latter end,
Angels around befriending virtue's friend ;
Sinks to the grave with unperceived decay,
Whilst resignation gently slopes the way ;
And all his prospects brightening to the last,
His heaven commences ere the world be past."

In these verses, I need not say with what melody, with what touching truth, with what exquisite beauty of comparison—as indeed in hundreds more pages of the writings of this honest soul—the whole character of the man is told—his humble confession of faults and weakness ; his pleasant little vanity, and desire that his village should admire him ; his simple scheme of good in which everybody was to be happy—no ·beggar was to be refused his dinner—nobody in fact was to work much, and he to be the harmless chief of the Utopia, and the monarch of the Irish Yvetot.   He would have told again, and without fear of their failing, those famous jokes* which

* " Goldsmith's incessant desire of being conspicuous in company was the occasion of his sometimes appearing to such disadvantage, as one should hardly have supposed possible in a man of his genius.   When his literary reputation had risen deservedly high, and his society was much courted, he became very jealous of the extraordinary attention which was everywhere paid to Johnson. One evening, in a circle of wits, he found fault with me for talking of Johnson as entitled to the honour of unquestionable superiority. 'Sir,' said he, 'you are for making a monarchy of what should be a republic.'

" He was still more mortified, when, talking in a company with fluent vivacity, and, as he flattered himself, to the admiration of all present, a German who sat next him, and perceived Johnson rolling himself as if about to speak, suddenly stopped him, saying, ' Stay, stay—Toctor Shonson is going to zay zomething.'   This was no doubt very provoking, especially to one so irritable as Goldsmith, who frequently mentioned it with strong expressions of indignation.

" It may also be observed that Goldsmith was sometimes content to be treated with an easy familiarity, but upon occasions would be consequential and important.   An instance of this occurred in a small particular.   Johnson had a way of contracting the names of his friends, as Beauclerk, Beau ; Boswell, Bozzy. . . . . . I remember one day, when Tom Davies was telling that Dr. Johnson said—'We are all in labour for a name to *Goldy's* play,'

had hung fire in London ; he would have talked of his great friends
of the Club—of my Lord Clare and my Lord Bishop, my Lord Nugent
—sure he knew them intimately, and was hand and glove with some
of the best men in town—and he would have spoken of Johnson
and of Burke, and of Sir Joshua who had painted him—and he
would have told wonderful sly stories of Ranelagh and the Pantheon,
and the masquerades at Madame Cornelis' ; and he would have
toasted, with a sigh, the Jessamy Bride—the lovely Mary Horneck.

The figure of that charming young lady forms one of the prettiest
recollections of Goldsmith's life. She and her beautiful sister, who
married Bunbury, the graceful and humourous amateur artist of those
days, when Gilray had but just begun to try his powers, were among the
kindest and dearest of Goldsmith's many friends, cheered and pitied
him, travelled abroad with him, made him welcome at their home,
and gave him many a pleasant holiday. He bought his finest clothes
to figure at their country-house at Barton—he wrote them droll
verses. They loved him, laughed at him, played him tricks and made

Goldsmith seemed displeased that such a liberty should be taken with his
name, and said, 'I have often desired him not to call me *Goldy*.'"

This is one of several of Boswell's depreciatory mentions of Goldsmith—
which may well irritate biographers and admirers—and also those who take
that more kindly and more profound view of Boswell's own character, which
was opened up by Mr. Carlyle's famous article on his book. No wonder that
Mr. Irving calls Boswell an "incarnation of toadyism." And the worst of it
is, that Johnson himself has suffered from this habit of the Laird of Auchinleck's. People are apt to forget under what Boswellian stimulus the great
Doctor uttered many hasty things :—things no more indicative of the nature of
the depths of his character than the phosphoric gleaming of the sea, when
struck at night, is indicative of radical corruption of nature ! In truth, it is
clear enough on the whole that both Johnson and Goldsmith *appreciated* each
other, and that they mutually knew it. They were, as it were, tripped up
and flung against each other, occasionally, by the blundering and silly gam-
bolling of people in company.

Something must be allowed for Boswell's "rivalry for Johnson's good
graces" with Oliver '(as Sir Walter Scott has remarked), for Oliver was
intimate with the Doctor before his biographer was,—and, as we all remember, marched off with him to "take tea with Mrs. Williams" before
Boswell had advanced to that honourable degree of intimacy. But, in truth,
Boswell—though he perhaps showed more talent in his delineation of the
Doctor than is generally ascribed to him—had not faculty to take a fair view
of *two* great men at a time. Besides, as Mr. Forster justly remarks, "he was
impatient of Goldsmith from the first hour of their acquaintance."—*Life and
Adventures*, p. 292.

him happy. He asked for a loan from Garrick, and Garrick kindly supplied him, to enable him to go to Barton : but there were to be no more holidays and only one brief struggle more for poor Goldsmith. A lock of his hair was taken from the coffin and given to the Jessamy Bride. She lived quite into our time. Hazlitt saw her an old lady, but beautiful still, in Northcote's painting-room, who told the eager critic how proud she always was that Goldsmith had admired her. The younger Colman has left a touching reminiscence of him (vol. i. 63, 64) :—

"I was only five years old," he says, "when Goldsmith took me on his knee one evening whilst he was drinking coffee with my father, and began to play with me, which amiable act I returned, with the ingratitude of a peevish brat, by giving him a very smart slap on the face : it must have been a tingler, for it left the marks of my spiteful paw on his cheek. This infantile outrage was followed by summary justice, and I was locked up by my indignant father in an adjoining room to undergo solitary imprisonment in the dark. Here I began to howl and scream most abominably, which was no bad step towards my liberation, since those who were not inclined to pity me might be likely to set me free for the purpose of abating a nuisance.

"At length a generous friend appeared to extricate me from jeopardy, and that generous friend was no other than the man I had so wantonly molested by assault and battery—it was the tender-hearted Doctor himself, with a lighted candle in his hand and a smile upon his countenance, which was still partially red from the effects of my petulance. I sulked and sobbed as he fondled and soothed, till I began to brighten. Goldsmith seized the propitious moment of returning good-humour, when he put down the candle and began to conjure. He placed three hats, which happened to be in the room, and a shilling under each. The shillings he told me were England, France, and Spain. 'Hey presto cockalorum !' cried the Doctor, and lo, on uncovering the shillings, which had been dispersed each beneath a separate hat, they were all found congregated under one. I was no politician at five years old, and therefore might not have wondered at the sudden revolution which brought England, France, and Spain all under one crown ; but as also I was no conjuror, it amazed me beyond measure. . . . . From that time, whenever the Doctor came to visit my father, 'I plucked his gown to share the good man's smile ;' a game at romps constantly ensued, and we were always cordial friends and merry playfellows. Our unequal companionship varied somewhat as to sports as I grew older ; but it did not last long : my senior playmate died in his forty-fifth year, when

I had attained my eleventh. . . . . In all the numerous accounts of his virtues and foibles, his genius and absurdities, his knowledge of nature and ignorance of the world, his ' compassion for another's woe' was always predominant; and my trivial story of his humouring a froward child weighs but as a feather in the recorded scale of his benevolence."

Think of him reckless, thriftless, vain if you like—but merciful, gentle, generous, full of love and pity. He passes out of our life, and goes to render his account beyond it. Think of the poor pensioners weeping at his grave ; think of the noble spirits that admired and deplored him ; think of the righteous pen that wrote his epitaph—and of the wonderful and unanimous response of affection with which the world has paid back the love he gave it. His humour delighting us still : his song fresh and beautiful as when first he charmed with it : his words in all our mouths : his very weaknesses beloved and familiar—his benevolent spirit seems still to smile upon us ; to do gentle kindnesses : to succour with sweet charity : to soothe, caress, and forgive : to plead with the fortunate for the unhappy and the poor.

His name is the last in the list of those men of humour who have formed the themes of the discourses which you have heard so kindly.

Long before I had ever hoped for such an audience, or dreamed of the possibility of the good fortune which has brought me so many friends, I was at issue with some of my literary brethren upon a point —which they held from tradition I think rather than experience—that our profession was neglected in this country ; and that men of letters were ill-received and held in slight esteem. It would hardly be grateful of me now to alter my old opinion that we do meet with good-will and kindness, with generous helping hands in the time of our necessity, with cordial and friendly recognition. What claim had any one of these of whom I have been speaking, but genius ? What return of gratitude, fame, affection, did it not bring to all ?

What punishment befell those who were unfortunate among them, but that which follows reckless habits and careless lives ? For these faults a wit must suffer like the dullest prodigal that ever ran in debt. He must pay the tailor if he wears the coat; his children must go in rags if he spends his money at the tavern ; he can't come to London and be made Lord Chancellor if he stops on the road and gambles away his last shilling at Dublin. And he must pay the social penalty of these follies too, and expect that the world will shun the man of bad habits, that women will avoid the man of loose life, that prudent folks will close their doors as a precaution, and before a demand should be made on their pockets by the needy prodigal. With what difficulty had any one of these men to contend, save that eternal and mechanical one of want of means and lack of capital, and of which thousands of young lawyers, young doctors, young soldiers and sailors, of inventors, manufacturers, shopkeepers, have to complain? Hearts as brave and resolute as ever beat in the breast of any wit or poet, sicken and break daily in the vain endeavour and unavailing struggle against life's difficulty. Don't we see daily ruined inventors, grey-haired midshipmen, baulked heroes, blighted curates, barristers pining a hungry life out in chambers, the attorneys never mounting to their garrets, whilst scores of them are rapping at the door of the successful quack below? If these suffer, who is the author, that he should be exempt? Let us bear our ills with the same constancy with which others endure them, accept our manly part in life, hold our own, and ask no more. I can conceive of no kings or laws causing or curing Goldsmith's improvidence, or Fielding's fatal love of pleasure, or Dick Steele's mania for running races with the constable. You never can out-run that sure-footed officer—not by any swiftness or by dodges devised by any genius, however great; and he carries off the Tatler to the spunging-house, or taps the Citizen of the World on the shoulder as he would any other mortal.

Does society look down on a man because he is an author? I suppose if people want a buffoon they tolerate him only in so far as he is amusing; it can hardly be expected that they should respect him as an equal. Is there to be a guard of honour provided for the author of the last new novel or poem? how long is he to reign, and keep other potentates out of possession? He retires, grumbles, and prints a lamentation that literature is despised. If Captain A. is left out of Lady B.'s parties, he does not state that the army is despised: if Lord C. no longer asks Counsellor D. to dinner, Counsellor D. does not announce that the bar is insulted. He is not fair to society if he enters it with this suspicion hankering about him; if he is doubtful about his reception, how hold up his head honestly, and look frankly in the face that world about which he is full of suspicion? Is he place-hunting, and thinking in his mind that he ought to be made an Ambassador, like Prior, or a Secretary of State, like Addison? his pretence of equality falls to the ground at once: he is scheming for a patron, not shaking the hand of a friend, when he meets the world. Treat such a man as he deserves; laugh at his buffoonery, and give him a dinner

and a *bon jour ;* laugh at his self-sufficiency and absurd assumptions
of superiority, and his equally ludicrous airs of martyrdom : laugh at
his flattery and his scheming, and buy it, if it's worth the having.   Let
the wag have his dinner and the hireling his pay, if you want him,
and make a profound bow to the *grand homme incompris,* and the
boisterous martyr, and show him the door.   The great world, the
great aggregate experience, has its good sense, as it has its good
humour.   It detects a pretender, as it trusts a loyal heart.   It is kind
in the main : how should it be otherwise than kind, when it is so wise
and clear-headed ?   To any literary man who says, "It despises my
profession," I say, with all my might—no, no, no.   It may pass over
your individual case—how many a brave fellow has failed in the race
and perished unknown in the struggle !—but it treats you as you merit
in the main.   If you serve it, it is not unthankful ; if you please it, it is
pleased ; if you cringe to it, it detects you, and scorns you if you are
mean ; it returns your cheerfulness with its good humour ; it deals not
ungenerously with your weaknesses ; it recognizes most kindly your
merits ; it gives you a fair place and fair play.   To any one of those
men of whom we have spoken was it in the main ungrateful ?   A king
might refuse Goldsmith a pension, as a publisher might keep his
masterpiece and the delight of all the world in his desk for two years ;
but it was mistake, and not ill-will.   Noble and illustrious names of
Swift, and Pope, and Addison ! dear and honoured memories of
Goldsmith and Fielding ! kind friends, teachers, benefactors ! who
shall say that our country, which continues to bring you such an
unceasing tribute of applause, admiration, love, sympathy, does not do
honour to the literary calling in the honour which it bestows upon *you !*

THE END.